Becoming an
# *Effective*
# Health Care
# Manager

Becoming an

# *Effective*
# Health Care
# Manager

## The Essential Skills of Leadership

Len Sperry, M.D., Ph.D.

 HEALTH
PROFESSIONS
PRESS

Baltimore • London • Winnipeg • Sydney

**Health Professions Press, Inc.**
Post Office Box 10624
Baltimore, Maryland 21285-0624

www.healthpropress.com

Typeset by Auburn Associates, Baltimore, Maryland.
Manufactured in the United States of America by
Versa Press, Inc., East Peoria, Illinois.

All cases described in this book are composites based on the authors' actual experiences. Individuals' names have been changed and identifying details have been altered to protect confidentiality.

All names and financial data in Chapter 11 are fictional and are provided only for illustrative purposes to demonstrate typical financial and business practices.

**Library of Congress Cataloging-in-Publication Data**
Sperry, Len.
    Becoming an effective health care manager : the essential skills of leadership / by Len Sperry.
      p.    cm.
    Includes bibliographical references and index.
    ISBN 1-878812-86-6
      1. Health services administrators.   2. Leadership.   3. Health facilities—Personnel management.   4. Health services administration.   I. Title.

    RA971.S72   2003
    362.1'068'3—dc21                    2003041655

British Library Cataloguing in Publication data are available from the British Library.

# Contents

# About the Author

**Len Sperry, M.D., Ph.D.,** is a physician who has practiced medicine and health care leadership for more than 20 years. He taught health care leadership courses at the Medical College of Wisconsin in Milwaukee and at Barry University in Miami Shores, Florida, where he was Director of the graduate program in Health Services Administration. He has written more than 300 professional publications, including 40 books. His latest publication is *Effective Leadership: Strategies for Maximizing Executive Productivity and Health* (Brunner-Routledge, 2001). Dr. Sperry has received lifetime achievement awards from the American Psychological Association and the Academy of Organizational and Occupational Psychiatry for his contributions to organizational development and leadership.

# Preface

"If there is one thing that keeps this place from being a first-class health care system, it's a lack of really effective managers."

I've heard countless hospital administrators and consultants make this and similar remarks. No doubt it is the reason why highly effective health care managers are in such high demand today. Such managers play an indispensable role in boosting productivity, quality of care, and cost savings as well as patient and employee satisfaction. Other business sectors are experiencing a similar shortage of highly effective managers but not as severely as in health care. Studies across all business sectors find that skilled leadership is *more* predictive of the financial viability of an organization than any combination of the other key indicators of financial viability, such as market share, reputation, and overall assets. Research also suggests that health care organization systems that actively focus on skill building in leadership development programs can dramatically increase productivity and employee commitment.

What skills are essential in increasing productivity and commitment? Technical skills? Analytic skills? Operational skills? Relational skills? It is assumed that managers would not be hired if they did not possess at least adequate levels of technical and job-related skills. Research studies and surveys, however, consistently reveal that relational, operational, and analytic skills are the most important and essential for increasing productivity and commitment.

Accordingly, this text can help to increase and enhance the leadership skills of managers in three key functional skill set areas:

1. Operational (team performance, commitment and motivation, delegation, and time and stress management)
2. Relational (communications, negotiation and conflict management, coaching, and counseling and interviewing)
3. Analytic (budgeting, managing financial and human resources, strategic thinking and decision making, and evaluating organizational and personal resources)

This book focuses on several skills within 12 core skill sets. A *skill set*, as the term implies, is a set or cluster of related skills. For example, communication is a skill set consisting of several specific skills such as listening, engagement, empathic responding, nonverbal communication, verbal presentations, and written communication.

This book focuses on the 12 skill sets that are essential to becoming an effective health care manager. These skills are described and illustrated in this learner-friendly approach to leadership development. Unlike other leadership and management books that simply describe the skills that effective managers and supervisors need, *Becoming an Effective Health Care Manager: The Essential Skills of Leadership* is designed to promote the learning and mastery of these skills. The discussion of each skill includes five learning sections:

1. A concise description of the skill
2. Skill-focused exercises for learning each skill
3. One or more case examples illustrating the successful use of the skill in a realistic, daily health care management situation
4. A set of review questions and related individual and group activities to assess learning outcomes for that skill
5. A self-assessment for identifying the learner's current skill level

The book is based on solid research findings and on the author's consultation, courses, and seminars in which managers have been taught these skills with this effective learning approach. It is a high-interest, high-impact, hands-on approach to learning. It includes self-assessment devices to evaluate current skill levels in each of the 12 skill sets, as well as a pre- and posttest assessment of the reader/learner's overall leadership skill competency. Finally, realistic individual and small-group learning exercises promote skill development.

*Becoming an Effective Health Care Manager: The Essential Skills of Leadership* will be useful in leadership and management courses and continuing education workshops and seminars for health care managers, as well as in undergraduate and graduate courses in health administration programs. It should also appeal to individual managers interested in developing these skills to increase their own effectiveness.

The structure of the book is straightforward and direct, and consists of three steps. Step I is preparatory. This section introduces the idea of skill building in leadership development and contains the Self-Assessment of Essential Leadership Skills: Pretest, which provides the learner with an assessment of his or her overall leadership skills competence level. In Step II, the learner explores the principles and practices of the 12 skill sets. Each chapter in this section focuses on one skill set and contains case examples, skill development exercises and activities, and a detailed self-assessment of that skill set. The goal of these chapters is to assist the learner in becoming a more effective manager. Finally, Step III progresses to an action plan for continuing the journey of *becoming* an effective manager and making the transition to *being* an effective manager, that is, achieving and maintaining mastery of the skills of effective leadership. Step III concludes with the Self-Assessment of Essential Leadership Skills: Posttest.

# Acknowledgments

Many individuals were instrumental in launching and finalizing this project, and I would like to acknowledge their contributions. I begin by recognizing my colleague, Dr. Alan Whiteman, for the material he contributed to the book. Likewise, several prominent health care executives have reviewed and provided valuable pre-publication feedback on the book. My deepest appreciation to Joseph Catania, CEO, Catholic Health Services, Inc., Miami, Florida; Fred Messing, COO, Baptist Health System of Florida; Dr. Harry Prosen, Chair, Department of Psychiatry, Medical College of Wisconsin; Dr. Chet Evans, Dean, School of Graduate Medical Sciences, Barry University; Dr. William W. Greaves, Director of M.P.H. Programs and the Division of Public Health at the Medical College of Wisconsin; John Johnson, President and CEO of Holy Cross Hospital, Fort Lauderdale, Florida; Dr. Jo Manion, President of Manion & Associates; and Sister John Karen Frei, O.P., Ph.D., Dean and Vice President of Research, Barry University. I'm most grateful to Mary Magnus, my editor at Health Professions Press, who championed this project from the outset, and to Amy Kopperude at Health Professions Press for her superb efforts in keeping this project on track. Finally, special thanks to Julia Thompson, my administrative assistant, for providing invaluable technical assistance.

# Becoming an Effective Leader in Health Care Management

*"Effective health care managers are skillful health care managers."*

The above statement captures the essence of this book. A quick glance through the business and management section of a large bookstore reveals a seemingly endless stream of titles on developing management skills, improving effective leadership, identifying talented managers, promoting leadership development, and the like. Why is this? Because skillful, effective managers are in short supply today, and many efforts are being made to address this situation. This shortage is particularly keen in health care organizations but can also be found in many corporations and organizations in America today. Because of the unprecedented changes under way in health care, the need for effective health care leaders is probably more critical now than at any other time in recent history.

This book addresses the need for skilled managers by providing the reader with a practical manual for developing and enhancing the essential skills needed to become a more effective and successful health care manager. This introductory section, Step I, sets the stage for acquiring these skills. It begins by describing the role of skill development in promoting effective leadership. It then describes the basis for identifying the 12 essential skills, or more accurately skill sets, of effective health care managers. Each of these 12 skill sets is described briefly. Finally, there is an overview of the rest of the book, as well as instructions for taking and scoring the *Self-Assessment of Essential Leadership Skills: Pretest* on pages 10–17. Before turning to these topics, it is necessary to clarify terminology, beginning with the terms *leadership* and *management,* and then contrast leadership *skills* with *talents* and *competencies.*

## HEALTH CARE LEADERSHIP OR MANAGEMENT?

Since the 1980s, the issue of distinguishing between leadership and management has been debated. Management typically has been associated with how individuals function under conditions of stability, that is, in transactional activities such as accomplishing objectives, monitoring compliance, and coordinating staff and workflow. In contrast, leadership is typically associated with how individuals function under conditions of instability and change, that is, in transformational activities such as envisioning, galvanizing commitment, and providing inspiration. Consultants to health care organizations often highlight this distinction, emphasizing that leadership is essential in revitalizing health care (Manion, 1999).

Research suggests that such distinctions are neither valid nor useful because effective management and leadership cannot be separated (Quinn, 2000; Tichy, 1999). "Leading change and managing stability, establishing visions and accomplishing objectives, breaking the rules and monitoring conformance, although paradoxical, are all required to be successful" (Whetten & Cameron, 2002, p. 16). From this perspective, leadership and management are complementary—a perspective that informs this book. Not surprisingly, the skills necessary to be an effective manager are also necessary to be an effective leader. Before turning to these necessary or essential skills, it is useful to clarify and define some common terms.

## SKILLS, KNOWLEDGE,
## TALENTS, AND COMPETENCIES

Unfortunately, the terms *skills, knowledge, talents,* and *competencies* are often used interchangeably. Because of their importance in understanding effective leadership, it is helpful to define and differentiate these key terms.

*Skills* are defined by Buckingham and Coffman as "the how-to's of a role" (1999, p. 82). Skills are capabilities that can be transferred from one person to another. For example, reading a balance sheet is a financial management skill. Similar to skills is *knowledge,* which is "what you are aware of" (Buckingham & Coffman, 1999, p. 82). Knowledge can be differentiated into factual knowledge and experiential knowledge. Factual knowledge represents concepts or ideas that are available to anyone. For example, the various provisions of the Americans with Disabilities Act (ADA) of 1990 (PL 101-336) are pertinent factual knowledge for human resources managers. Experiential knowledge is what we learn subjectively through firsthand experience. Both types can be learned and transferred from one person to another.

*Talents* are natural abilities that influence an individual's "recurring patterns of thought, feeling, or behavior" (Buckingham & Coffman, 1999, p. 83). For example, precision is a talent associated with effective accountants and computer programmers. These abilities are inborn traits, which means that they cannot be learned. It is possible to train someone who does not have a particular talent, such as precision, to follow a protocol that may increase his or her skill for attention to detail (which is one aspect of precision), but the outcome of this training will never instill precision in an individual.

For example, in more than 30 years as both an executive and a consultant, I have learned that good judgment is really an inborn talent that cannot be approximated easily. I have observed that individuals with good judgment can intuitively make split-second decisions under duress that turn out to be excellent decisions about people or tasks. Other individuals who have been taught a problem-solving protocol may be able to follow the protocol and systematically think through a problem reasonably well when there is sufficient time and little or no duress. However, these individuals are at a great disadvantage when they are forced to make quick decisions under fire.

On the basis of their leadership research, Buckingham and Coffman (1999) indicated that the capacity to discover talent in others is an important capability for executives. They note that "the best managers are adept at spotting a glimpse of talent in someone and then repositioning him so that he can play to that talent more effectively" (p. 83). Such leaders are talent hunters and talent developers and do not confuse talents with skills. Jack Welch, the retired chief executive officer (CEO) of General Electric (GE) who described himself as GE's best talent scout, exemplifies this view of leadership.

*Competencies* can be defined as capabilities that many corporations use to describe expected behaviors in leaders. Unfortunately, Buckingham and Coffman noted that some competencies (e.g., "remaining calm when under fire") may actually be talents, other competencies (e.g., "implementing basic operational systems") may actually be skills, and still others may be "part skills, part knowledge and part talent" (1999, p. 89). They urged executives to be very clear about the actual requirements of specific competencies because if a talent-based competency is specified as an expected behavior for a given individual, unless the individual possesses that talent, the expected behavior will never be achieved.

The ideal is to establish "pure" competencies, that is, those that are primarily skill based and not talent based. It seems that the most discerning and effective executives are those who establish skill-based competencies. It is critically important for leaders to clearly distinguish talents from skills and competencies when selecting individuals for positions and when doing coaching or planning leadership development activities. In other words, the best leaders are those who know how to search out needed talents in others and coach for needed skills and competencies.

## LEADERSHIP SKILLS

### The Key to Corporate Success

Why do corporations consider leadership skills so important? Because leadership skills are the key to a corporation's success. Mounting evidence has shown that skillful leaders are the key determinant of corporate success. Whether organizations are public or private, in the manufacturing, the health care, or the service sector, the "research findings now make it almost unquestionable that if organizations want to succeed, they must have competent, skillful managers" (Whetten & Cameron, 2002, p. 4).

Although many would agree that competent leadership is an important and significant factor in corporate success, some would balk at the suggestion that skillful leadership is more important than other factors, such as market share or assets. Surprisingly, research does not support that viewpoint. For example, in a study of the factors that accounted for the financial success of corporations, five factors were identified that predicted success: market share, capital intensity, size of assets, industry average return on sales, and effective leadership. Interestingly, this research indicated that the ability to manage effectively was *three times* more important than the other four factors combined (Hanson, 1986). Successive studies seem to offer further support for Hanson's conclusion, namely, that effective leadership fosters corporate financial success whereas ineffective leadership fosters financial failure. One might reasonably conclude that successful corporations are successful because they have managers with well-developed leadership and management skills.

Surveys of CEOs and other executives and managers consistently show that poor leadership is the factor most responsible for business failure and that the best way to ensure corporate success is to provide better leadership. The obvious question is, What is the best way to provide better leadership? The answer is clear: Develop effective leadership and management skills. Whetten and Cameron concluded that "management skills are more important than industry, environment, competition and economic factors combined" (2002, p. 5).

## The Building Blocks of Effective Leadership

What is the relationship between skills and effective leadership? Leadership skills are the building blocks on which effective leadership is based. Therefore, this book is focused on developing leadership skills rather than talents, competencies, or even knowledge. As building blocks, leadership skills are the means by which managers translate their own leadership style, talents, and competencies into practice.

## THE ESSENTIAL SKILLS AND
## SKILL SETS OF LEADERSHIP

What are the essential leadership skills necessary for effective health care leadership? This book focuses on several skills within 12 core skill sets. A *skill set*, as the term implies, is a set or cluster of related skills. For example, communication is a skill set consisting of several specific skills such as listening, engagement, empathic responding, nonverbal communication, verbal presentations, and written communication. Similarly, the skill set of coaching involves several specific skills including engagement, listening, assessment, advising, education, monitoring, and evaluation.

The 12 skill sets described and illustrated in this book were chosen based on current research and survey findings. In a study of the attributes associated with successful, effective leadership, Whetten and Cameron (1998) found, to their surprise, that the most common attributes of successful leadership were basic leadership skills. They surveyed 402 managers who were rated as highly effective leaders by senior managers in their organizations. These organizations encompassed the health care, business, education, and government sectors. These highly effective managers were interviewed to determine which attributes were associated with leadership effectiveness. The 10 most frequently cited attributes were all basic leadership skills: verbal communication, time and stress management, decision making, problem solving, motivation, delegation, vision and goal setting, self-awareness, team building, and conflict management. Other studies suggest similar skills.

It is also instructive to note the results of studies focusing on attributes of managers who are considered ineffective. A study of the perceptions of 830 managers as to why managers fail reported that the most common reasons were skill deficits. The five most common skill deficits, in order of magnitude, were ineffective communication skills, poor interpersonal skills, failure to clarify expectations, poor delegation, and inability to develop teamwork. Comparing these skill deficits with the skills of highly effective leaders (as reported by Whetten & Cameron, 1998) provides an interesting picture. Basically, leaders who are ineffective and fail lack the essential skills that highly effective leaders possess.

In my consulting experience with senior leaders in health care organizations, I have informally surveyed hundreds of individuals about the attributes of effective leaders. There seems to be considerable overlap between these attributes and the 10 skills identified in the Whetten and Cameron (1998) study. Some of these senior health care executives I surveyed mentioned that some additional skills were essential for effective health care leadership. These included budgeting, financial analysis, coaching, counseling, and life–work balance. Because many health care managers have risen through the ranks or have clinical backgrounds, they are unlikely to have formal training in accounting and financial management. The skills of budgeting and financial analysis are essential skills for these managers. Also, unlike other sectors of the workplace, in which coaching and counseling are considered required leadership skills, health care is just beginning to recognize the need for and value of such skills and skill sets.

Table 1 identifies the 12 essential skill sets covered in this book by type: operational, relational, and analytic. Table 2 briefly describes the 12 essential skill sets. Some contain very basic or core skills that are requisite for the development of other skills of effective leadership. For example, basic to the communication skill set are active listening, two-way communication, and engagement, which are requisite core skills for most skill sets, especially coaching, team building, and delegation. Similarly, the strategic thinking and decision making skills are involved in most of the analytic skill sets, particularly budgeting and finance. Furthermore, basic skills in the skill set of commitment and motivation are essential for all other skills that emphasize productivity and performance.

**Table 1.** Skill sets by categories

**Operational**
   Galvanizing commitment and motivation
   Maximizing team performance
   Delegating to maximize performance
   Managing stress and time effectively

**Relational**
   Communicating effectively and strategically
   Negotiating and managing conflict and difficult people
   Coaching for maximum performance and development
   Counseling and interviewing for maximum performance and development

**Analytic**
   Thinking and deciding strategically
   Mastering the budget process
   Mastering and monitoring financial and human resources
   Assessing corporate and personal resources

**Table 2.**   The 12 skill sets of the effective leader

| | |
|---|---|
| Commitment and motivation | Prepares the manager with several skills and strategies for assessing the causes of decreased commitment and motivation and skills for increasing employee commitment and triggering their motivation to improve performance |
| Team performance | Provides the manager with skills and strategies for influencing the process of team development and team building to maximize individual and team performance, job satisfaction, and commitment to the organization |
| Delegation and empowerment | Provides the manager an understanding of empowered delegation (i.e., a set of skills for delegating/assigning an employee a task while simultaneously empowering that employee to successfully complete the task) |
| Effective, strategic communication | Provides the manager several skills and strategies for improving productivity, interpersonal relationships, and job commitment through strategic communication. This set includes core skills such as engagement, active listening, and interpersonal communication as well as advanced skills such as effective writing, verbal presentations, and conducting effective meetings. |
| Negotiating conflict and difficult people | Provides the manager with skills in assessing and managing conflict, as well as measures to prevent it. Skills and strategies are also included for effectively dealing with angry, negative, and uncooperative employees. |
| Coaching | Prepares managers to enhance their skills in coaching employees to achieve optimal performance. Three sets of coaching skills are described: skill-based, performance-based, and developmental coaching. |
| Counseling and interviewing | Provides the manager with specific interviewing skills and strategies to maximize outcomes in employment, exit, appraisal, and disciplinary and counseling interviews |
| Strategic thinking and decision making | Provides the manager a strategy for learning to think strategically (i.e., "outside the box"). One related skill is strategic planning, which, in its best sense, is an application of strategic thinking. |
| Budgeting | Prepares managers to review past performance and budgets in order to effectively plan, implement, and then evaluate a unit budget |
| Monitoring financial and human resources | Provides the manager sufficient knowledge and understanding to critically review financial statements and other financial reports for making informed decisions |
| Evaluating self–job/ organization–family fit | Provides the manager a strategy for assessing various personal and organizational resources and evaluating the impact of these resources—or lack thereof—on the manager in terms of the degree of "fit" among self, job, organization, career, and family |
| Time and stress management | Enhances the leader's capacity to control and cope with stress on and off the job. It emphasizes several specific skills and strategies for the long-term and immediate management of work stress, job strain, and time stressors. |

## STRATEGY FOR
## BECOMING AN EFFECTIVE LEADER

There are two critical ingredients in becoming an effective manager: skills and "fit." The first ingredient, skills, indicates that effective managers are successful at what they do because they have developed competence in the core set of leadership skills. The core set of skills includes the various operational, relational, and analytic skills described and illustrated in this book as well as the requisite technical skills that are specific to the manager's position. The second ingredient is level of "fit." The basic premise is that it is easier for an individual to function as an effective manager if he or she is in the right place at the right time and works with the right managers and co-workers. In other words, although skills are a necessary condition for effectiveness, having an adequate "fit" or match with a job and an organization that prizes such skills is the sufficient condition. Truly effective managers are able to develop, enhance, and maintain their leadership skills because their work environment not only "permits" managers to use these skills but requires and rewards their utilization. Over time, truly effective managers move from the "becoming" mode to the "being" mode. These managers find that they have gained sufficient mastery of the requisite leadership skills and apply them almost effortlessly. Step III of this book describes this shift from becoming to being.

## ORGANIZATION OF THE BOOK

The book is a personalized approach to skill mastery. This first step concludes with an overall self-assessment of current leadership skills that directs the reader to those skill areas that need improvement. In Step II, each skill chapter covers 1 of the 12 essential leadership skills utilizing the following personalized skill-learning format:

1. Learning principles and guidelines for applying the skill
2. Case examples of successful skill performance
3. Individual and group skill development exercises
4. Self-assessment of level of skill and related attitudes
5. Review activities

In Step III, the focus shifts from "becoming" to "being" an effective manager. That section provides some suggestions and guidelines for maintaining and further enhancing the requisite skills for effective leadership and also contains the *Self-Assessment of Essential Leadership Skills: Posttest.*

## CONCLUDING NOTE

This section began with the statement, "Skillful health care managers are effective health care managers," and it ends with the same declaration. There is no question that the demand for highly effective, skillful leaders in health care far exceeds the supply. Developing the essential skills of effective leadership should be one of the top priorities of senior management in health care today. Unfortunately, developing these skills has yet to achieve that status in many parts of the health care sector. Instead, senior health care managers seem to be more focused on low census, low productivity, and poor employee morale, as well as high turnover rates, apparently unaware of the role that highly effective leadership has in reversing these situations. At Intermountain Health Care, a health care organization based in Utah with more than 23,000 employees, highly effective leadership has fostered high levels of productivity, quality, morale, and employee commitment, and turnover is very low. *Modern Healthcare,* a business newsweekly, honored Intermountain Health Care in January 2000 as the number one integrated health care system in the United States. Hopefully, this book can help you become a similarly effective health care leader.

## SELF-ASSESSMENT OF
## ESSENTIAL LEADERSHIP SKILLS: PRETEST

**Directions:** This assessment will help you evaluate your current level of skill and attitudes regarding several leadership skills. Use the following statements to assess your attitudes and skills by circling the number that is closest to your experience: 1 = never, 2 = sometimes, 3 = often, and 4 = always. Respond in a way that reflects your skills today, rather than those you hope to have in the future. Answer as honestly and realistically as you can because this inventory will help you tailor your learning to your particular needs. Instructions on scoring and interpreting the results are provided in the analysis section at the end of the assessment.

## MOTIVATION

1. I try to persuade and influence employees rather than force them to do what I want.   1   2   ③   4

2. I design work assignments so they are interesting and challenging.   1   ②   3   4

3. I strive to match an employee's ability and talent with job responsibilities.   1   2   ③   4

4. Knowing that employees have different needs and wants, I try to personalize rewards and feedback.   1   ②   3   4

5. I provide immediate positive feedback and other forms of recognition for work that is well done.   1   2   ③   4

## COMMITMENT

6. Many of my professional needs are met in my current job.   1   ②   3   4

7. I would not be satisfied working for another health care organization.   1   2   3   4

8. I try my best and give full effort in my current job.   1   2   ③   4

9. Emotionally, it would be difficult for me to leave my current job.   ①   2   3   4

10. Other health care organizations can't compare with mine.   ①   2   3   4

## TEAM PERFORMANCE

11. I allow the team to have input in any
decision that affects team performance.     1   2   (3)   4

12. I strive to show team members that I trust
them implicitly.    1   (2)   3   4

13. I set high standards of team performance
and outcomes.    1   2   (3)   4

14. I strive to foster a culture that values
teams and team development.    1   2   (3)   4

15. I lay out a clear vision and specific short-
term goals of what our team can
accomplish.    1   (2)   3   4

## DELEGATION

16. I try to do only the work that must be
done by me and delegate the rest.    1   2   3   4

17. I am regarded by my superior as a good
delegator.    1   2   3   4

18. I delegate with the thought that it helps
staff grow to their fullest potential.    1   2   3   4

19. When I delegate responsibility, I make
sure that staff have the full authority to
perform the task properly.    1   2   3   4

20. I review my job every 3–6 months to see
whether I can increase my delegation to
staff.    1   2   3   4

## COMMUNICATION

21. I strive to be an "active listener" by using
eye contact, head nods, smiles, "uh-
huhs," restatements, and leaning forward.    1   2   3   (4)

22. If staff haven't understood my message, it means I haven't communicated effectively.    1   2   ③   4

23. My staff members tell me about bad news (e.g., problems, mistakes, delays) as well as good news.    1   2   ③   4

24. I draft reports that are clear, concise, persuasive, and well structured.    1   2   3   ④

25. Throughout my presentation, I make eye contact with all segments of the audience.    1   2   ③   4

## NEGOTIATION

26. In attempting to resolve a conflict, I look for common areas of agreement.    1   ②   3   4

27. When there is conflict, I try to clarify the interests of both parties and create an agenda for resolving the dispute.    1   2   ③   4

28. I try to keep the discussion focused on problems rather than on personalities.    1   2   ③   4

29. I encourage parties to generate possible solutions and spell out the benefits of each.    1   ②   3   4

30. I help the parties to come to agreement on the best solution.    1   2   3   4

## COACHING

31. Being a manager means coaching employees.    1   2   ③   4

32. I revise performance plans with the employee and provide additional coaching as needed.    1   2   3   4

33. I communicate a positive attitude when coaching to convey my belief in employees' ability to achieve their goals.　1　2　3　④

34. When coaching, my focus is on current performance and potential achievement.　1　2　3　4

35. My superiors consider me to be an effective coach.　1　2　3　4

## COUNSELING AND INTERVIEWING

36. During interviews, I put the individual at ease and attempt to maintain a relaxed, friendly tone.　1　2　③　4

37. I start interviews by being direct and specific about my agenda or my concerns.　1　②　3　4

38. I try to listen actively and use good eye contact and positive body language to communicate my respect, interest, and concern.　1　2　3　④

39. I view the outcomes and success of counseling as dependent on the individual's involvement, so I encourage his or her full participation.　1　2　③　4

40. To avoid any possible misunderstanding on my part, I check out my perceptions of the situation or concern with the individual.　1　②　3　4

## STRATEGIC THINKING AND DECISION MAKING

41. I follow a multistep decision-making model to ensure a sound decision.　1　2　3　4

42. I make my decisions in a timely fashion
    and ensure that they are implemented.        1    2    3    4

43. My superiors consider me a strategic
    thinker.                                      1    2    3    4

44. I combine analytical methods and
    creative approaches in making decisions.      1    2   (3)   4

45. I constantly check to ensure that my team
    operates within the strategy.                 1    2    3    4

## BUDGETING

46. I develop my goals and objectives for the
    coming year before I prepare my budget.       1    2    3    4

47. I adjust my budget periodically to correct
    for changes in projections.                   1    2    3    4

48. I study the budget manual and follow it
    closely in preparing my budget.               1    2    3    4

49. I prefer a flexible budget so that my
    projections can be corrected for changes.     1    2    3    4

50. I communicate budget issues directly
    with my staff and get their input.            1    2    3    4

## FINANCIAL AND HUMAN RESOURCES MONITORING

51. I use management accounting reports to
    manage my unit.                               1    2    3    4

52. I use benchmarks in monitoring
    performance.                                  1    2    3    4

53. I use accounting ratios to analyze
    financial information.                        1    2    3    4

54. I know how my organization's mission and goals relate to its overall financial management.　　1　2　3　4

55. I can read and analyze my organization's financial statements.　　1　2　3　4

## ORGANIZATIONAL AND PERSONAL RESOURCES AND "FIT"

56. I maintain balance in my personal and professional life by pursuing hobbies and interests.　　1　2　(3)　4

57. I can arrange my work life so it doesn't spill over into my personal life.　　1　2　(3)　4

58. I have made the most of my talents and abilities.　　1　(2)　3　4

59. My values match the organization's core values.　　(1)　2　3　4

60. There is a good fit among me and my job, family, and organization.　　(1)　2　3　4

## TIME AND STRESS MANAGEMENT

61. I feel reasonably calm and centered even if I am under pressure.　　1　(2)　3　4

62. I undertake only as many tasks as I can handle at once.　　1　(2)　3　4

63. I know and practice several immediate stress reducers such as mindfulness and deep breathing.　　1　(2)　3　4

64. I deal with tasks by prioritizing my work load.　　1　2　(3)　4

65. I would say that, for the most part, I am able to cope with my work load.　　1　2　(3)　4

## Self-Assessment Analysis: Global

Add your circled scores together to arrive at your total score. Then, refer to the following scoring ranges to identify your level of skill and attitudes toward leadership. For the assessment as a whole, if you scored in the range

221–260      You are in the top quartile.

191–220      You are in the second quartile.

120–190      You are in the third quartile.

119 or below    You are in the bottom quartile.

## Self-Assessment Analysis: Specific Skill Sets

Now compute your scores for the specific sets of skills. Enter each score on the line provided.

1. _____   Commitment and Motivation

2. _____   Team Performance

3. _____   Delegation

4. _____   Communication

5. _____   Negotiation

6. _____   Coaching

7. _____   Counseling and Interviewing

8. _____   Strategic Thinking and Decision Making

9. _____   Budgeting

10. _____   Financial and Human Resources Monitoring

11. _____   Organizational and Personal Resources and "Fit"

12. _____   Time and Stress Management

## Interpretation of Scores

For each specific set of skills, the following scoring ranges suggest that

16–20       You appear to have highly developed skills in this area.

11–15       You appear to have reasonably well-developed skills in this area.

10 or below   Your skills in this area appear to need improvement.

# Mastering the 12 Essential Skills

*"Our management schools need to identify the skills managers use, select students who show potential in these skills, put students in situations where these skills can be practiced, and then give them systematic feedback on their performance."*

—Henry Mintzberg

# Skill 1

# Galvanizing Commitment and Motivation

Here, as in subsequent chapters of this book, skills are operational as the capacity to consistently implement specific strategies grows. The objectives of this chapter are to

- Describe the value and necessity of commitment and motivation to health care organizations
- Describe the relationship between commitment and motivation
- Differentiate four common theories of motivation
- Define and illustrate the skill of engendering commitment
- Define and illustrate the skill of motivating employees
- Assess your attitudes and skills regarding commitment and motivation
- Provide skill development exercises and activities to develop or enhance skills in engendering commitment and motivation

## COMMITMENT

What is commitment? O'Malley (2000) notes that commitment is commonly defined as "the state or an instance of being obligated or emotionally impelled" (p. 27). In other words, individuals who are committed feel connected and are motivated to maintain that connection. Committed health care employees are pleasant, hardworking individuals who look forward to going to work, put in a full day's effort, are productive, act in the organization's best interest, and stay with the organization. Conversely, uncommitted employees tend to be remote and aloof, may pursue their own interests irrespective of the organization's mission, take full advantage of time off, and never seem to be around when they are needed. Their work output barely meets minimum standards; they can be confrontational, defensive, and oppositional; and, if a better opportunity arises, they will move to another organization (O'Malley, 2000).

Commitment has become a critical problem for corporations today, particularly for health care organizations. According to O'Malley (2000), surveys report that among first-year employees, some 43% indicate that they are highly committed to their jobs. By the second and third years of employment, however, this percentage begins to drop. By the fourth year, the expressed level of commitment has fallen to a level of 34%. This level of commitment remains the same for employees who spend at least 20 years with the same employer. Job commitment appears to be decreasing in every sector of the workplace. O'Malley also noted that a survey conducted by the Hudson Institute and published in 2000 found that only 42% of employees believe that their employers were deserving of the employees' allegiance. This decline in commitment comes at a time when major shortages of skilled workers are being predicted. Some corporations are expecting to lose more than half of their workforce to retirement by 2005. In addition, a 1998 Harris poll revealed that more than 50% of workers will leave their jobs within 5 years for various reasons (O'Malley, 2000).

Employee turnover rates are a telling marker of commitment levels. Turnover rates in the health care sector are often in the 25%–40% range. This means that each year between 2 and 4 employees of 10 must be replaced. Although turnover is higher in some other sectors (i.e., 75% for fast-food restaurants), replacement in those sectors is less problematic. Replacing skilled nursing and other professional personnel in health care settings is a major concern.

Why do employees leave or stay in their jobs? Several employee turnover studies offer a possible answer: The major factor accounting for employee retention is the quality of employee–manager relationships. Essentially, employees who work for managers who are caring and concerned about their careers and provide them with challenging work are more likely to remain in that organization than to leave. Relationships appear to be key both to employee commitment and to productivity and performance.

## Levels of Commitment

Commitment is not a binary phenomenon in which one is either committed or not committed. Rather, there are varying degrees or levels of commitment. Macher (1988) described a continuum of commitment ranging from extremely low to extremely high levels of commitment. Seven levels can be described, beginning with very high and proceeding to very low:

1. *Deep commitment:* These employees possess the highest level of commitment. They find a deep sense of purpose and meaning in their work and exert themselves in ways that really make a difference.
2. *Personal ambition:* These employees work hard and know how to "work the system" to achieve their own personal goals and ambitions. Achieving the corporation's mission is a secondary consideration.
3. *Concerned but limited sense of power:* These employees are technically competent and care about quality but feel victimized by the system. As a result, they limit their effort and commitment to their job and the organization.
4. *Formal commitment:* These employees do only what is required and will not extend themselves beyond the minimum.
5. *Retired on the job:* These employees actively dodge work and responsibility and regularly make excuses for poor performance or nonperformance. They may appear to be going through the motions but achieve at or below the minimum.
6. *Alienated:* These employees exhibit considerable mistrust of the organization, their co-workers, and customers or patients. Although they may not take overt action to sabotage the orga-

nization's mission, they tend to complain, feel resigned, and minimally meet performance standards and are dubbed as "unmotivated."

7. *Actively hostile:* These employees possess the lowest level of commitment. They vigorously—although subtly, to avoid being fired—work against the organization's basic mission. They tend to be antimanagement, and their only commitment is to receiving a salary and benefits.

## Conditions that Foster Commitment

Table 1 is derived from O'Malley's (2000) research on commitment. It describes five basic conditions that facilitate the development of commitment—fit and belonging, status and identity, trust and reciprocity, emotional reward, and economic independence—and fulfill the five most basic needs of employees—acceptance, esteem, security, growth, and sustenance, respectively.

## Strategies that Foster and Enhance Commitment

An effective way of establishing and maintaining high levels of employee commitment is to foster what this book calls a "cul-

**Table 1.**   Conditions that foster commitment and fulfillment of employee needs

| Condition | Description |
| --- | --- |
| Fit and belonging | The extent to which employee and organizational values and interests are compatible, and the degree to which employee feels that he or she belongs and develops friendships. This fulfills the employee's need for *acceptance.* |
| Status and identity | The extent to which the employee's self-concept is influenced by the organizational affiliation. This fulfills the employee's need for *esteem.* |
| Trust and reciprocity | The extent to which the organization acts in such a way that the employee and organization become indebted to each other. This fulfills the employee's need for *security.* |
| Emotional reward | The extent to which the employee experiences the job and work environment as satisfying and supportive. This fulfills the employee's need for *growth.* |
| Economic interdependence | The extent to which the employee believes that compensation is fair and to which compensations benefit the employee in such a way that he or she remains in the organization. This fulfills the employee's need for *sustenance.* |

*Source:* O'Malley (2000).

ture of commitment," meaning an organizational culture that places a high priority on employee–manager relationships based on trust, belonging, esteem, growth, and economic interdependence as well as productivity and performance. In short, it is the quality of relationships between employees and their managers that keeps employees committed to a health care organization. This section presents four strategies for fostering and enhancing commitment.

1.  *Foster a leadership style and culture focused on employee need.* Unfortunately, commitment cannot be instilled in employees. Rather, commitment must be evoked. Instead of being commanded of employees, it emerges from a leadership style and culture that meets employees' needs of trust, acceptance, esteem, security, growth, and sustenance.

2.  *Recruit and hire employees compatible with a culture of commitment.* Establishing and maintaining a culture of commitment requires that prospective employees not only have the capacity to meet performance expectations but share the organization's basic values and mission. If candidates do not have both of these attributes, they may not be compatible with a culture of commitment and probably should not be hired.

3.  *Socialize employees to the culture of commitment.* Efforts to foster commitment do not cease after employees are hired who are compatible with the culture of commitment. In addition to presenting standard human resources policies and filling out paperwork, formal orientation programs need to emphasize the importance of the organization's basic values and mission in the daily life of the employee and his or her work team. Organizations that excel in fostering commitment utilize various means to socialize new employees. For example, some pair a new employee with a co-worker or a mentor to instill the culture over the first 6 months or so of employment.

4.  *Foster relationship management.* Organizations must endeavor to maintain healthy relationships with employees over time. O'Malley described the need for "preventive maintenance to keep relationships moving in a mutually desirable direction as well as corrective maintenance to resurrect relationships that are faltering" (2000, p. 221).

# MOTIVATION

## Commitment and Motivation

What is the relationship between commitment and motivation? Commitment and motivation are intimately related in that commitment is a component or dimension of motivation. Motivation can be defined as behavior that is energetic and goal directed. Although there is little agreement among motivation researchers on the source of this energy, there is growing consensus that motivation involves three factors: ability, commitment, and a goal (O'Malley, 2000).

## Theories of Motivation

Since the 1940s, research into human behavior has suggested that people are motivated by a number of different needs, at work and in their personal lives. Recognizing and satisfying these needs will help managers to get the best from their employees. Six motivation theories are briefly described in this section. Each theory offers managers a valuable insight into increasing employee performance. Table 2 highlights the key points of each of these theories.

*Reinforcement Theory*    B.F. Skinner is associated with the reinforcement theory of motivation. According to this theory, a behavior that is reinforced or rewarded is likely to be repeated, and, depending on how rewards are provided, behavior can be shaped in a predictable fashion. When a behavior is not reinforced, it tends to disappear or be extinguished. Reinforcement is distinguished from punishment, in which a noxious or negative response, rather than a reward, is provided. Reinforcement theory has many applications in the workplace. Knowing that employees are motivated by rewards and respond in ways they find most reinforcing, managers should provide the kinds of rewards (e.g., a "thank you" or some type of personal recognition) that are meaningful or salient to employees. Usually, rewards that follow the expected behavior as immediately as possible and are salient are most likely to be effective.

*Expectancy Theory*    Previously it was noted that having a goal was one of the three key components in motivation. The expectancy theory of motivation emphasizes the importance of goals and the expectation of achieving specific goals. This theory, developed by Victor Vroom in the 1960s, is based on the premise that individuals are motivated to act because of the expectation that their behavior will lead to a specific reward that is valued by them. For instance, an individual decides how hard he or she must work to get a promotion. Then, he or she must decide if it is possible to sustain that level of effort. Finally, the individual decides how much he or she values that reward (i.e., the promotion). In other words, three factors determine the level of effort an individual is willing to expend: expectancy, valence, and instrumentality. As shown in the following formula, the interaction of these three factors indicate the individual's level of motivation according to the expectancy theory:

$$\text{Motivation} = \text{expectancy} \times \text{valence} \times \text{instrumentality}$$

Expectancy is the individual's view of whether his or her efforts will lead to the required level of performance necessary to attain a reward. Valence indicates how valued the reward is to the individual. Instrumentality is the individual's view of the link between performance level and the expected reward. In short, an individual will

**Table 2.** Six common theories of motivation relevant to management

| Theory | Key idea |
| --- | --- |
| Reinforcement theory | Individuals are motivated by rewards and respond in ways that they find most reinforcing, and behavior can be shaped by controlling rewards and other reinforcers. |
| Expectancy theory | Individuals are motivated by the expectation that behavior will lead to a specific reward and that reward is valued by the individual. |
| Theory X and Theory Y | Individuals are motivated by external control and discipline according to the Theory X view of human nature, as contrasted with the Theory Y view in which individuals seek responsibility and opportunities to be productive and creative. |
| Hierarchy of needs | Individuals are motivated by a hierarchy of needs. Each lower level of need must be satisfied before the next higher level of need can be operative. |
| Two-factor theory | Individuals are motivated by "motivating" factors such as recognition, responsibility, and challenge rather than by "hygiene" factors such as salary and job security. |
| Learned needs theory | Individuals are motivated by the need for achievement, the need for affiliation, or the need for power. The dominant need varies by individual. |

deliver only the level of performance needed to achieve a valued reward. According to this theory, managers can foster motivation by increasing the links among expectation, performance, and reward.

*Theory X and Theory Y*     Douglas McGregor described two sets of assumptions that he found managers to hold about human nature and that determine their view of motivation. He called one set of assumptions Theory X and the other set Theory Y. The Theory X view is that employees dislike work and avoid it whenever possible because they have little ambition and must be directed or coerced if they are to be even minimally productive. This is because individuals are inherently irresponsible and motivated only by external control. The Theory Y view is that work is a natural activity and individuals will work willingly without external controls. This is because they seek rather than shun responsibility and opportunities to be productive and creative. In short, Theory X is a pessimistic, distrustful way of looking at employees, whereas Theory Y is more optimistic and trusting.

The implications for management are clear. If a manager believes that employees are inherently lazy, irresponsible, and resistant to change, motivated only by money and selfish desires and responding only to being threatened or controlled, that manager will act on those assumptions. Conversely, a manager who believes that employees are inherently active, responsible, mature, and capable of self-direction and self-actualization when challenged to achieve corporate goals will act on those assumptions.

*Hierarchy of Needs*     Consistent with the Theory Y view, Abraham Maslow speculated that given the chance and the right circumstances, employees will work productively and positively. He proposed that individual needs were the motivational forces of behavior. Needs are the forces or factors that drive individuals to seek satisfaction or fulfillment. Maslow noted five sets of needs: 1) physiological, 2) safety, 3) social and belonging, 4) self-esteem, and 5) self-actualization needs. His research indicated these needs were hierarchically arranged such that once needs at a lower level (e.g., physiological and safety needs) are satisfied, needs at the next higher level (e.g., social and belonging needs) become motivators. A corollary finding was that once a lower need had been satisfied, it would no longer be an immediate motivator until it resurfaced for some reason.

The hierarchy of needs is particularly relevant in the work-place because individuals require more than a salary to meet basic physiological needs and a safe working environment to meet safety needs; they also seek out interaction to meet social and belonging needs and respect to meet self-esteem needs. When designing jobs, working conditions, and organizational structures, managers must bear in mind the full range of needs in the hierarchy. Doing this will cost no more, but it will undoubtedly generate higher psychological and economic rewards all around.

*Two-Factor Theory*   Frederick Herzberg developed a "two-factor" theory of motivation based on "motivators" and "hygiene factors." He believed that only those needs that corresponded with self-esteem and self-actualization levels (i.e., "psychic income" such as recognition, advancement, and growth) were "motivators," whereas needs at lower levels (i.e., "actual income" such as salary and benefits) would not motivate employees. Based on his research, Herzberg concluded that hygiene factors, such as salary, job security, and working conditions, do not, in and of themselves, motivate employees to higher levels of productivity. In fact, subsequent researchers have called hygiene factors "demotivators." Nevertheless, failure to meet them causes dissatisfaction. These factors can be as seemingly trivial as a parking space or as vital as sufficient vacation time. Interestingly, Herzberg found that the most important hygiene factor is money. Because money is such an important factor, managers should strive to meet their employees' financial needs. Individuals require certain pay levels to meet basic physiological and safety needs, so limiting or eliminating pay raises or incentive programs can easily demotivate employees. Not surprisingly, job insecurity serves as a powerful demotivator for many employees today.

The second of Herzberg's factors is a set of motivators that actually drive employees to achieve. To maintain a productive workforce, managers should focus on motivators such as recognition, a sense of achievement, opportunities for learning and career development, meaningful responsibility, stimulating and challenging work, and supportive relationships and being part of a good work team. How much a person enjoys achievement depends purely on its recognition. In turn, the ability to achieve is dependent on having an enjoyable job and meaningful responsibilities. The greater those responsibilities, the more the employee can experience the satisfaction of advancement. Motivators are built around deriving personal growth and self-actualization from tasks. Managers can raise motivation in employees by increasing their job responsibilities, thereby enriching their work experience.

*Learned Needs Theory*    According to this motivation theory proposed by David McClelland, needs are developed or learned over time. Three core needs—power, achievement, and affiliation—are present in everyone, although one of these three is dominant in any given individual. As a need, achievement drives job performance. Employees with a dominant need for achievement like challenges, excel in a competitive environment, and will seek out ways to increase production and improve work processes. Consequently, to ensure that they perform at high levels, these employees should be provided with challenging jobs and ongoing feedback.

Individuals with a dominant need for power like to be in charge of situations and individuals. They gravitate to jobs of influence and status and can become very effective managers when they are willing to exercise their influence through others to drive both productivity and quality. Managers who recognize the dominant power need in employees will provide these individuals with increasing control over their jobs and allow them to participate in decisions that have an impact on them.

Individuals with a dominant need for affiliation want to feel that they belong and are liked by others. They are motivated by the social aspects of work and easily develop relationships with others. Although they make effective and loyal team members, they tend to steer away from positions of leadership. Managers of employees who exhibit this dominant need will recognize that these individuals should not routinely be assigned to work on tasks alone but should be assigned to team activities. They are also the ones to call on to train new employees or to function as mentors.

## Indicators of Motivation in Employees and Teams

Motivation can be recognized in a number of ways. For example, employees who feel useful and optimistic and are productive are likely be motivated employees. Similarly, teams that can combine their individual efforts to achieve team goals as well as look after each other's interests are likely to be motivated teams. Effective managers routinely assess levels of motivation in their employees and immediately address specific indicators of declining motivation. Some key indicators for assessing employees' or teams' level of motivation include the following: 1) the degree to which they are productive and work to achieve their best effort, 2) the degree to which they freely volunteer effort and ideas, 3) the degree to which they respond positively to requests and new assignments, and 4) the degree to which they appear to be happy and satisfied with their work. To establish a more formal assessment, managers can rate each of these indicators on a 5-point scale in which 1 equals very low and 5 equals very high.

## STRATEGIES FOR ENHANCING MOTIVATION

Five strategies are offered to guide managers in increasing motivation in their work units:

1. Establish clear performance expectations.
2. Facilitate outcomes by coaching and by removing obstacles to goal achievement.
3. Provide rewards tailored to employee need.
4. Provide feedback and rewards in a timely manner.
5. Tap into employee passion and enthusiasm.

### Establish Clear Performance Expectations

As emphasized in expectancy theory, individuals are motivated by the expectation that their efforts will lead to a specific reward. The manager's initial effort in enhancing motivation should be to establish clear goals and expectations for employee and team performance. It goes without saying that goals and expectations must be understood and accepted by employees if they are to be accomplished. Research shows rather consistently that employees are more likely to "own" goals if they believe they have been sufficiently involved in the goal-setting process. Furthermore, these goals and expectations must be formulated in such a way that they are sufficiently specific and consistent as well as appropriately challenging for an employee or team.

## Facilitate Outcomes by Coaching and by Removing Obstacles to Goal Achievement

After setting goals and expectations, managers can shift their attention to facilitating the process of goal achievement. This may involve providing the necessary training or coaching, providing resources, engendering the support of other individuals or units, and removing barriers. As noted previously, motivation is dependent on a goal, ability, and commitment. In other words, motivated employees are "willing" and "able." Even though employees take ownership of the goals and are sufficiently committed (i.e., "willing"), it cannot be assumed that employees have the requisite ability (i.e., "able"). That is, a barrier to goal achievement may be employee inexperience or skill deficits. For that reason, skill-based coaching and/or training may be necessary.

## Provide Rewards Tailored to Employee Need

Trying to motivate employees is challenging because of the variations among them and the way they interact with the personality and motivation of their manager. Thus, it is valuable to tailor or match rewards and feedback to individuals based on their unique needs and expectations. Tailoring begins with assessment of individual differences.

Individual differences involving motivation are noted in personality needs, age, gender, and position on the career ladder. Of these factors, managers would do well to identify the dominant personality needs of their employees (i.e., power, achievement, or affiliation). For example, while achievement can be its own reward, it is rarely sufficient. Achievers also want recognition. Providing a simple "thank you" is an important and underused reward that can mean a lot to an achiever. Employees with high affiliation needs will value inclusion in activities that involve small group efforts to plan recreational activities, parties, or outings. Employees with high power needs are attracted by appointments to strategic planning task forces or other committees on which they make input to and have contact with top management. Employees with high power needs also react positively to being involved in decisions about budgets, targets, and other goals.

Tailoring also involves finding the right combination of target and reward, that is, the kind that will maximize productivity. No approach to linking rewards to goals can work well unless both aims and thresholds are realistic and fair. For instance, a manager attempting to reduce costs should advise the team of present cost levels, give them a target to shoot toward that is realistic, and reward them fairly for the degree of cost reduction achieved.

Recall that many incentives can motivate individuals, but each can have a different effect depending on individual differences. Commonly used financial incentives include salary increases, annual bonuses, and immediate bonuses. Nonfinancial incentives include recognition, parking spaces, days off, and other perks. If a manager is not in a position to offer financial incentives such as immediate bonuses, it is possible to motivate staff by providing nonfinancial incentives that are attractive to the potential recipient (e.g., a dedicated parking space near the employee entrance for an employee to whom status is important). Nonfinancial rewards may be less expensive and may have a higher valence for particular employees than cash rewards.

## Provide Feedback and Rewards in a Timely Manner

Up to this point, we have noted that it is essential that employees understand and accept performance expectations and that managers assist employees in achieving these expectations by coaching, removing barriers, and providing tailored feedback and rewards. Although these are necessary efforts for increasing productivity and performance, they are not sufficient in and of themselves. The timeliness of providing accurate feedback and tailored rewards is an essential factor that cannot be understated.

Evaluative feedback needs to be specific and forthright for it to be effective. Furthermore, it is important to minimize the time delay between performance and feedback and rewards. Generally speaking, the longer the delay in providing rewards, the less value they have and the greater the likelihood that they will reinforce undesirable behavior, such as grumbling and complaining.

Effective managers recognize the value of accurate feedback and immediate rewards. In a timely fashion, they will communicate with an individual or team in person, by e-mail, or by short memo. They understand that whereas the annual formal performance appraisal focuses on long-term goal setting and productivity review, the brief, weekly performance review is essential to make course corrections and provide feedback and recognition in the short term.

## Tap into Employee Passion and Enthusiasm

Passion can be thought of as a strong desire for a particular activity. Employees who are passionate or enthusiastic about a personal or professional interest or some aspect of their job can have a positive impact on co-workers. One powerful key to enhancing workplace motivation is to tap into employee passion and enthusiasm.

Nearly every employee is passionate about some aspect of his or her job or personal or professional life. An employee who is an expert at some aspect of his or her job may enjoy the attention derived from being turned to for advice by both co-workers and superiors. Some employees are passionate about teaching others in seminars or in one-to-one situations. Other employees have a propensity for creativity or problem solving. When opportunities arise that tap into these passions or talents, these employees typically give 110% effort.

Just as the effective manager carefully observes individual differences in employees (i.e., their dominant power, achievement, or affiliation needs) in order to tailor rewards and feedback, the manager should also be attentive to the particular passions of each of his or her employees. The effective manager will find ways of tapping those passions in order to enhance motivation and increase productivity and performance.

*North Shore Health Systems is a regional medical center with some 3,500 employees. It has served the community for more than 60 years and has garnered several awards over that period of time. The most recent honor was being named one of the best health care systems in the region last year by a prominent weekly news magazine. The criteria for this award included service to the community, patient satisfaction, and bed occupancy and productivity, as well as employee morale, absenteeism, and retention rates. In terms of regional and national benchmarks, North Shore was well ahead of other health care institutions in all categories. It is notable that employee absenteeism and turnover rates were among the lowest in the nation, averaging just more than 2% for each of the previous*

*5 years. Survey data showed that the majority of salaried employees would not leave the regional medical center unless they were offered jobs with 25% salary increases and 30% benefits increases. Interviews with North Shore employees revealed four themes: 1) management is perceived as being very concerned about employees, 2) the work environment fosters productivity and high-quality clinical care, 3) North Shore attracts and retains highly competent and caring employees, and 4) employee values match the medical center's values and mission. North Shore exemplifies a health system of committed, motivated employees.*

## EXERCISES FOR SKILL DEVELOPMENT

### Individual Exercise

Using the five strategies for enhancing motivation, design a specific plan for managing a new employee or a new phase of an existing work relationship (i.e., an employee about to begin work on a new project). Write out specific directives on how you would implement each of the five strategies. Now consider meeting with this employee to discuss this plan, including asking for his or her suggestions on implementing this plan. Predict how you would proceed and how the employee is likely to respond.

### Group Exercise

Divide into groups of four to discuss the North Shore Health Systems case example. As a small group, discuss the following elements:

1. Focus first on commitment. Using the four strategies for increasing commitment, suggest how North Shore developed and maintains its high level of commitment.

2. Next focus on level of motivation. Estimate the overall level of motivation for North Shore employees on the four indicators (based on a 1–5 scale).

3. Then, utilizing the five strategies for enhancing motivation, suggest how North Shore developed and maintains its high levels of productivity and quality.

After 30 minutes, return to the large group and compare observations.

## SELF-ASSESSMENT OF SKILL 1:
## GALVANIZING COMMITMENT AND MOTIVATION

**Directions:** This assessment will help you evaluate your level of skill and attitudes toward commitment and motivation. Use the following statements to assess your attitudes and skills by circling the number that is closest to your experience: 1 = never, 2 = sometimes, 3 = often, and 4 = always. Respond in a way that reflects your skills today, rather than those you hope to have in the future. Answer as honestly as you can. Instructions on scoring and interpreting the results are provided in the analysis section at the end of the assessment.

1. I try to persuade and influence employees rather than force them to do what I want.    1    2    3    4

2. I rotate or combine work assignments so employees can use different kinds of skills.    1    2    3    4

3. I design work assignments so they are interesting and challenging.    1    2    3    4

4. I believe that providing adequate resources to employees is a prerequisite to improving their job performance.    1    2    3    4

5. I involve people in issues at the earliest possible opportunity.    1    2    3    4

6. I carefully assess the causes of poor job performance before offering coaching or taking disciplinary action.    1    2    3    4

7. I strive to match an employee's ability and talent with job responsibilities.    1    2    3    4

8. I change benchmarks to keep targets at stimulating levels.    1    2    3    4

9. I review the workflow process in order to remove obstacles to performance.    1    2    3    4

10. I look at assignments and moves as ways
to develop my employees.　1　2　3　4

11. I encourage employees to act on their
own initiatives.　1　2　3　4

12. Knowing that employees have different
needs and wants, I try to personalize
rewards and feedback.　1　2　3　4

13. I reward, recognize, and promote on merit
alone.　1　2　3　4

14. I establish clear standards of expected
performance.　1　2　3　4

15. I ensure that employees feel fairly and
equitably treated.　1　2　3　4

16. I approach performance problems by first
determining whether they are caused by a
lack of ability or lack of motivation.　1　2　3　4

17. I provide immediate positive feedback
and other forms of recognition for work
that is well done.　1　2　3　4

18. I enjoy telling others about the hospital
for which I work.　1　2　3　4

19. Many of my professional needs are met in
my current job.　1　2　3　4

20. I consider my workplace to be the best in
the region.　1　2　3　4

21. I would not be satisfied working for
another health care organization.　1　2　3　4

22. I try my best and give full effort in my
current job.　1　2　3　4

23. Disagreements between my employer
    and me are handled constructively.        1    2    3    4

24. Emotionally, it would be difficult for me to
    leave my current job.                     1    2    3    4

25. Other health care organizations can't
    compare with mine.                        1    2    3    4

### Self-Assessment Analysis

Add your circled scores together to arrive at your total score. Then, refer to the following scoring ranges to identify your level of skill and attitude toward commitment and motivation. You may want to refer back to sections of this skill chapter for suggestions on increasing and honing your commitment and motivation skills.

76–100    You appear to have highly developed commitment and motivation skills and attitudes that facilitate employee performance and professional development. Continue to enhance and maintain these skills.

51–75     You appear to have reasonably well-developed commitment and motivation skills, but certain areas could be improved. By further developing these skills, you can become even more effective in increasing productivity and performance.

25–50     Your commitment and motivation skills appear to need improvement. It may also be that some of your attitudes toward commitment and motivation may hinder employee performance and professional development. You might focus on improving selected skills and attitudes (i.e., items that you scored as 1 or 2).

## REVIEW ACTIVITIES

1. Indicate the level of commitment in your unit and in your health care organization. Suggest which of the five determinants of commitment account for this level of commitment.
2. Based on O'Malley's five determinants of commitment, propose a plan for increasing commitment in your unit.

3. In a sentence or two, describe the relationship between commitment and motivation.
4. In some ways, Theory X versus Theory Y views about work and motivating employees are akin to the "big stick" versus "carrot" approach to motivation. Which view, Theory X or Theory Y, is closer to your experience? What impact does this view have on your leadership and unit effectiveness?
5. Provide a one-sentence summary for the six common theories of motivation. Then, indicate which feature(s) or factor(s) of each theory can be relevant for you in increasing motivation in your unit.
6. Based on your overall score on the Self-Assessment of Skill 1, devise a plan for increasing your motivation skills.

## FOR FURTHER INFORMATION

Manion, J. (1998). *From management to leadership: Interpersonal skills for success in healthcare.* Chicago: American Hospital Publishers.

Manion, a management consultant to health care organizations, makes a strong case for health care managers' focusing on building relationships and increasing commitment among staff. Chapter 3, "Building Commitment: Getting Others to Follow," nicely complements the discussion of commitment in the present chapter.

Kinlaw, D. (1999). *Coaching for commitment: Interpersonal strategies for obtaining superior performance from individuals and teams* (2nd ed.). San Francisco: Jossey-Bass.

This second edition of Kinlaw's text continues to emphasize individual and team coaching as the most direct leverage that managers have in increasing both commitment and performance. The book provides a step-by-step protocol for building commitment.

O'Malley, M. (2000). *Creating commitment: How to attract and retain talented employees by building relationships that last.* New York: John Wiley & Sons.

The basic reference book on the determinants of commitment by an internationally known consultant, this is an indispensable resource for the most current research on employee commitment.

# Maximizing Team Performance

The objectives of this chapter are to

- Discuss the advantages and disadvantages of teams in health care organizations

- Describe the four stages of team development

- Illustrate four different team player styles and their impact on the team process

- Describe the process of team building

- Define high-performing teams and indicate several characteristics of such teams

- Describe eight strategies for effective team leadership

- Assess your attitudes and skills regarding maximizing team performance

- Provide skill development exercises and activities to develop or enhance skills in maximizing team performance

## TEAMS IN HEALTH CARE ORGANIZATIONS

What are teams, and what are the different types of teams? A useful working definition is that a team is "a small number of people with complementary skills who are committed to a common purpose, performance goals, and approach for which they hold themselves mutually accountable" (Katzenbach & Smith, 1993, p. 45).

There are several types of teams in organizations today. *Primary work teams* are ongoing teams organized around the primary work or function of a unit. For example, teams in a medical laboratory department are usually designed around specialized functions such as microbiology, hematology, and chemistry. *Ad hoc teams* are temporary teams that perform a particular task, such as a project team whose purpose is to plan a new medical service, and then dissolve when the task is completed. *Management teams* are formed to provide collective leadership to a department or the entire organization.

Since the 1980s, teams have been a dominant force in increasing productivity and commitment in corporations. Historically, health care organizations were somewhat reluctant to adopt the concept of working in teams, with the exception of surgical teams and the like. Today, these organizations utilize teams in virtually all areas of health care, recognizing that, although not a panacea, teams are particularly useful in dealing with procedures, productivity, quality, relationships, and problem solving. Other benefits of teams in health care settings are notable. For example, team effort often can surpass the efforts of members working independently, employee turnover is decreased when employees are members of teams, and teams lessen dependence on individuals. This means that services do not suffer as much when one member of a team is absent or not available.

However, there are some disadvantages of teamwork in health care settings. In certain situations, teams are not always needed or viable. For instance, specialists can deal with specific situations more expediently without the need to consult with or get approval from other team members. Thus, although employees do depend on each other in most parts of health care, teams are less viable where there are no obvious interdependencies. Furthermore, because considerable time and resources are needed to build a smooth-functioning, effective team, some health care organizations that are financially challenged and operating in a crisis management mode may be less receptive to team building.

## STAGES OF TEAM DEVELOPMENT

Every team moves through a predictable pattern of stages in its development. Various changes in team behaviors, relationships, and leadership demands are associated with these evolving stages. Thus, it is incumbent on managers to understand and be able to recognize these stages. Research reveals four such stages, which were described and labeled by Tuckman (1965). In order of development, they are forming, storming, norming, and performing. Although some research has suggested that the second and third stages are reversed, they are described here in the order originally proposed by Tuckman. Table 1 provides a capsule summary of these four stages.

### Forming

This is the beginning stage of development in which team members start becoming acquainted with each other, with the team's purpose, and with its boundaries. At this stage, members tend to experience a sense of anticipation along with uncertainty resulting from a lack of boundary and rules. Accordingly, they may focus attention on leaders and demonstrate some degree of dependency on such leaders. The goal is not so much to be productive as to establish a sense of purpose. The main task of this stage is to orient members, establish relationships, and develop a sense of trust. The basic task of team leaders is to provide clarity of direction.

### Storming

At this stage of team development, members start feeling more independence and a sense of individuality. In the process, they begin reacting against their dependency on the team leaders and each other. Accordingly, teams must contend with competition among

**Table 1.** Four stages of team development

| Stage | Key task |
|---|---|
| Forming | Become acquainted and establish direction |
| Storming | Manage conflict and growing pains |
| Norming | Create cohesiveness and enhanced commitment |
| Performing | Continue improvement |

members, dissension, testing of rules and boundaries, negativity, and violations of team expectations. The main task of this stage is to effectively manage conflicts and turn negative dependence into interdependence. This stage truly tests the mettle of team leaders because the very viability of the team is at stake. In order to emerge from this very trying but necessary stage, effective leadership is essential. Accordingly, team leaders must strive to foster consensus building, recognize team achievement while legitimizing productive expressions of individuality, and encourage win–win relationships.

## Norming

At this stage of its development, the team is faced with reestablishing a sense of stability, loyalty, and focus that was challenged in the storming stage. To become highly effective, a team must share a common vision and develop a cohesive team culture. As a team increases its commitment and clarifies norms and expectations, members experience increasing peer pressure to adhere to those norms and expectations. Not surprising, dealing with the tendency toward groupthink (i.e., the agreement by the team not to disagree), as well as exclusivity (i.e., decreasing receptivity to diversity and "outsiders"), are major challenges for the group at this stage. The main tasks of this stage are to foster empowerment and participation, increase and maintain a sense of cohesion, and provide feedback to members on their performance. The leader's tasks are to foster cooperation and commitment to a common vision, provide supportive feedback, and manage tendencies toward groupthink.

## Performing

At this stage of its development, the team is able to experience high levels of efficiency and effectiveness because it has worked through the challenges of the previous stages of development. It has developed high levels of trust, loyalty, and morale, and team members have a strong personal commitment to the team. Because it has overcome the tendencies to groupthink and of exclusivity and can function interdependently, it is on its way to becoming a "high-performing team." The main tasks at this stage are to foster a culture of innovation and continuous improvement, encourage creative problem solving, and capitalize on core competencies. The leader's basic task is to upgrade and elevate team performance such that the group becomes a high-performing team.

## TEAM PLAYER STYLES

Effective and high-performing teams maximize the talents, skills, and personal styles of their members. Research indicates that there are four basic personal styles that contribute in different ways to the success or downfall of a team. Parker (1996) described four such "team player styles" and their unique contributions to team process and team functioning. A brief description of these team player styles is presented here. Table 2 summarizes the main contribution of each style to team functioning.

**Contributor:** The contributor is a task-oriented team member who can be expected to provide other team members with input in the form of data, suggestions, and feedback. Individuals with this team player style typically challenge the team to set high performance standards and to utilize human and financial resources wisely. They tend to be logical, dependable, responsible, organized, and resourceful individuals.

**Collaborator:** The collaborator is a goal-oriented team member who can be expected to keep the team focused on its vision and goals. Individuals with this team player style can be expected to be open to new ideas, to follow through on commitments, and to share the limelight with others. They tend to be imaginative, cooperative, generous, and confident individuals.

**Communicator:** Of all the team player styles, the communicator is the most process oriented. These individuals have the capacity to listen well, to provide feedback, to encourage others' involvement, to resolve conflict, and to build consensus. They can be

Table 2.   Four personal styles among team members

| Style | Main contribution to the team |
| --- | --- |
| Contributor | Provides input and high performance standards |
| Collaborator | Maintains the team's focus on its vision and goals |
| Communicator | Fosters a positive, relaxed work environment |
| Challenger | Encourages the team to take risks and act ethically |

expected to create a relaxed, informal environment. They tend to be pleasant, patient, tactful, considerate, and genuinely helpful individuals.

**Challenger:** The team member who is most likely to question the team's direction, motives, and actions is the challenger. These individuals take risks and encourage other team members to do the same. They are willing and able to disagree with those in authority. They tend to be candid, adventurous, and highly ethical.

Of the many factors that contribute to a team's effectiveness and success, a balance of team player styles is an important factor. Effective teams tend to be composed of a balance of all four styles. Managers will do well to consider personal styles when selecting team members in order to achieve a good balance among the styles. Parker (1996) provided a useful self-assessment inventory, The Team Player Survey, that managers can use to determine the basic team player styles of their employees. In addition, he described and illustrated how each of these styles has an impact on and is influenced during each of the four stages of team development.

## TEAM BUILDING

Team building is a systematic process for unifying the efforts and galvanizing the commitment of a group of employees with common objectives into an effective and efficient functioning work team. The goals of team building are quite lofty in that team building attempts to foster increased productivity while maintaining high levels of quality as well as improving work relationships, commitment, and job satisfaction.

Team building is a continuous process that requires a number of basic changes in manager attitudes and behavior, employee attitudes and behavior, reward systems, and corporate culture. Successful team building requires both shared power and authority, and increased employee participation.

The basic premise of team building challenges traditional managerial attitudes regarding control and command. Not surprising, then, team building is bound to fail if managers insist on exerting control over a team and its members. Similarly, team building requires a high degree of cooperation and collaboration among team members. Employees who prefer to work alone and compete with their co-workers for rewards and recognition may find team-building efforts exasperating and threatening. An inability or un-willingness to cooperate on the part of a team member is a prelude to failure of the team. In addition, organizational culture can either foster or inhibit team-building efforts. A culture that fosters competition and individual accomplishment, and downplays the value of information sharing among individuals and units, cannot support team-building efforts.

## Implementing and Maintaining the Team-Building Process

Implementing team building in a health care organization begins at the top. First of all, top management must visibly demonstrate its commitment to and support for a team approach. At a minimum, this requires a concerted effort to educate managers and employees about teams and modify management attitudes, reward systems, and organizational culture so that they facilitate rather than impede the team-building process. In addition, employees must be expected to take responsibility for the success of team building. They must be willing and able to cooperate and collaborate with other team members.

How is the team-building process actually initiated? Ideally, a manager with previous successful experience in team building initiates the process on site by selecting appropriate team members and coaching them about what it means to function as a team. Alternatively, an internal or external consultant is asked to initiate this process in conjunction with the manager. In the past, the team-building process was facilitated by a consultant who utilized various group process methods (e.g., group trust exercises, "rope courses," river rafting) to help the members of a new—and sometimes an already established—team learn to become comfortable working with one another. This type of off-site "retreat" is less common today.

As a team continues to develop, it is essential for its members to meet periodically, usually for a day or so quarterly, to formally address the team-building process and issues involving goals and performance. The more team building becomes an integral part of a team's operations, the more likely the team is to increase its effectiveness and productivity.

Here are some effective tactics that managers should consider in the ongoing process of building and maintaining a team:

- Articulate high standards for the team.
- Role-model the behavior expected from team members.
- Assess for complementarity of skills and personal styles in selecting new members.
- Keep the team size to between 8 and 12 members to optimize team functioning.
- Reward high-performing team members.

# CHARACTERISTICS OF HIGH-PERFORMING TEAMS

It has been estimated that more than 80% of employees are involved in some form of teamwork. Although teams are being used extensively today, not all teams are particularly effective. Teams with very high levels of effectiveness are designated as high-performing teams. Such teams share a number of common characteristics (see Table 3), as described by Hackman (1990) and Katzenbach and Smith (1993). The reader will note that these characteristics are integrally related.

**Shared vision**—Team members share a specific purpose and vision. The specificity of this vision and the team's short-term goals serve as a source of both motivation and commitment to their mutually coordinated efforts.

**Outcomes oriented**—The primary focus is on achieving results or outcomes. The expected outcome is the central preoccupation of the team from initial planning through implementation and on to monitoring performance. Achieving this result requires a high degree of single-mindedness and closely coordinated team effort.

**Table 3.**   Characteristics of a high-performing team

Shared vision
Outcomes oriented
Coordination
Quality
Competency

*Source:* Hackman (1990) and Katzenbach and Smith (1993).

**Coordination**—Work roles are shared and coordinated in such a manner that the outcome is a team accomplishment rather than a set of individual accomplishments. Such a level of coordination requires a high degree of mutual trust and commitment. It also requires that team members possess high-level technical, conceptual, and interpersonal skills.

**Quality**—Team members seek to achieve the highest levels of quality and ongoing or continuous quality improvement. Their goal is to achieve a level of quality above the expected standard of performance and then to supersede that level in subsequent efforts. This requires very high levels of commitment, coordination, and competency.

**Competency**—Team members exhibit very high levels of skills and competencies. These include interpersonal skills such as empathy, two-way communication, and conflict resolution; conceptual or analytical skills such as strategic thinking, problem solving, and decision making; and finely honed technical skills.

## STRATEGIES FOR EFFECTIVE TEAM LEADERSHIP

1. *Foster an organizational culture that values teams.* One aspect of creating such a team-friendly culture is to review and reconsider reward structures as well as policies and procedures that may foster individual achievement and competition.

2. *Foster team decision making.* A manager who is successful in team building recognizes that giving team members a voice in decision making is not a sign of weakness or an abrogation of the manager's responsibility but rather demonstrates the manager's confidence in his or her employees. Team decision making increases the team member's ownership of those decisions and improves their commitment to productivity as well as to the organization.

3. *Select job candidates who have proven team skills.* Not all job candidates have the desire or capability for being an effective team member. Some individuals prefer to work alone. It cannot be assumed that because a candidate has the requisite technical skills, he or she can learn to work collaboratively on a team. Instead, in addition to technical skills and experience, look for

candidates who have the requisite interpersonal and decision-making skills to function as a team member.

4. *Clarify the mission and articulate a vision and goals for the team.* Articulating a motivating vision for a team is a manager's main task, because a vision gives a sense of direction, evokes commitment, and serves to bind a team together. Flowing from this vision is a particular mission and set of goals that the manager must clarify and routinely reassert. It can be quite useful to draft a team mission statement, for example: "Our team is committed to providing quality care at low cost to cardiac by-pass patients. Staff maintain their expertise and commitment through continuing education and team-building retreats."

5. *Provide training to develop or enhance team skills.* Training that increases requisite team skills such as supportive communication, empowerment, active listening, and decision making increases the likelihood that a team will be committed, efficient, and productive.

6. *Provide teams opportunities for autonomy.* Managers who need to exert command and control over a team cannot fathom a team functioning with autonomy. However, autonomy is essential for a team to become highly effective and efficient. Thus, managers need to provide teams with opportunities to function independently as well as interdependently. Delegation of given tasks and specific decisions, such as letting the team select new members, fosters autonomy.

7. *Demonstrate integrity and credibility.* Being believable, honest, trustworthy, and fair are characteristic of an individual with a high degree of credibility. Integrity, a prerequisite of credibility, refers to the soundness of one's moral character. Credibility is considered the essential requirement for leadership effectiveness (Kouzes & Posner, 1987). Credibility increases not only an employee's confidence in a leader but also the leader's influence over the employee. A manager who is not viewed as credible is unlikely to develop a high-performance team.

8. *Be readily available to team members.* Availability and visibility reinforce a manager's commitment to the team and provide assurance of assistance and support. Managers who seem to be tied up perpetually with meetings or special projects or frequently are gone are not viewed by employees as true team members. A manager who is not available is not likely to succeed at building an effective team.

*Celebration Health, part of the Florida Hospital Systems, is an experiment in re-visioning health care. Since 1998, the inpatient hospital wing has become a learning lab for other hospitals throughout the nation. Celebration's vision is "care for the whole person for the person's whole life." This relatively new hospital subscribes to the belief that truly effective health care must be focused as much on helping individuals create healthy lifestyles as on dealing with disease. As a bold experiment, Celebration adopted a unique integrated services approach in which inpatient hospital rooms are specially constructed and licensed as "universal rooms," meaning that any hospital room can be used for multiple purposes, such as intensive or critical care or labor and delivery, as need and patient census dictate. This design permits maximum staffing flexibility while minimizing costs.*

*Celebration Health anticipated that getting traditionally trained staff to "buy into" this new approach would be a major challenge. Accordingly, they instituted an intensive educational program emphasizing team building. Today, ongoing staff education and the team-building process continue, with one day in each quarter devoted to both education and team building in order to reinforce and refine the change process. The results of these efforts have been a 10%–15% increase in staff productivity, substantial cost savings, and increased patient satisfaction. In short, successful implementation of this bold experiment in health care was made possible because of ongoing team building.[1]*

## EXERCISES FOR SKILL DEVELOPMENT

### Individual Exercise

Consider the following case example:

*Julie Snow had been the Director of Nursing for a small community hospital for only 1 week before she learned firsthand that nurses, nursing assistants, and secretaries on one of the medical-surgical units were constantly in conflict. For example, nursing assistants complained that nurses assigned them to all of the difficult patients and then were unwilling to help them when needed.*

---

[1]A detailed account of Celebration Health is found in Linda Gambee Henry & James Douglas Henry's (1999) book, *Reclaiming Soul in Health Care: Practical Strategies for Revitalizing Providers of Care.*

*Conversely, the nurses contended that the nursing assistants were not answering call lights or assisting with patients. The nurses also alleged that unit secretaries withheld information from them when patients left the floor for lab tests or if their assigned patients needed assistance. In turn, the secretaries said that nurses refused to help transcribe physician orders, schedule tests, and answer phones. This led the nurses to assert that the secretaries spent an inordinate amount of time on personal tasks and expected nursing staff to do much of the unit secretaries' work.*

*Ms. Snow observed that nurses and nursing assistants usually attended to their own assigned duties but did not help out when others were swamped. She also learned, to her dismay, that this unit had functioned this way for nearly 3 years, a situation her predecessor had ignored.*

Now analyze the case in terms of the following issues:

1.  Describe the situation on the medical-surgical unit. Include speculation about the team's stage of development and leadership issues.

2.  Outline a plan for team building in this unit. Indicate how you would proceed to unify the efforts of team members. Draft a suitable unit mission statement.

3.  Indicate the role you believe Julie Snow could take to best facilitate the team-building process. If Snow chooses not to address the problem, as did her predecessor, predict the likely long-term consequences.

### Group Exercise

In small groups of four, consider the following case example:

*Jordon Smeely is the vice president in charge of several projects at a large, upscale long-term care facility. He had assigned Emilio Cruz, one of his managers, to develop a new staffing plan for the facility. Cruz had been hired 6 months earlier and led a team of six employees drawn from the nursing facility. Smeely had met with Cruz on several occasions about the project. In their last meeting, Smeely had expressed his exasperation with Cruz's difficulty in getting the team to do its work. It seemed to Smeely that the team had been at an impasse for at least a month and nothing was getting done. Three members had recently quit the team after a shouting match with Cruz, and the other were quite de-*

*moralized. When Cruz said that Smeely had failed to assign re-*
*placement members to the team and to support and back up his*
*actions, Smeely's anger erupted. He berated Cruz for his con-*
*stant complaining, lack of team leadership, and ongoing overde-*
*pendency on Smeely for advice and direction.*

Now analyze the case in terms of the following issues:

1. Estimate the stage of development of Cruz's team. Offer documentation for your answer. Specify the tasks that a team is expected to address at this stage. Indicate the tasks that Cruz, as team leader, is probably not addressing.

2. Propose a plan of action for Cruz that would move this team forward. Be specific in proposing a mission statement, indicating who should choose replacement members and so forth.

3. Suggest how Smeely might respond more effectively to Cruz and the situation.

## SELF-ASSESSMENT OF SKILL 2:
## MAXIMIZING TEAM PERFORMANCE

**Directions:** This assessment will help you evaluate your level of skill and attitudes toward maximizing team performance. Use the following statements to assess your attitudes and skills by circling the number that is closest to your experience: 1 = never, 2 = sometimes, 3 = often, and 4 = always. Respond in a way that reflects your skills today, rather than those you hope to have in the future. Answer as honestly as you can. Instructions on scoring and interpreting the results are provided in the analysis section at the end of the assessment.

1. I give my team precise goals and
   communicate them clearly.　　　　　　　1　2　3　4

2. I strive to match my leadership style to
   suit team need and circumstances.　　　1　2　3　4

3. I encourage team members to talk with
   me about any problems.　　　　　　　　1　2　3　4

4.  I allow the team to have input in any decision that affects it.             1   2   3   4

5.  I share the leadership function with other team members.                    1   2   3   4

6.  I spend time with the team outside work hours to build team spirit and informally discuss matters.       1   2   3   4

7.  I am clear and consistent in what I want the team to accomplish.            1   2   3   4

8.  I strive to show team members that I trust them implicitly.                 1   2   3   4

9.  I look for underlying causes of problems that affect our team.             1   2   3   4

10. As long as it is not confidential, I pass on all relevant information to our team.    1   2   3   4

11. I strive to eliminate conflict arising from overlap of role responsibility in our team.    1   2   3   4

12. I use various methods to foster unity and cohesion among team members.      1   2   3   4

13. I make sure that team meetings are planned well in advance and always provide agendas.    1   2   3   4

14. I promptly address personal problems and issues that arise in the team.     1   2   3   4

15. I encourage team members to think "outside the box."                        1   2   3   4

16. I stress the importance of strategic thinking, and I model it for the team.    1   2   3   4

17. I frequently monitor team morale.           1   2   3   4

18. I am firm but fair in dealing with problems
    in our team.                                                        1   2   3   4

19. I monitor the projects worked on by
    individual team members.     1   2   3   4

20. I set high standards of team performance
    and outcomes.     1   2   3   4

21. I offer encouragement and coaching to
    team members to improve their
    performance.     1   2   3   4

22. I lay out a clear vision and specific short-
    term goals of what our team can
    accomplish.     1   2   3   4

23. I recruit job candidates who have proven
    team skills.     1   2   3   4

24. I strive to foster a culture that values
    teams and team development.     1   2   3   4

25. I use a variety of methods to facilitate
    task accomplishment in the team.     1   2   3   4

### Self-Assessment Analysis

Add your circled scores together to arrive at your total score. Then, refer to the scoring ranges below to identify your level of skill performance and attitudes toward maximizing team performance. You may want to refer back to sections of this chapter for suggestions on increasing and honing your team performance skills.

76–100    You appear to have highly developed team performance skills and attitudes that facilitate employee performance and professional development. Continue to enhance and maintain these skills.

51–75    You appear to have reasonably well-developed team performance skills, but certain areas could be improved. By further developing these skills, you can become even more effective in increasing productivity and performance.

25–50　　Your team performance skills appear to need improvement. It may also be that some of your attitudes toward team performance may hinder employee performance and professional development. You might focus on improving selected skills and attitudes (i.e., items that you scored as 1 or 2).

## REVIEW ACTIVITIES

1. Describe the use of teams in your unit as well as in your health care organization. What organizational and personal factors seem to facilitate or delimit their use?
2. Propose a plan for increasing the utilization of teams in your unit.
3. Summarize the key points for each of the four stages of team development.
4. Identify the team player styles of yourself and your employees. Indicate how the mix of these styles has a positive or negative impact on your unit's performance.
5. Team building is becoming more widespread in health care organizations. How could team building be incorporated in your unit or organization? Sketch a brief action plan.
6. List the characteristics of high-performing teams. Now evaluate one or more teams with which you are familiar—in or outside your health care organization—on these characteristics, using a 5-point scale in which 1 = very low and 5 = very high.
7. List the eight strategies for effective team leadership. Now evaluate one or more team leaders who are familiar to you— you may include yourself—with regard to these strategies, using a 5-point scale in which 1 = very low and 5 = very high.
8. Based on your overall score on the Self-Assessment of Skill 2, devise a plan for increasing your team performance skills.

## FOR FURTHER INFORMATION

Parker, G. (1996). *Team players and teamwork: The new competitive business strategy.* San Francisco: Jossey-Bass.

Parker not only describes the four team-player styles, but he shows how these styles relate to and influence the four stages of team development: forming, storming, norming, and performing. A short, but very informative, book.

Katzenbach, J., & Smith, D. (1993). *The wisdom of teams: Creating the high-performance organization.* Boston: Harvard Business School Press.

An award-winning book that makes the case that high-level productivity cannot easily be achieved without teams and team development. Probably the best of Katzenbach's books on teams.

Manion, J., Lorimer, W., & Leander, W. (1996). *Team-based health care organizations.* Gaithersburg, MD: Aspen.

One of the few books on team development that focuses specifically on teams in health care settings. The senior author, Jo Manion, is the author of the acclaimed book *From Management to Leadership: Interpersonal Skills for Success in Health Care* (American Hospital Publishers, 1998).

# Delegating to
# Maximize Performance

Delegation requires a broad range of management skills, including engagement, communication, empowerment, and monitoring skills. The objectives of this chapter are to

- Describe the value and utility of delegation and empowerment in health care organizations

- Define and illustrate the skill of empowered delegation

- Assess your attitudes and skills regarding delegation

- Provide skill development exercises and activities to develop or enhance skills in delegation

## THE NEED FOR EMPOWERED DELEGATION

This chapter addresses the manager's role with regard to empowered delegation. Empowered delegation is a strategy by which managers assign an employee a task while simultaneously empowering that employee to successfully complete the task (Whetten &

Cameron, 2002). Unfortunately, the current climate in health care is not particularly compatible with empowerment, and, as a result, managers are less likely to foster empowered delegation. To the extent that they face shorter deadlines and increased demands for productivity, managers are likely to feel threatened and seek more power and control over people and situations. Nevertheless, health care organizations are less likely to succeed without empowered employees.

Why is empowered delegation important? Fostering a sense of empowerment in others and delegating in ways that empower employees result in several important outcomes for health care organizations.

> Empowered employees are more productive, psychologically and physically healthy, proactive and innovative, persistent in work, trustworthy, interpersonally effective, intrinsically motivated, and have higher morale and commitment than employees who are not empowered. (Whetten & Cameron, 2002, p. 437)

Thus, learning how to become an empowering manager who can effectively delegate is critical for managers.

## DELEGATION, EMPOWERMENT, AND EMPOWERED DELEGATION

### Delegation

Traditionally, delegation is understood as entrusting an employee with a task for which the manager remains ultimately responsible. Delegation can range from a major appointment, such as the leadership of a Joint Commission on the Accreditation of Healthcare Organization accreditation preparation team to one of any number of smaller tasks in the everyday life of the health care organization, such as arranging a continuing medical education (CME) or continuing education (CE) program or interviewing a job candidate.

Two basic issues involved in the process of delegation are control and autonomy. The first issue, control, is the matter of authority and influence for manager and employee. How much authority will the delegated employee be able to exercise without referring back to the manager, and how far should the manager exercise direct influence over the work of the employee? When choosing a delegate, the manager assesses whether a given employee is capable of performing the task with available resources and can, in fact, perform the task. The second issue is autonomy. Will the employee be given sufficient autonomy to undertake the task in his or her own way?

Delegation has a number of benefits. First and foremost, delegation allows managers to unburden themselves of less essential management tasks and free up time for more essential management tasks and functions. With more streamlined workloads, they are more available to engage in essential managerial tasks such as coaching, encouragement, and monitoring performance. In other words, delegation increases a manager's efficiency but not necessarily his or her effectiveness.

## Empowerment

Empowerment is a strategy for helping others to act and feel more competent and confident. A manager does not directly empower employees but, rather, creates situations in which employees can empower themselves. Empowerment results when managers are successful in fostering five attributes in others: self-efficacy, self-determination, personal control, trust, and a sense of meaning (Whetten & Cameron, 2002). Self-efficacy is the sense of possessing the capacity and competence to perform a task successfully. Self-determination is the sense of having a choice and the freedom to initiate and be involved in tasks of one's own choosing. Personal control refers to the capability to effect change and exert a measure of control over the external environment. Trust is a sense of security and the assurance of being treated fairly. A sense of meaning refers to the sense of a purpose to, involvement in, and caring about the activities in which one engages.

How can managers actively foster empowerment? Several strategies are suggested:

1. Articulate a vision and goals that specify desired outcomes.
2. Assist employees in mastering challenges or problems.
3. Model the correct behavior.
4. Provide social and emotional support.
5. Replace negative emotions with positive emotions.

6. Provide resources needed to accomplish the task.
7. Connect efforts to outcomes.
8. Create a sense of confidence in the trustworthiness of the manager.

## Empowered Delegation

Empowered delegation stands in contrast to the traditional view of delegation wherein burdensome tasks are basically shifted from managers to employees, which may result in resentful feelings and a sense of disempowerment. As noted previously, empowered delegation is a strategy by which managers assign a task while simultaneously empowering employees. Whetten and Cameron (2002) indicated that empowered delegation typically develops employees' knowledge base, capabilities, and sense of personal mastery. They noted research indicating that empowered delegation also increases employee involvement, commitment, and job satisfaction. Unlike the traditional view of delegation, wherein only the manager's efficiency is increased, empowered delegation increases productivity and effectiveness as well as efficiency.

Whetten and Cameron suggested some guidelines that managers can employ to empower employees:

1. Begin with the end in mind.
2. Allow employee participation in the assignment of tasks.
3. Establish parity between authority and responsibility.
4. Focus accountability on results.
5. Delegate consistently.
6. Clarify consequences.

## BARRIERS TO DELEGATION

Whereas some managers are in favor of delegation, others are not. Barriers preventing delegation are often based on negative feelings of insecurity and mistrust. Lack of confidence in employees is a common barrier to delegation. Managers who subscribe to the philosophy that "if you want it done right, do it yourself" are basically asserting their lack of trust that employees are sufficiently resourceful and responsible to handle delegated tasks. Even though managers may be more proficient and efficient at many tasks than their staff, efforts to do too many of those tasks inevitably lead to being overburdened. As a result, these managers have less time to spend on the higher level tasks that cannot be delegated. Furthermore, employees cannot increase their proficiency and efficiency unless they are given the opportunity to learn and perform a broader range of tasks.

There are also organizational barriers to delegation. Such barriers usually reflect the organization's systems of incentives, delegation practices of senior management, and the culture of the organization. When incentives are based solely on measures such as quarterly productivity targets and do not recognize the value of developing employee competence and commitment, managers may be less inclined to delegate, particularly if senior management does not model empowered delegation. Furthermore, health care organizations that have adopted a crisis management culture tend to downplay delegation, regarding it as time consuming and diverting managers' attention away from "more important matters." Similarly, organizational cultures that are highly competitive or individualistic may reinforce managers' belief in doing things themselves so that they are done right. Conversely, health care organizations that are receptive to empowerment are most likely to favor and support delegation.

## THE DECISION TO DELEGATE: WHAT AND TO WHOM

### What to Delegate and to Retain

The decision to delegate begins with a determination of what tasks and responsibilities a manager can and probably should delegate and what tasks and responsibilities he or she cannot delegate. This decision process involves the manager assessing his or her time and that of employees and grouping and prioritizing his or her current responsibilities. Table 1 lists examples of tasks that managers can and cannot delegate.

Tasks that managers cannot delegate include key areas such as controlling overall performance and confidential human resources matters (i.e., how employees are rewarded, appraised, promoted, informed, coached, and counseled), as well as negotiating the unit's

**Table 1.** Delegable and nondelegable responsibilities

| Can be delegated | Cannot be delegated |
| --- | --- |
| Tactical | Strategic |
| • Planning operational initiatives<br>• Implementing strategic initiatives | • Clarifying the unit's vision<br>• Establishing key goals, targets, and implementation plan |
| Staff functions | Leadership functions |
| • Drafting routine administrative reports<br>• Compiling and analyzing data; program development<br>• Selected project management tasks<br>• Writing proposals<br>• Preparing CME/CEU (continuing medical education/continuing education unit) and other training programs | • Overall responsibility for providing direction and stewardship to a project or work unit<br>• Negotiating the annual budget<br>• Representing the unit's needs with management<br>• Developing and challenging staff to maximize their performance |
| Personnel | Personnel |
| • Serving on search committees<br>• Proposing and/or examining salary, bonus, benefits and nonfinancial rewards criteria<br>• Performing feasibility studies | • Hiring decisions<br>• Performing annual performance reviews<br>• Coaching employees<br>• Disciplinary actions<br>• Setting parameters for salaries/bonuses and significant nonfinancial rewards |
| Outcomes and quality | Outcomes and quality |
| • Collecting and analyzing productivity, performance outcomes, and quality data | • Setting goals<br>• Monitoring progress toward goals<br>• Setting quality standards and ensuring standards are met |
| Less sensitive tasks | Highly sensitive tasks |
| • Other routine tasks | • Confidential personnel and operational matters, often involving contract negotiations, legal, or compliance issues |

annual budget with superiors. Nondelegable tasks also include strategic responsibilities such as setting key goals and targets and ensuring that key initiatives are achieved. Certainly, they include challenging and developing staff to perform their best. Managers also may need to handle all dealings with important customers.

Tasks that primarily involve daily operations are most likely to be delegated—in part or totally—to staff. These include compiling data and routine administrative reports, handling technical duties, and setting work schedules and work flow.

## To Whom to Delegate

Having clearly defined the tasks involved, the manager must carefully consider the qualities of all members of his or her team and begin thinking about which delegable responsibilities may suit each individual, taking into account his or her strengths and potential. For important tasks, the manager should choose employees who are able and willing, meaning those who possess the requisite skills and competence as well as those who are motivated to undertake the task. These tend to be empowered employees and represent the best bet for delegation, assuming that they are available or can be freed up for the task. For less important tasks or responsibilities in which time is not of the essence, the manager should look to employees who may be less able although highly willing, that is, less experienced individuals who are highly motivated. These employees will need coaching to develop the necessary level of skill and competence required for the task.

It is important for managers to recognize the challenges presented by delegating responsibilities to employees who are able but not particularly willing or who are both unable and unwilling. Often, considerable coaching, and even counseling, may be necessary with these individuals before they can be expected to successfully handle a delegated responsibility. Here, the task is to increase their willingness and sense of empowerment.

## SIX STEPS TO EFFECTIVE DELEGATION

The process of delegation begins with the manager's decision to delegate a given responsibility and the selection of the employee to whom the responsibility will be delegated. Assuming the employee agrees to take on the delegated responsibility, the process of delegation moves into high gear. An initial meeting is held to formalize the delegation, followed by ongoing meetings to review progress. A six-step protocol is provided in Table 2 to guide that initial meeting, in which the first five steps should be accomplished, as well as the follow-up meetings.

**Table 2.** Six-step delegation protocol

| Steps | Description |
|---|---|
| 1. Specify the task and expectations for performance | Describe the task and its purpose, its importance, and your expectations for 1) work product or deliverables and 2) performance standards |
| 2. Define the parameters and boundaries | Indicate the specific direction and limits you want heeded in terms of 1) timeline (i.e., deadlines), 2) budget, and 3) decisional authority |
| 3. Provide the necessary resource allocation | Together with the employee, discuss resources needs and allocation, that is, personnel, adjustment in priorities and duties, training or coaching, expenses, materials, and so forth. |
| 4. Recap the employee's understanding of the task | Check the employee's understanding of the task and expectations by saying, "Please recap for me what you're being asked to do and the expectations for it." Asking "Did you understand what I want you to do?" will not elicit such an understanding. |
| 5. Schedule progress reviews | Set up a schedule of checkpoint meetings to regularly monitor progress. The newer the assignment to an employee, the more frequently meetings should be scheduled |
| 6. Evaluate and provide feedback | Each checkpoint meeting recognizes the progress made. Provide both positive and negative feedback, as indicated, to keep the task on course. |

An initial delegation meeting usually takes 10–30 minutes. In preparation for this meeting, the manager could use the six-step protocol to think about expectations, consider parameters, and project anticipated resource allocation and reallocation. The following case example provides a detailed account of how such a meeting would proceed.

> *Gerry is the Director of Program Development for the university medical center. For the past few years, the medical center's executive committee has wanted to establish a distance learning capacity to extend its continuing education programs to nursing and medical personnel throughout the region who are unable to take time off and travel to the university medical center to attend these training programs. Gerry's department of three program specialists and an administrative assistant already had oversight of nearly 60 CEU/CME programs offered on site annually. She has been asked to prepare a proposal for a small pilot project. Gerry reviewed her*

*staff and turned to Jesse, a program specialist who had, at his last performance appraisal review, expressed interest in "stretching" beyond his current job responsibilities. Although Jesse had been involved in completing feasibility studies, he had not been involved in proposal writing. Gerry arranged to meet with Jesse to discuss the delegated task, utilizing the six-step delegation protocol to structure the meeting. Here is how that meeting proceeded.*

*Step 1: Gerry described the proposed distance learning project in general terms. It was to target primarily nurses and physicians in need of CEU/CME units for license renewal. It would coordinate the efforts of current on-site CEU/CME programs and selectively reconfigure some of them in a distance learning format. The purpose of the delegation was to develop a cost-effective program proposal. Gerry then outlined the results she expected:*

*Work products: These include a detailed proposal containing the results of a feasibility study, program outlines, implementation plan, and budget projections for translating two existing on-site nursing and two medical continuing education courses. The final draft proposal would be presented by Gerry and Jesse to the executive committee at their next monthly meeting.*

*Performance standards: These include a clear and precise proposal with executive summary, rationale, results of the feasibility and marketing study, outlines of the four courses, implementation time lines, and detailed staff, equipment, and budget projections.*

*Step 2: Gerry established the following parameters:*

*Time line: The first draft of the proposal was due in 90 days. It would be jointly reviewed, and a final proposal would be due 2 weeks later.*

*Budget: This includes the cost of preparing a mailed survey and other efforts to establish the feasibility of the project and buy-in by current nursing and medical faculty who might be involved in working with the distance learning effort, as well as a data analysis budget.*

*Decisional authority: Ann, Gerry's administrative assistant, would assist Jesse as he saw fit in preparing the proposal. In his fact-finding meetings and discussions, Jesse was to talk only of the possibility—not the inevitability—of a distance learning format.*

*Step 3: Gerry would send a memo to the other department staff briefing them on Jesse's new responsibility. She would also meet with the other program specialists to redeploy some of Jesse's other responsibilities. She also agreed to coach Jesse on proposal writing.*

*It was agreed that at least 0.5 full-time equivalent (FTE) release time was needed for Jesse for 3.5 months. Ann would be available up to 0.25 FTE to assist Jesse.*

*Step 4: Jesse was able to summarize the project goals and expectations. He was pleased to be asked to head up the project and expressed his eagerness to get started.*

*Steps 5 and 6: Gerry suggested they meet weekly for the duration of the project to review progress. Jesse agreed to develop a list of checkpoints for the project with a timeline and Gantt chart for the next 4 months. They both agreed that the feasibility survey was the first priority and needed to be designed, printed, and mailed within 3 weeks. The review meetings would focus on progress toward meeting the checkpoints. Coaching on proposal writing would begin as soon as the survey was mailed.*

## EXERCISES FOR SKILL DEVELOPMENT

### Individual Exercises

1.   Make a list of your job responsibilities. Label those items that you need to keep with a *k*, those that you can completely reassign with an *r*, and those that you can partially reassign with a *p*.

2.   Recall a past experience of delegating or being delegated a task. How well was the delegation process handled? Compare the process with the six-step protocol presented here. Indicate which steps were effectively addressed and which were not.

3.   Plan how you will delegate a responsibility to one of your employees. Indicate which task will be delegated and how you chose it, as well as whom you chose as the delegate and why you chose that person. Then, lay out a game plan based on the six-step protocol for conducting the initial meeting and checkpoint follow-up meetings.

### Group Exercises

Divide into groups of four, and discuss the following case example:

*As director of hospital security, Andrews took pride in the fact that reported crime and safety incident statistics had declined during each of the 3 years he had been in charge of security. Several months ago, he had proposed a shuttle service for employees on the second and third shifts who parked their cars in a distant lot, but it was questionable whether funds would be available for both a shuttle vehicle and a driver. Andrews was pleasantly surprised when the board of directors approved the purchase of a small shuttle bus, although they did not give approval for a driver. Andrews believed that his own security force could drive the shuttle, and delegated the task of coordinating that effort to Roosevelt, the captain of the day shift and a long-time member of the security force. Roosevelt agreed to take on this responsibility. They met and Andrews laid out his view on how this security measure could be implemented. In the following week, Andrews was pleased to see that a driving schedule had been developed for the second and third shifts. A week later, he met with Roosevelt and learned that things seemed to going smoothly with the project. Every now and then, when Andrews saw Roosevelt and asked him how things were going, the answer was "pretty good."*

*When the next quarterly security report was being readied for the hospital administrator, Andrews noticed there were no statistics reported on shuttle bus usage or employee satisfaction with the service. He called Roosevelt to get the figures, only to learn that they were not being collected. On further inquiry with the captains of the second and third shift, Andrews learned that Roosevelt had only once met with the night shift staff and had never mentioned anything about collecting statistics on employees using the shuttle. In checking the employee newsletter, Andrews was not able to find any stories about the shuttle service, nor did he find any posted notices about the services. He specifically recalled telling Roosevelt to advertise the service and to arrange to have usage and satisfaction statistics collected. When Andrews met face to face with Roosevelt, he expressed his dismay about how this delegated task was handled.*

1. In your small group, analyze the case using the six-step delegation protocol. Indicate what the chief of security did and did not do to ensure that the delegated project would succeed.

2. Now role-play the first meeting between Andrews and Roosevelt following the first five steps of the six-step protocol. Divide into pairs, with one person playing Andrews and the other Roosevelt.

Plan on 10 minutes for the role play. Reverse roles and role-play the scenario again.

3. Return to the large group and discuss the role-play experience.

## SELF-ASSESSMENT OF SKILL 3: DELEGATING TO MAXIMIZE PERFORMANCE

**Directions:** This assessment will help you evaluate your level of skill and attitudes toward delegation. Use the following statements to assess your attitudes and skill by circling the number that is closest to your experience: 1 = never, 2 = sometimes, 3 = often, and 4 = always. Respond in a way that reflects your skills today, rather than those you hope to have in the future. Answer as honestly as you can. Instructions on scoring and interpreting the results are provided in the analysis section at the end of the assessment.

1. When I delegate tasks, my staff are clear about standards of performance and time frames.     1   2   3   4

2. I give my staff the benefit of the doubt but act quickly if I must replace a delegate.     1   2   3   4

3. I try to do only the work that must be done by me and delegate the rest.     1   2   3   4

4. I coach my staff if they lack the skills or experience, which permits me to avoid doing many tasks myself.     1   2   3   4

5. I am regarded by my superior as a good delegator.     1   2   3   4

6. I take great care with the structuring and reviewing of delegation.     1   2   3   4

7. I treat my staff as equals when establishing the best course of action.     1   2   3   4

8.  I ensure that delegates understand the
    extent of their accountability.                        1   2   3   4

9.  I ensure that there are no overlaps in
    responsibility among delegates.                        1   2   3   4

10. I am able to appoint or replace delegates
    quickly when required.                                 1   2   3   4

11. I delegate with the thought that it helps
    staff grow to their fullest potential.                1   2   3   4

12. I appoint the best individual for a task
    regardless of age, experience, or
    seniority.                                             1   2   3   4

13. I involve my delegate in the process of
    preparing a full and detailed brief.                  1   2   3   4

14. I ensure that there is adequate backup
    available for delegates when needed.                  1   2   3   4

15. I have adequate time for planning,
    meetings, and special problems.                        1   2   3   4

16. I encourage delegates to use their
    initiative when confronted with problems.             1   2   3   4

17. I ensure that I provide regular, positive
    feedback to my delegates.                              1   2   3   4

18. I ask for feedback from staff and react
    positively to what I learn.                            1   2   3   4

19. I use an agenda when reviewing progress
    with a delegate or team.                               1   2   3   4

20. I keep an up-to-date log of which tasks—
    and to whom—I have delegated.                          1   2   3   4

21. When I delegate responsibility, I make
    sure that staff have the full authority to
    perform the task properly.                             1   2   3   4

22. I make myself available to my staff and
deal with any problems they might have.　　1　2　3　4

23. I consider all possible alternatives before
reclaiming a delegated task.　　1　2　3　4

24. I make opportunities to thank delegates
for all tasks successfully completed.　　1　2　3　4

25. I review my job every 3–6 months to see
whether I can increase my delegation to
staff.　　1　2　3　4

### Self-Assessment Analysis

Add your circled scores together to arrive at your total score. Then, refer to the scoring ranges below to identify your level of skill performance and attitudes toward delegation. You may want to refer back to sections of this chapter for suggestions on increasing and honing your delegation skills.

76–100　You appear to have highly developed delegation skills and attitudes that facilitate employee performance and professional development. Continue to enhance and maintain these skills.

51–75　You appear to have reasonably well-developed delegation skills, but certain areas could be improved. By further developing your delegation skills, you can become even more effective in increasing productivity and performance.

25–50　Your delegation skills appear to need improvement. It may also be that some of your attitudes toward delegation may hinder employee performance and professional development. You might focus on improving selected skills and attitudes (i.e., items that you scored as 1 or 2).

## REVIEW ACTIVITIES

1. Why are delegation and empowerment particularly important in health care organizations?

2. Define delegation and empowerment. Describe the relationship between them. Now give a definition of empowered delegation.

3. Describe the five characteristics of empowerment. Cite examples of particular employees or units that show evidence of empowerment.

4. Devise a plan for how you could facilitate empowerment in your work setting.

5. Describe your experience with delegation. What personal or organizational barriers influence your willingness to delegate?

6. How do you anticipate applying the knowledge and skills of this chapter in your job? How might you incorporate the six-step delegation protocol in your work as a manager?

## FOR FURTHER INFORMATION

Nelson, R.B. (1994). *Empowering employees through delegation.* New York: Irwin Professional.

Emphasizing the value of empowerment, Nelson provides a step-by-step method of delegating by communicating responsibility in a way that ensures that all parties know exactly what is expected of them. The book provides a number of examples of how, what, and when to delegate effectively.

Roebuck, C. (1999). *Effective delegation.* New York: AMACOM.

If you have never read a book on delegation, this is a good one to choose. It is only 96 pages long but covers all aspects of the delegation process. It emphasizes delegation as an effective strategy for improving team performance.

<table>
<tr><td>Skill 4</td><td># Communicating Effectively and Strategically</td></tr>
</table>

# Communicating Effectively and Strategically

Skill 4

*with Alan Whiteman, Ph.D.*[1]

The objectives of this chapter are to

- Distinguish three levels of communication in health care organizations and describe the role of communication as a management tool

- Define engagement as a requisite skill for other management skills

- Specify the value and role of active listening in health care settings

- Demonstrate effective oral communication

- Demonstrate effective written communication

- Demonstrate the effective use of presentation skills

- Plan and implement strategic communication

- Assess your attitudes and skills regarding communicating strategically verbally, in writing, and in oral presentations

- Provide skill development exercises and activities to develop or enhance skills in strategic communication

---

[1]Alan Whiteman, Ph.D., is Associate Professor and Director of the Health Services Administration program at Barry University, Miami Shores, Florida.

## THE COMMUNICATION PROCESS

The ability to communicate with others is the basic component of all relationships that occur in our lives, whether they are personal or work related. For managers, communication skills are of paramount importance. A failure to communicate can be critical, and in health care it could be fatal. Four important elements should always be considered in all communication: the relationship between the communicating individuals, the communicators themselves, organizational culture, and the dialogue itself (Parsons, 2001).

Interpersonal communication is dependent on both the sender and receiver involved in the communication (see Figure 1). The relationship of the parties will determine the type and level of communication. For example, communication that occurs between a manager and an employee or a peer may be conducted on a casual basis. A conversation between a manager and his or her immediate superior or a member of the board of directors will be handled in a different manner because of the formal relationship between such individuals. The relationship that exists between the individual participants also has a distinct impact on the effectiveness of the communication. The communication will be affected by the receiver's respect for and trust in the sender. The most effective communication occurs when the individuals who are communicating have a strong, positive relationship.

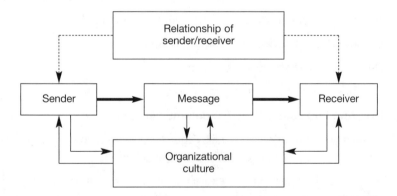

**Figure 1.** Communication and relationship. (Key: ■■■ indicates the direct flow of verbal communication [the sender encodes the message, which then flows to the receiver]; ——— indicates the indirect nature of communication that is "filtered" through the relationship that exists between the sender and receiver and its impact on the message [e.g., if there is a positive relationship, the message is likely to be positively encoded with meaning, above and beyond the message itself, and vice versa]; ----- indicates the influence of culture on both the sender and receiver.)

Organizational culture also influences the accuracy and effectiveness of communication. Not surprisingly, a culture that values and fosters respect and teamwork will more positively have an impact on communication than a culture that fosters distrust and competitiveness among individuals and units. In addition, the message will be interpreted by the receiver based on what is communicated, how it is communicated, the level of language used, and the comfort level that exists between the individuals. How we make a statement is as important as what we say. Facial expressions, body language, and eye contact all play an important role in the way the message is received. If the sender appears interested and attentive, the message may have a very positive reception. Conversely, if the sender appears distracted, rushed, or disinterested, the other party may not pay attention or may disregard the message because the sender is conveying a sense of minimal importance along with the message.

Finally, the message itself is of paramount importance. It is imperative that the message be planned and organized in a fashion that meets the level of understanding of the receiver. This is further complicated by the cultural differences that exist in our society today. What we communicate and how we communicate are critical to the success of communication.

## EFFECTIVE COMMUNICATION AS A MANAGEMENT TOOL

The ability of managers, at all levels, to communicate effectively is crucial to both individual success and the success of the organization. Compared with other organizations, health care organizations are faced with some unique communication challenges. Besides communicating with their employees, vendors, and customers, health care organizations must also effectively, efficiently, and compassionately communicate with a very wide range of professional staff, with the media, and with "customers" who may be seriously ill and dying, along with their often anxious and concerned families and relatives. Effective communication is essential in the following situations in health care management:

- Daily interaction with staff
- Talking to patients and families
- Telephone calls

- Writing memos
- Making presentations at team or unit meetings
- Coaching personnel
- Interviewing prospective job candidates

There are three levels of communication in a health care organization: the interpersonal level, the team and unit level, and the organizational level. Supervisors have primary responsibility for interpersonal- and team-level communication; middle managers have primary responsibility for communication at the interpersonal and team and unit levels; and senior managers have primary responsibility at all three levels. In order to function effectively, all managers must develop competency in a variety of communication skills. Not surprisingly, successful health care organizations in today's environment expect such mastery of their managers.

All managers communicate repeatedly throughout the day in various modalities: oral, written, and formal presentations. This communication is received and processed differently by various individuals, sometimes resulting in unexpected and disastrous consequences. These can range from simple misunderstandings or hurt feelings to serious conflicts and reduced productivity and morale. Accordingly, managers must not only be skilled communicators but also strategically plan their communication in order to be clearly understood and effective.

This chapter focuses on five communication skills that managers must utilize effectively: engagement, listening, oral communication, written communication, and presentation. It emphasizes the value of strategic communication and discusses some strategies for external as well as internal communication in health care settings.

## ENGAGEMENT:
## THE PREREQUISITE LEADERSHIP SKILL

Any time a health care manager meets with an individual to be interviewed for a job or promotion, to negotiate a raise, to discuss the delegation of a responsibility, to evaluate annual performance, or to provide coaching, there are three possible outcomes: circumstances will get better, get worse, or remain the same. The key difference between circumstances getting better versus getting worse or remaining the same is the level of engagement between the manager and the individual.

Engagement refers to the degree of trust and level of agreement among two or more individuals to work together toward a common goal. More specifically, engagement requires staff to trust and accept the influence of their manager to work with them in a manner that is respectful and helpful to them. The building of trust and respect is key to developing commitment of staff to a work unit, their manager, and the organization. Although trust and respect are necessary for commitment, they are not sufficient. In addition, both parties must have or develop the intention of cooperating to discuss a matter and possibly agree on a common objective.

In other words, engagement is an active process involving two parties agreeing to discuss a common issue or concern in an atmosphere of trust and respect, even though they may view the matter very differently and may not agree on a common course of action or outcome. Thus, although engagement is a prelude to a successful outcome, it does not guarantee one. Only when there is a moderate to high degree of engagement is it possible for delegation, coaching, team development, interviewing or counseling, or interpersonal communication to be successful. The reader will note that, in other chapters, engagement is described as a requisite skill to the development of many of the management skills described in this book.

## LISTENING

Listening is the most basic of communication skills, but many managers fail to understand effective listening. To communicate with another individual, one must really listen to what that person is saying and how he or she is saying it. Many difficult situations and problems can be averted if managers take the time to listen to employees and, just as important, patients—a skill managers fail at frequently. Covey (1990) stated that individuals listen at one of four levels and that this level of listening determines the effectiveness of their actions. These levels are 1) ignoring the other party, 2) pretending to hear the other party, 3) selectively choosing what we want to hear, or 4) attentively listening to the other party's communication. A fifth level called empathic listening, which very few individuals practice, is listening with the intent to really understand what is being said (Covey, 1990).

It is of the utmost importance for managers to prepare to actively listen to verbal communications. The following series of techniques can be applied to facilitate this process (Hiebert & Klatt, 2001):

1. Set the physical and mental stage for good listening by preparing a site that will be conducive to listening and by clearing your mind of all clutter at the same time so that you can focus on the communication.
2. Prepare your ears and eyes for listening. You must pay attention to tone, body language, eye contact, and so forth.
3. Keep appropriate silence.
4. Ask good questions.
5. Listen for content.
6. Listen for process. This means listening to how the individual is solving the problem.
7. Listen for emotions.

It is important to remember that, when we are communicating with others, they may not be listening to what we are saying. Thus, it is important to always confirm the information one is sharing (i.e., ask the listener to summarize what was said), especially in a situation in which miscommunication can have serious consequences.

*Mary Smith, R.N., works in the emergency room of the hospital. She has had a very hectic morning and is totally frazzled. Just before noon, Mary calls the housekeeper assigned to the area and tells her that the patient in Room 1 has been quite ill, soiling the room. The housekeeper tells Mary that she will clean the room as soon as possible.*

This communication was not planned, and Mary has failed to clearly explain to the housekeeper that the patient in Room 1 may have a contagious disease and that the housekeeper should follow the appropriate safety and sanitation procedures. This simple failure could have dire consequences. The housekeeper, in turn, was not listening to what Mary was telling her and does not understand the need to clean the room immediately. It is a managers' responsibility to communicate clearly and to ensure that employees understand the communication clearly.

## EXERCISES FOR SKILL DEVELOPMENT

### Individual Exercise

Select a friend, family member, or co-worker, and present him or her with a scenario that can be solved through a verbal response. Using the seven-step process described previously, listen carefully to the response. After completing this task, ask the individual how well he or she thought you had listened to the solution. Also, critique yourself based on the seven-step process.

### Group Exercise

Break into two-member teams for the following exercise in utilizing effective listening and communication techniques.

1. Each person develops a brief communication that contains instructions from a manager to an employee regarding a specific assignment.

2. One team member delivers his or her communication to the other team member.

3. The team members change roles, and the other person presents his or her communication.

After presenting the communication, compare each message sent with the corresponding message received, and critique the effectiveness of each.

## Review Questions

1. Why is it important to be an effective listener?
2. After giving an employee instructions, what should be the next step taken by the manager?
3. What role do interpersonal relationships play in the communication process?

## ORAL COMMUNICATION

*Bill Brown, Director of Information Systems at ABC Hospital, has been plagued recently by computer system failures throughout the hospital. It is 6:00 A.M., and he has been working all night trying to solve the most recent problem—the scheduling program is not accessible by outpatient admitting. Leslie Hernandez, the admitting clerk working in outpatient admitting this morning, is newly hired and has recently moved to the United States from South America. Bill cannot find the admitting supervisor, storms into the department, and finds Leslie trying to help a patient. Bill does not introduce himself and gruffly announces in front of the patient, "You can't use the computer because the controller is out and the motherboard died." Bill rushes out, leaving Leslie totally confused with no idea how to assist the patient, who is very stressed over the outpatient procedure she is scheduled to receive.*

If they are to succeed in their careers, managers must be effective in all of their communication. The most basic skill is oral communication. From infancy, individuals have verbal communication with family, friends, teachers, and others. Many individuals do not realize that there is a significant difference between social and business communication. People communicating in a social setting tend to use casual language that may be culturally or geographically linked or in some other way uniquely tied to the particular individuals involved. In a business setting, all verbal communication must be clear, direct, and simple to understand. Managers must think before they speak. Effective communication does not occur by accident; it is planned.

As stated previously, listening is a key factor in effective communication. We must listen to what is being said and what is not being said. At times, the silent message is of paramount importance, and the individual is more comfortable conveying his or her message in a covert fashion.

The next critical step is planning the message intended for delivery. It is important to deliver a single, clear message in communication. The speaker must make sure that the message is complete, that it is understood, and that it represents a single item for the receiving individual to process. It is important to not deliver mixed or convoluted messages. Managers should remember that in today's environment, they are communicating with individuals who may speak English as a second language and, therefore, may not be proficient in the slang expressions and alternative meanings of certain words that are common in English. Another parameter that enters into the communication process is gender. Communication to women and men must be structured and delivered in formats that are designed to meet gender-specific issues. Women, for the most part, listen more effectively than men and tend to look for more meaning in the communication, whereas men tend to accept more direct communication but more frequently fail to listen to the true content of the message.

Health care managers work in a technologically advanced environment. Verbal communication requires that effective voice mail communication be a part of the everyday routine. Voice mail communication needs to be planned because they are not two-way communication. The sender has no means to ensure that the receiver understands the message and the follow-up that may be required. Therefore, it is important for the sender to either follow up at a later time to be sure the message was understood or conclude the message with an instruction to call the sender with questions or for clarification of the message.

Good verbal communication requires managers to pay continuous attention to what they say. To ensure that a message gets communicated, managers should consider the following points (Brownell, 1999):

- Own your messages by using "I" statements such as "I need," "I want," or "I feel."
- Be specific and make your messages complete.
- Make your verbal and nonverbal messages congruent. Don't smile if you feel angry.
- State your point not just once, but in two or more ways.
- Ask for feedback.
- Present single ideas.
- Avoid making judgment by providing feedback without evaluation or judgment.

## EXERCISES FOR SKILL DEVELOPMENT

### Individual Exercise

Prepare a set of oral instructions on a specific task, such as retrieving an item that has been stored out of sight. You must give these oral instructions to a friend, family member, or colleague. The instructions should be thorough and brief, following the guidance provided in this section of the chapter. Observe the individual who has received the instructions and make sure that he or she has completed the task. Ask the individual to critique your instructions.

### Group Exercise

Use the following exercise to practice effective oral communication techniques:

1.  The instructor prepares a specific assignment that the group must complete during the session, and each member of the group receives a different aspect of the assignment.

2.  Each member of the group prepares and presents a 2-minute oral communication based on the assignment, which requires the development of instructions to the group.

3.  The group critiques each oral presentation on an evaluation sheet.

## Review Questions

1.  What are the barriers to oral communication?
2.  What is the importance of feedback in oral communication?
3.  List the differences between business and social communication.
4.  Why should a manager always plan his or her communication with subordinates?

## WRITTEN COMMUNICATIONS

Written communication presents another challenge to health care managers. The nature and complexity of health care organizations requires that managers communicate in writing in a variety of formats (e.g., e-mail, memos, letters, reports, meeting minutes). This communication must be easy to understand and follow, must be direct, and must effectively address the issues of importance.

*Jerry Jones is the Director of Housekeeping at ABC Hospital, a general acute-care hospital serving a blue-collar neighborhood in a large city. The hospital has adopted new security measures to deal with rising crime in the immediate area around the hospital. The hospital's chief executive officer has directed all department heads*

*to prepare a memo to supervisors, followed by department meet-
ings, explaining what each employee can do to enhance security.
Jerry Jones' department supervisors and employees are primarily
speakers of other languages with minimal formal education. Jerry
plans the memo to his supervisors carefully.*

*TO: Housekeeping supervisors*

*FROM: Jerry Jones, Director of Housekeeping*

*SUBJECT: Security*

> *In recent weeks, there has been a rise in crime around the hospital.
> ABC Hospital is very concerned about the safety of our patients, vis-
> itors, and employees. Attached is a copy of the new security proce-
> dures from administration. Please explain these new procedures to
> each of your employees by Friday. You must be sure that they fully
> understand the procedures. If any employees have difficulty under-
> standing the procedures, make sure that they are translated for those
> employees. A department meeting has been scheduled for Monday at
> 3:00 P.M. to review the rules, and all employees must attend.*

This memo is an example of simple written communication that
is clear and to the point. In written communication, it is very important to convey the intent of the message in the first paragraph, telling
the reader "what" and "why." The balance of the memo or the letter
should be an explanation and supporting material for the issues at
hand. The reader should never be forced to hunt for the message
being sent. An easy way for managers to test their writing skills is to
ask someone to read a document they have written and explain what
the document says. They might be surprised at the response.

Because it is important to write for the reader, writers must focus
on conveying information in a way that speaks to the reader's experience and needs. Finally, it is important to write clearly and concisely;
use correct grammar, spelling, and punctuation; use technical terms
appropriately; avoid acronyms; and eliminate unnecessary detail.

## EXERCISES FOR SKILL DEVELOPMENT

### Individual Exercise

Write a business letter to a friend, family member, or colleague asking
him or her to assist you in preparing a training manual for the employ-

ees you supervise. Explain in the letter the specific help you are requesting and the reason for preparing the manual. After the receiver has read the letter, ask him or her to tell you if it conveyed the proper message.

### Group Exercise

Break into pairs for the following exercise on effective written communication:

1. Each member of the pair prepares a memorandum on a topic assigned in class.

2. Each member of the pair exchanges his or her memorandum with the other person, and each writes a brief response to the exchanged memorandum.

3. The instructor meets with each pair briefly to review the quality and effectiveness of the communication.

Return to the large group to discuss the exercise.

## Review Questions

1. What are the goals of a written communication?
2. What is the proper length for a written communication?
3. How many topics should be covered in an effective written communication?
4. When writing a letter, when is it okay to use acronyms?

## PRESENTATION SKILLS

*Linda Lowrey, R.N., M.S., administrator at Shady Pines Retirement Center, is busy preparing a 10-minute presentation for the Brownsville Town Council. Linda was asked by a member of the council to attend the next monthly meeting and make a presentation regarding the recent growth of her facility. She is very excited to have this opportunity to talk about long-term care in the United States, her facility, and problems facing the long-term care industry. She is also excited about this chance to display her knowledge and show off the presentation skills she developed in graduate school. Geoffrey*

*Smith, president of Brownsville Savings & Loan Association, is busy preparing questions for Linda regarding the recent additions to her building. Geoffrey has been receiving complaints from local residents about the "eyesore" that has been created by these additions.*

Managers, by the nature of their jobs, are required to make presentations at various levels within a health care organization. These presentations may be as simple as a brief discussion with staff or as complex as a presentation to upper management. How managers organize their presentations, how well they prepare, and how well they know the subject matter will determine their success. In the previous case example, Ms. Lowrey will not be prepared for Mr. Smith because she did not prepare for her audience.

Most individuals get jittery when they are required to make presentations. This is a good response to the situation because it tends to keep individuals more alert and focused on the task. The secrets to good presentations are quite simple:

- Be well prepared—rehearse your presentation.
  - Limit the problem.
  - Assess the external climate.
  - Evaluate the corporate culture.
- Select and organize information.
- Have an outline of the material being presented.
  - If possible, use visual aids that are simple and uncluttered.
  - If asked questions, think through your response before answering or tell the questioner you will get back to him or her with an answer—and do so.
  - Know about your audience and what they expect.
    - Primary (actual) expectations
    - Hidden expectations
    - Decision maker(s)
  - Have a specific time frame.
    - Determine when the primary message should be delivered.
  - Do not bore your audience with too long of a presentation.
    - Limit your information.
  - Never read your visual aids to the audience—just discuss them.

- Relax.
- Obtain and evaluate feedback.

Remember, well-prepared professional presentations will make an individual more credible, effective, and persuasive in his or her career.

## Review Questions

1.  Why is it important to know your audience before making a presentation?
2.  Why is it an ineffective practice to read to your audience?
3.  Explain the importance of visual aids.
4.  Why is it a poor practice to convey a great deal of information to the audience?
5.  What is the best way to begin a presentation?

## STRATEGIC COMMUNICATION

Strategic communication is a way of thinking about how to get the message from inside our heads and hearts into the heads and hearts of those whom we wish to inform or influence. This requires some forethought about the purpose and outcome of the message: how it relates to the needs of staff, the unit's mission, and deadlines.

Strategic communication is a way of connecting that keeps managers and staff on track. In short, it is an intentional process of presenting ideas in a clear, concise, and persuasive way that contrasts with the off-the-cuff oral and written communication that characterize the communication efforts of too many managers. How does a manager learn to communicate strategically? First of all, he or she must master the requisite communication skills outlined earlier in this chapter. Second, he or she must make an intentional effort to use these communication skills in a strategic manner, that is, in ways that are consistent with the organization's values, mission, and strategy.

The worksheet in Figure 2 provides a way of planning strategic communication in any organizational setting. It provides managers with a methodology for thinking through how to effectively communicate with staff, peers, and superiors. The outline can serve

| Outcome<br>The specific result that you want to achieve | |
|---|---|
| Context<br>The organizational impor-tance of the communication | |
| Messages<br>The key information that your staff needs | |
| Tactical reinforcement<br>Tactics/methods to rein-force the message | |
| Feedback<br>The way the message was received and its impact on the individual, team, unit, or organization | |

**Figure 2.** Strategic communication planning sheet.

as a guide to preparing an effective plan for oral and written communication or formal presentations.

*Xavier Triton is the manager of a geriatric outpatient medicine clinic in a large medical center. The medical center has just adopted a "Code of Professional Conduct" in an effort to increase compliance with state and federal laws and regulations and reduce the medical center's spiraling liability costs. Xavier's responsibility is to see that the code is implemented in his units.*

*Before he started to think strategically about communicating with his staff, Xavier would routinely set aside a few minutes to draft memos or prepare a staff meeting agenda and send it off. He gave little thought to the importance of memos, letters, and meeting agendas in relation to the organization's overall strategy; his unit's implementation of that strategy; and the impact of these communications on his staff. Now, he spends a few extra minutes thinking strategically as he plans not only his written communication but his oral communication as well. Figure 3 shows how Xavier used the planning sheet to develop his strategic communication. Based on this worksheet, Xavier not only will draft a memo that will be attached to the code that will be delivered to all of his staff, but he will also put into motion the first of several initiatives to successfully implement the code, which hopefully will result in winning the incentive award for his unit.*

| | |
|---|---|
| **Outcome**<br>The specific result that you want to achieve | My staff will<br>1. understand and accept and, most importantly,<br>2. implement the medical center's new Code of Ethics, particularly the section on billing irregularities (as per Health Insurance Portability and Accountability Act regulations) |
| **Context**<br>The organizational importance of the communication | 1. A very high level of adherence to the Code will greatly reduce the hospital's legal liability and federal sanctions. (Last year the medical center was fined $6 million for being out of compliance with Medicare regulations alone.)<br>2. Code adherence is so important that the CEO has announced an incentive: An annual award for the unit with the highest level of compliance includes three extra personal days for those employees. |
| **Messages**<br>The key information that your staff needs | Since staff are likely to balk at another set of regulations, I need to<br>1. Emphasize our past success with compliance issues<br>2. Explain that we're most vulnerable to noncompliance with billing problems<br>3. Reiterate that we need to focus on billing issues<br>4. State that we should be able to win the new award—and staff should start thinking about what they'll do with the extra personal days off |
| **Tactical reinforcement**<br>Tactics/methods to reinforce the message | 1. Post a copy of the Code and this memo on all bulletin boards.<br>2. Plan to meet in two days to have an open discussion with the whole staff.<br>3. Include Code adherence as a written performance standard for my staff. |
| **Feedback**<br>The way the message was received and its impact on the individual, team, unit, or organization | 1. Ask Jack W. to review the memo for clarity and tone before it's finalized and sent out.<br>2. Encourage staff to e-mail me with their ideas for implementing the Code—ideas that will be discussed at our next staff meeting.<br>3. Listen to staff discussion of Code, gauge their reactions, and incorporate their ideas in an implementation plan. |

**Figure 3.** Xavier Triton's completed strategic communication planning sheet.

## EXERCISES FOR SKILL DEVELOPMENT

### Individual Exercise

Use the planning sheet shown in Figure 1 to guide you to think strategically about one of your forthcoming communication activities. It may be a memo, a meeting agenda, a brief presentation, or a meeting with a vendor.

### Group Exercise

Conduct two role plays of staff meetings. Select one participant to be Xavier Triton. In the first role play—approximately 15 minutes—Xavier Triton's staff has just received a short memo from Xavier saying only that top management expects that all units will implement the new code of conduct. In the second role play—approximately 15 minutes—the staff has received Xavier's strategically planned memo, and some participants have already sent him ideas by e-mail for responding to the challenge of implementing the code. Compare and discuss the difference between the two memos and the resulting staff meetings.

## INTERNAL AND EXTERNAL COMMUNICATION

All of the previous discussion has focused primarily on communication internal to the organization. For managers at all levels in a health care organization, communication will be made both internally, to other parts of the organization, and externally, to the community, including contact with a vast number of other organizations. It is important to remember that the same rules, suggestions, and concepts presented earlier with regard to internal communication apply to external communication as well.

External communication adds a new dimension to the communication process. External communication can include letters, telephone calls, e-mail, various media presentations, and even data that become public information under federal and state law. It is crucial to remember that the various forms of communication external to the health care organization represent the organization in the public's eye. Managers must be sure that the desired message is the message being received. A poorly written communication or a public statement that has not been well planned can create significant damage to an organization and its public image.

> *Don Rembrowski, Business Office Manager at Happy Valley Hospital, is very excited. The local newspaper has just called him and requested an interview regarding the hospital's patient billing procedures. Don is busy writing notes for his upcoming interview. He plans to tell the reporter about the new ASP system that is used to bill HMOs and PPOs. The reporter meets with Don and is totally confused. He asks Don exactly what he means and Don gets frustrated. The paper decides not to publish the article because the staff is sure the readers will be confused. Don's immediate supervisor calls Don and reprimands him for losing an opportunity to get free publicity.*

The problem presented in this case is very common in the health care industry. Don is so excited about the opportunity to share his knowledge and tell about all the good things the billing department does, he has forgotten the basic fact that if he wants to share information with the public, he must put the information in terms that everyone can understand.

The health care industry is notorious for utilizing technical terminology, acronyms, and buzzwords. Communication outside of the organization must add an extra planning step in the preparation process. This step encompasses reviewing the written or oral communication to make sure that the topic is explained in terms that non–health care personnel can understand. If necessary, the communicator may have to add additional text or additional narrative to bring the other party(ies) to a level at which the communication makes sense to them.

Many health care managers do not perceive themselves as marketers, constantly selling a product. In reality, as individuals and as agents of their respective organizations, managers are constantly selling themselves and their entity. The messages conveyed to the community, regardless of the communication modality, present an image of the service that is being offered. If ineffective communication is the norm, the health care entity may suffer significant damage to its public image.

Bienvenu (2000) suggested that in developing communication for either internal or external use, the communicator should analyze the communication environment and understand the existing situations, the target audiences, and the desired objectives with these audiences. Even though these factors all function together, it is important to analyze each factor individually and to thoroughly understand all of the nuances associated with each.

Prior to engaging in any form of external communication, it is extremely important that a manager fully understand the health care organization's policy on external communication. Most likely, there are expressed policies of what managers/employees are permitted to communicate and how this information may be disseminated. Most health care facilities have an individual who is trained and responsible for communicating with the media and approving materials prior to public release. This is critical because certain information, improperly represented, could do irreparable damage to the organization. The best way to effectively communicate on behalf of the organization is to fully understand policy and procedure before undertaking activities outside the entity.

## EXERCISES FOR SKILL DEVELOPMENT

### Individual Exercise

You are the Director of Radiology at a 250-bed, not-for-profit, general acute-care hospital. You live in a city of 76,234 residents, composed of primarily middle-income families. Your hospital has recently purchased a positron emission tomography (PET) scanner, and the administration wants to tell members of the community about this exciting technological advance that will soon be operating at their local hospital. Prepare a two-paragraph press release and ask a friend, family member, or colleague to read the document and critique it for you. Ask the individual what message he or she received by reading the document.

### Group Exercise

Each member of the group prepares a press release according to the directions for the previous individual exercise, and then reads his or her press release to the group. The group members critique and comment on each presentation.

## Review Questions

1. Explain the key differences between internal and external communication.
2. List the key components of good internal and external communications.
3. What are some common barriers to effective communication in health care organizations?

## SELF-ASSESSMENT OF SKILL 4: COMMUNICATING EFFECTIVELY AND STRATEGICALLY

**Directions:** This assessment will help you evaluate your level of skill and attitudes toward effective and strategic communication. Use the following statements to assess your attitudes and skills by circling the number that is closest to your experience: 1 = never, 2 = sometimes, 3 = often, and 4 = always. Respond in a way that reflects your skills today, rather than those you hope to have in the future. Answer as honestly as you can. Instructions on scoring and interpreting the results are provided at the end of the assessment.

1. I avoid "listening traps" such as letting myself be turned off by the other person's delivery, voice, appearance, ethnic background, or gender.      1    2    3    4

2. I strive to be an "active listener" by using eye contact, head nods, smiles, "uh-huhs," restatements, and leaning forward.      1    2    3    4

3. I listen for both the message and the feeling expressed by the sender.      1    2    3    4

4. When listening, I may ask relevant questions to increase my understanding and show my interest.      1    2    3    4

5. I observe body language such as facial expressions, tenseness, and yawning to

increase my understanding of the
sender's message.      1   2   3   4

6. I communicate fully to staff so that
rumors and the grapevine don't become
a problem on my unit.      1   2   3   4

7. I try to communicate my interest in and
caring about others in order to build trust
and open communication.      1   2   3   4

8. Because I know that my communication
can result in distortions and disagreements, I ask for feedback to check for
understanding.      1   2   3   4

9. If staff haven't understood my message,
it means I haven't communicated
effectively.      1   2   3   4

10. My staff tell me about bad news
(i.e., problems, mistakes, delays) as well
as good news.      1   2   3   4

11. I draft reports that are clear, concise,
persuasive, and well structured.      1   2   3   4

12. I hand out written directions that give
pertinent information on a task.      1   2   3   4

13. I do thorough research before putting out
a written proposal or plan.      1   2   3   4

14. I apply the guidelines of effective writing
to all external and internal
communication.      1   2   3   4

15. I get reliable, critical feedback on
important memos and reports before
finalizing them.      1   2   3   4

16. I get the audience's attention right from
the start of my presentation.      1   2   3   4

17. I organize material for my presentations around key points.      1   2   3   4

18. I choose visual aids that illustrate and reinforce the key points of my presentation.      1   2   3   4

19. Throughout my presentation, I make eye contact with all segments of the audience.      1   2   3   4

20. My replies to questions are to the point and hold others' interest.      1   2   3   4

21. I think carefully about my message before deciding how to communicate it.      1   2   3   4

22. I solicit feedback about my communication skills.      1   2   3   4

23. I believe that trust, respect, and the intention to cooperate between both parties are essential for communications to succeed.      1   2   3   4

24. I place a high priority on communicating regularly with my staff.      1   2   3   4

25. I have a strategy for communication and check activities against this plan.      1   2   3   4

### Self-Assessment Analysis

#### *Section I*

Add your circled scores together to arrive at your total score. Now that you have computed your total score, refer to the scoring ranges below to identify your overall level of skill performance and attitudes regarding communication. You may want to refer back to sections of this chapter for suggestions on increasing and honing communication skills.

76–100    You appear to have highly developed communication skills that facilitate employee performance and professional development. Continue to enhance and maintain these skills.

51–75　　You appear to have reasonably well-developed communication skills, but certain areas could be improved. By further developing your communication skills, you can become even more effective in increasing productivity and performance.

25–50　　Your communication skills appear to need improvement. It may also be that some of your attitudes toward communication may hinder employee performance and professional development. You might focus on improving selected skills and attitudes (i.e., items that you scored as 1 or 2).

### *Section II*

This section breaks out the specific communication skills and attitudes covered in the self-assessment. Sum up your scores for each of the following item sets:

Items 1–5　　_____　　Listening Skills

Items 6–10　　_____　　Oral Communication Skills

Items 11–15 _____　　Written Communication Skills

Items 16–20 _____　　Presentation Skills

Items 21–25 _____　　Strategic Communication Skills

You can now compare your scores on each of these five areas against the following criteria:

11–20　　You appear to have a high level of skill in this area.

11–18　　You appear to have a moderate level of skill in this area, but certain areas could be improved.

1–10　　You appear to have a limited level of skill in this area. You might focus on improving selected skills and attitudes (i.e., items that you scored as 1 or 2).

## FOR FURTHER INFORMATION

Parsons, P. (2001). *Beyond persuasion: The healthcare manager's guide to strategic communications.* Chicago: Health Administration Press.

A useful guide for managers to improve written and oral communication at the three levels of corporate communication: interpersonal, team, and organization-wide, this book provides powerful exercises and strategies for dealing with the topics described in this chapter as well others (e.g., answering e-mail, fielding questions from the media).

Covey, S. (1990). *Seven habits of highly effective people: Powerful lessons in personal change.* New York: Simon & Schuster.

A classic book with several sections focusing on strategies for communication in organizational settings, this text is also a valuable resource for information on applying communication skills to one's personal life and family.

# Negotiating and Managing Conflict and Difficult Employees

Health care managers routinely face conflicts and difficult employees. Conflicts arise because of increased workloads, high turnover, fear of layoffs, and the relentless demands for higher productivity and tighter deadlines. Alongside these conflictual demands and circumstances are difficult employees. Managers are expected to effectively manage these conflicts and difficult employees with negotiation skills and people skills. This chapter addresses both.

The objectives of this chapter are to

- Describe the importance of negotiation and some guidelines for employing negotiation strategies
- Distinguish "difficult employees" from "different employees," "troubling employees," and "troubled employees"
- Provide two effective strategies for dealing with "difficult employees"
- Assess your attitudes about and skills for dealing with conflict and with difficult employees
- Provide skill development exercises and activities to develop or enhance skills in negotiation and dealing with difficult employees

## NEGOTIATING AND MANAGING CONFLICT

Conflict can be defined as differences or disagreements between or among individuals and groups that can lead to demoralization and decreased productivity or to positive feelings and increased productivity, depending on how the conflict is handled. Disagreements that are resolved and lead to win–win outcomes are important in organizations because they lead to improved relationships and service improvement, and often prevent inappropriate actions or serious mistakes.

The major causes of conflict in health care organizations tend to be poor communication, unclear expectations and guidelines, chronic friction between shifts or departments, and even staffing changes. It is not unusual for disputes to arise over personnel, work and vacation schedules, or the utilization of space, funds, or equipment. Sometimes the cause of conflict may be difficult to determine because the surface issues camouflage the real, underlying cause or because the cause is multidimensional.

When conflicts arise and are not quickly resolved, disputing parties can become angry, frustrated, and demoralized. Blaming, attacking, and bitterness are seldom helpful, and, if left unchecked, the consequences for the organization can be significant. Increased absenteeism, turnover, stress, and tardiness are common, along with decreases in productivity, loyalty, and commitment. Occasionally, sabotage and violence are noted.

## Conflict Resolution Strategies

The five common conflict resolution strategies are summarized in Table 1. The strategies of accommodation and avoidance result in lose–lose situations for both parties, and the competition strategy allows one party to win at the expense of the other. The strategies of compromise and collaboration provide a win for both parties. The outcomes of each strategy are worth considering. In the competition strategy, one party always "loses" and often feels badly treated. In the accommodation and avoidance strategies, one party also "loses" by deferring to the party who is perceived as more powerful. Only in the compromise and collaboration strategy is there sufficient cooperation so that neither party feels that they have lost or been humiliated.

**Table 1.** Common conflict resolution strategies

| Strategy | Description |
|---|---|
| Accommodation | A *lose-lose strategy* in which harmony is maintained |
| | Marked by nonassertive and noncooperative behavior |
| | One party cooperates to let the other win by deferring to the needs of the other. |
| Avoidance | A *lose-lose strategy* in which conflict is essentially avoided |
| | Marked by both nonassertive and noncooperative behavior |
| | Interpersonal problems are unresolved, which causes continued frustration. |
| Competition | A *win-lose strategy* in which one party gets their way |
| | Marked by assertive or aggressive behavior without cooperation |
| | One party feels vindicated whereas the other is defeated and possibly humiliated. |
| Compromise | A *partial-win strategy* in which an agreement is reached quickly |
| | Marked by assertive and cooperative behavior in that all parties achieve some gain and some satisfaction |
| | Common in union-management agreements |
| Collaboration | A *win-win strategy* in which a dispute is mutually resolved |
| | Marked by assertiveness and a high degree of cooperation |
| | It encourages a search for mutual goals and a creative solution, resulting in a mutual sense of fairness and satisfaction. |

Most managers have a primary and secondary style or strategy in managing conflict. Whether a manager utilizes his or her primary or secondary strategy depends largely on the nature of the problem, time parameters, or even the personality of the other party or parties involved. For example, a manager whose primary strategy is collaboration and whose secondary strategy is compromise may opt to utilize his or her secondary strategy when time is of the essence, such as when a group of employees threatens the "blue flu" if a safety issue is not immediately resolved.

Although each strategy is appropriate in a given situation, generally speaking, the collaboration strategy is the most effective. In collaboration, both parties strive for a solution that is neither a quick fix, nor a surrender, nor a humiliation of one of the parties. Rather, it is a joint consensus-seeking effort in which a win–win solution is achieved, that is, one that meets the goals, needs, and interests of both parties. The guiding question of the collaborative strategy is: "What can we do collectively to resolve an issue that allows both parties and the organization to come out ahead?"

Needless to say, collaboration is not the most common conflict management strategy in health care organizations. Why is that? Effective use of this strategy requires a relatively high level of engagement skills, that is, active listening and two-way communication (as described in the skill titled Communicating Effectively and Strategically) and the skill of mutual problem solving. Also, this strategy usually requires more time than the other four strategies. This may delay decisions and resolutions, adding to the frustration the parties may experience as they seek consensus. Although the collaboration strategy has been shown to resolve conflict with the fewest undesirable side effects, the other four strategies have their place.

## Guidelines for Effective Negotiation

The following guidelines for effective negotiation have been derived from Fisher and Ury's (1988) win–win model and Albrecht and Albrecht's (1993) added value negotiating model. Six steps are proposed:

1. *Prepare for the negotiation.* Begin by analyzing the situation. Identify the focus and source of the conflict, the situational variables (see Table 2), and the consequences—current and anticipated—if the conflict is not effectively managed in a timely manner. Try to find out what the parties want, what they are likely to propose, and what advantage(s) they have.

2. *Clarify needs and focus on interests.* Begin by asking the parties how they view the situation and what is important to them. Focus on their real interests rather than on stated positions that only engender endless wrangling. Accept that strong emotions and very different perceptions exist and are barriers to resolution if they become the focal point. Thus, it is essential to separate people from the problem.

3. *Emphasize points of agreement.* Focus on areas of agreement first and work from there. Only revisit the problem after a resolution is reached.

4. *Specify potential options or solutions for mutual gain.* With interests specified, it is possible to assess the elements of value (i.e., money, property, actions, rights, or risks). Consider these questions: What can one party give that the other needs, and vice versa? How can the parties mutually add value to the negotiation?

**Table 2.**   Factors in analyzing conflict and selecting a management strategy

**Focus of conflict**
People
Issues

**Nature of conflict**
Personal differences
  • Differing perceptions and expectations, particularly involving gender, ethnicity, and cultural values
  • Difficult to resolve since they are very value laden
Information deficiencies
  • Misinformation and misrepresentation of information
  • Indicates the need to restructure or repair communication system
Role incompatibility
  • Results from conflicting job expectations, goals, responsibilities, or pressures
  • Requires reconciling incompatible goals and responsibilities
Environmental stress
  • Results from resource scarcity, rapid change, or economic uncertainty
  • Suggests addressing resource allocation: personnel, budget, space, and so forth

**Situational variables in deciding on the conflict management strategy**
Importance of the disputed issue (i.e, extremely important versus limited importance)
Importance of the relationship (i.e., critical such as an ongoing partnership versus single transaction)
Relative power of the parties (e.g., boss–employee versus employee–employee; labor versus management)
Presence or absence of a union(s)
Time constraints (i.e., urgent versus nonurgent)

---

5.   *Agree on the best option or solution and insist on objective criteria.* Try for the option that represents a win–win solution. If a complete agreement cannot be reached, be willing to compromise. Attempt to identify a fair, rational, objective standard (i.e., market value, law, custom, or expert professional opinion) as the basis for agreement rather than subjective opinion or power position.

6.   *End on a positive note, if possible.* Review and document the agreed-on resolution.

## EXERCISES FOR SKILL DEVELOPMENT

### Individual Exercise

Consider the following case example:

*Jennifer and Amanda are patient education specialists who report to Sara, a nurse practitioner and director of the hospital's home health care program. Jennifer has mentioned to Sara, on at least three occasions over the past year, that she is being bullied by Amanda. Jennifer cited some examples, such as Amanda "forcing" her to fill out the program's monthly service report rather than sharing the task. Sara, whose office is in an adjoining building, had not observed such behavior and had not really taken Jennifer's complaints seriously. That all changed recently when, because of renovations in her office suite, Sara temporarily shared office space with the patient education program staff. It was an eye opener for her. Amanda was bullying not only Jennifer but most of the other staff as well. This brought to Sara's mind a recent exit interview in which one of the departing staff from that program had complained about Amanda's harassing behavior. It became clear to Sara how stressful this conflict has become for everyone in that program. Both Jennifer and Amanda are valued for their home health care expertise and experience, and Sara did not want to lose either of them. Sara realizes that she needs to manage this conflict, the sooner the better. She decides she will serve as a mediator between Jennifer and Amanda.*

1. Work up a plan for managing this conflict. Begin by specifying a) the focus of the conflict, b) the source of it, c) the consequences if it continues, and d) the most appropriate conflict management strategy (specify the benefits and likely downsides of the competition, compromise, avoidance, and accommodation strategies).

2. Following the six guidelines for conflict management, specify how you would advise Sara to proceed to mediate this conflict.

### Group Exercise

This exercise utilizes the case study of Jennifer and Amanda noted in the previous individual exercise.

1. Divide the participants into groups of three and role-play the conflict resolution meeting involving Sara, Jennifer, and Amanda. Assume that Sara utilizes the collaboration strategy, discuss the conflict, and generate solutions (following the guidelines for effective negotiation). Allow 30 minutes for the role plays.

2. Return to the large group to discuss the role plays. Have the participants comment on their role-play experience and suggest

ways for Sara to follow up with Jennifer and Amanda to keep the solution on track.

## DEALING WITH DIFFICULT EMPLOYEES

Most employees arrive for work on time, do their work, cooperate, meet deadlines, and otherwise act responsibly. These are referred to as good employees. There are also some employees who seem out of step with others in the organization. They may goof off, procrastinate, miss deadlines, or respond argumentatively, or they may be chronic complainers. They may have difficulty relating to others and typically do not listen to another's viewpoint or will predictably disagree with it. Or, they may object to the way management does things and can be an obstacle to the achievement of the manager's goals. These individuals are referred to as "problem people" or "difficult employees."

It is important to distinguish "difficult employees" from "troubling employees" and "troubled employees." *Troubling employees* are those whose behavior violates the health organization's rules or policies. Troubling behaviors include chronic tardiness, absenteeism, and stealing. Managers must deal with these behaviors quickly and decisively. Guidelines for dealing with troubling employees are provided in the "Disciplinary Interview" section of Skill 7, Counseling and Interviewing for Maximum Performance and Development. By contrast, *troubled employees* are individuals with personal issues or concerns that can have an impact on their workplace behavior and performance. Such personal issues can include marital and family problems, health and mental health problems, grief and bereavement, and alcohol and substance use problems. The "Counseling Interview" section of Skill 4, Counseling and Interviewing for Maximum Performance and Development, focuses on strategies that managers can use to deal with troubled employees.

The key distinguishing characteristic of *difficult employees* is that they do not respond to conventional methods of correction such as warnings, threats, or even heartfelt discussion. Needless to say, difficult employees can be an unwelcome challenge for managers, but they do not have to be. This section describes two sets of strategies for dealing effectively with difficult people.

## Strategy I: Personality-Types Focus

One common way of dealing more effectively with difficult people is to understand the personality and behavior patterns of these individuals. The basic assumption of this personality-types approach is that all individuals engage in rather predictable, patterned ways of thinking, feeling, and acting. It follows that managers who can recognize and understand these predictable behavior patterns of difficult people can respond in a more effective manner. Fortunately, the behavior patterns that seem to be the most disruptive or frustrating are relatively few in number. These have been carefully analyzed and described along with effective strategies for neutralizing or redirecting these problematic patterns. The most widely regarded personality-types approach has been described by Dr. Robert Bramson (1981), a consulting psychologist. Bramson described seven basic types, with variants; four of the most common types recognized in health care settings are presented here.

*Aggressors*    These individuals engage in various aggressive behaviors when things do not go their way. They use cutting remarks, bullying, tantrums, domination, pushiness, angry outbursts, and arrogance to control others. Aggressors act as they do because they view the world in win–lose terms. They must win at all costs, and winning means always having control and defending themselves. Specifically, they seek to control other people, time, resources, and space. Their worst fear is being vulnerable and out of control.

Two subtypes can be distinguished: secure and insecure. Secure aggressors look up to those who stand up to them. Thus, they will back off if someone stands up to them verbally. The opposite is true with insecure aggressors. When another individual stands up to or otherwise challenges an insecure aggressor, the insecure aggressor becomes more aggressive.

### Strategies for Dealing with Aggressors

- Stay cool, try not to take their behavior personally, and give them time to let off steam.
- Break into conversation if necessary because aggressors will talk incessantly as a means of showing their dominance.
- When dealing with secure aggressors, stand up to them, call their bluff, and forcefully state your opinion. Remember, they respect those who stand up and push back.

- When dealing with insecure aggressors, avoid head-on confrontations and do not challenge them. Instead, tactfully redirect them.

*Negativists*    These individuals find fault with any idea or plan. They will reflexively object with statements such as "It won't work" or "It's impossible." They are everyday "devil's advocates" who find fault with everything. Their negative attitude effectively deflates any optimistic feelings that others around them have. Negativists are motivated by power and control but in a different way than aggressors. Negativists derive a sense of power by making everyone else feel demoralized and less powerful. Because they believe that others—particularly authority figures such as managers—are conspiring to block their personal goals and efforts, they even the score by spoiling everyone else's efforts.

*Strategies for Dealing with Negativists*

- First and foremost, avoid getting dragged down by their negativity.
- Make realistically optimistic statements about past successes in solving similar problems.
- Assist negativists to distinguish between a problem analysis that is helpful and one that is based on their worst fears.
- Push their limits of negativity by drawing out their worst-case scenario of a situation; do not argue or agree, just listen and summarize.
- Do not show feelings of exasperation or demoralization, and do not confront their negativity at the same level of intensity at which it is expressed; rather, process it at a matter-of-fact level.

*Know-It-Alls*    These are the "superior" people around us who sincerely believe—and want us to recognize and acknowledge—that they know everything there is to know about anything that's important to know. Accordingly, they come across as arrogant, condescending, pompous, and imposing. The more ignorant and uninformed they make others feel, the better they feel. Two types can be identified: those who are indeed experts and those who are not but act as if they are. Know-it-alls believe they are intellectually superior to others, and they amass data and develop expertise, remarkable memories, and analytical abilities as a defense against the ambiguity and unpredictability in life, which to them is frightening. Not surprisingly, they view challenges to their expertise as personal attacks.

*Strategies for Dealing with Know-It-Alls*

- Without directly challenging their expertise, lead them to consider alternative plans or explanations.
- Acknowledge the legitimacy of their knowledge or their espoused position.
- Before responding to know-it-alls, have your homework done and be prepared to lay out your position or observation in a logical fashion.
- Do not expect credit for your bright ideas; anticipate that they may steal your ideas and present them as their own in a subsequent meeting.
- To "normalize" conversations that seem to be getting out of hand, ask a hypothetical question such as "Based on what you've stated, if we hypothesize that . . . ."

**Indecisives**　Indecisives are individuals who seldom, if ever, give a clear and unqualified response to a question. Instead of "yes" or "no," their expected answer is "maybe." They find decisions—both big and little—very anxiety producing, and they stall and procrastinate so long that the decision is made for them. They employ a variety of runarounds and dodges to keep others waiting for answers that never seem to come. Indecisives act this way out of a need to please everyone. They view themselves as ineffectual and unable to deal with risks and conflict. Therefore, they avoid risks and conflict and at the same time seek out others to take care of them, including making their decisions for them.

*Strategies for Dealing with Indecisives*

- Help them surface their concerns in a safe environment where they can indicate their reservations to your idea or proposal.
- When possible, support them in their concerns.
- Help them sort out their concerns, but avoid getting hooked into making their decisions for them.
- If it appears that lack of confidence in you is one of their concerns, make it safe for indecisives to be at least somewhat direct in responding to you.
- You can reduce their need for avoiding risk taking and thus draw them out by formally taking full responsibility for any problems associated with your plan recommendation.

## Strategy II: Solution Focus

Whereas the behavior pattern or personality types approach appeals to some health care managers and may even work well for them, this approach seems unnecessarily complicated or unappealing to other managers. These managers may find the solution-focused approach more to their liking. This approach is based on the principles of solution-focused therapy, a well-regarded approach to brief counseling developed by Lucy Gill (1999), a management consultant and research affiliate at the Mental Research Institute of Palo Alto in California.

The basic premise of this approach is that it is futile to use conventional methods of correction or discipline with difficult people. It replaces seemingly logical and reasonable solutions to "correct" difficult behavior, such as discussion, written performance standards, warnings, or threats, with nontraditional solutions. The basic assumption of this approach is that traditional solutions actually reinforce and perpetuate problems and conflicts. The solution-focused approach involves three steps:

Step 1: Specify the real issue or problem.
Step 2: Identify and avoid the problem-solving method that perpetuates the conflict or problem.
Step 3: Choose a different method that effectively solves the problem and keeps it solved.

This is a straightforward and relatively easy-to-use method, and many managers have found this three-step approach to be extremely effective in dealing with difficult people. However, it does require that the user be willing to examine and change his or her behavior and thinking, which some managers find threatening. Each of the three steps is fully described and illustrated in this section.

*Step 1: Specify the Real Issue or Problem*    The first task is to focus on the main complaint, the real issue or problem that is the most troublesome or will make the most difference if it is resolved. Achieving this focus is not as easy as it may appear. People often think in generalities (e.g., "My wife is selfish."). Such a generality may obscure the problem because most individuals are not selfish in every situation all of the time. It is more useful to specify when a person is selfish or rude, about what, and what problem or effect this behavior creates.

The first step in changing troublesome behavior is to carefully specify it. A helpful way of specifying a problem is to answer the *who, what, to whom,* and *how* questions: Who is doing what that presents a problem to whom, and how is the behavior a problem? To successfully use this approach, one must carefully analyze the underlying problem, not some surface manifestation or symptom of it.

WHO: Indicate the problematic individual by name.

WHAT: Come up with a specific description of what the individual actually says and does in the course of the problem—rather than symptoms, state reasons why it is a problem or the motive of the individual involved.

- The description should specify actual behavior, not labels for behavior. Labels such as "she is very rude" should be translated to "she constantly interrupts me when I'm talking."
- The description should point to behaviors that can be seen or heard.

TO WHOM: Specify who is being affected by this behavior. It may be you, one of your employees, or the whole work team.

HOW: Indicate how the difficult, troublesome behavior is a problem. Indicate what specific problem or effect the described behavior causes.

*Sharice Simmons, Director of Admission Services at a large community hospital, was at a loss attempting to deal with Larry Noen, a supervisor in the department. He was an intelligent, hard-working employee whose negative attitude seemed to be taking its toll on department morale. Whenever an idea or proposal was made at a staff meeting, Larry consistently found a reason why it could not work. Although his comments usually had merit, they seemed to have dampened staff initiative. Sharice had tried everything she could think of to diffuse the situation, but nothing seemed to help. With consultation, she agreed to try the three-step approach. First, she defined the problem:*

WHO: Larry

Is doing what: Constantly pointing out flaws in every proposal or idea

To whom this is a problem: Sharice and department staff

How this is a problem: Larry's negativity is ruining the team's morale and reduces its ability to solve problems, plan, and provide initiatives for new solutions and programs.

*Step 2: Identify and Avoid the Problem-Solving Method that Perpetuates the Conflict or Problem*  This step involves identifying our usual and typical solution(s), which, although they appear to be natural and reasonable, have not worked. The following questions must be answered:

- What unsuccessful solutions have you tried?
- What is the theme of these unsuccessful solutions to resolve the problem, that is, the basic statement you make to yourself or others about what you—or they—should or should not do, should or should not think, and should or should not feel?
- Were there any temporary successes (i.e., exceptions) in your efforts to solve the problem or conflict?

*Sharice reviewed her failed efforts. She noted that she had*

*Privately asked Larry to stop being so negative*

*Cautioned him that others' ideas were reasonable and that he must give the staff a chance to explore them*

*Warned him that his career could be damaged if he failed to change his behavior*

*Attempted to use formal "brainstorming" rules that discourage criticism, but he ignored them anyway*

*In desperation, yelled at him to shut up*

*Step 3: Choose a Different Method that Effectively Solves the Problem and Keeps It Solved*  The main value of Skill 2 is the insight—usually the painful insight—that many of the solutions we have practiced and perfected over the years just do not work. Perhaps a manager has used a particular solution repeatedly over weeks, months, and even years, convinced that it should work. The purpose of choosing a new solution is to allow managers to discard previous ineffective solution(s) in favor of more successful solutions.

Once the manager is able to specify what he or she is trying to change, and identify specifically what solutions do not work, it is possible to choose a different solution, presumably one that will have the intended effect. In one sense, choosing a new solution is easy because the new solution is sometimes the opposite of the old solution. Sometimes the new solution will be straightforward and other times it will be more complex. Answering the following questions should help identify an effective method:

- What is the *opposite* of what you are doing unsuccessfully now, or represents a significant shift in direction? What solution would stop you from repeating your ineffective solution?
- What would you *say and do differently* to put your new solution into practice? Would you need to introduce or explain your change of behavior?
- What *indicators of positive change* in the difficult person will you observe (i.e., small initiation changes) that indicate that things are beginning to improve?

There are a number of effective solution types or strategies from which to choose; Gill (1999) listed several. Among the most useful strategies are the following:

- The opposite strategy
- The unexpected strategy
- The outrageous strategy
- The ordinary strategy

Each of these solution types is based on the same rule: *Stop doing more of the same and do something significantly different.* Potentially, any of these solution types can be successful because they all avoid the problem-solving process that does not work.

*Sharice decided that she would try using the "opposite" strategy. This meant she would tell Larry that he should be even more negative rather than less negative. She planned to initiate this strategy at the next staff meeting. After quickly noting the meeting's agenda, Sharice said, "I've realized it's a mistake to quell critical comments that could really be beneficial. We should carefully consider all the things that could go wrong with any plan we propose. This will inevitably save us money and time. So I'm appointing Larry to be our critic in these meetings. You're good at critiquing ideas and plans, and I want you to share your criticisms on everything, even if you aren't certain it's that important a point. More criticism is better than less." Larry yawned and said he thought that was a lame idea. Sharice thanked him and said, "That's precisely what I had in mind." Throughout that and subsequent meetings, she didn't wait for his negativity to sidetrack the staff; Sharice was proactive in eliciting Larry's opinions. By the third meeting, Larry had become unusually quiet, except to answer Sharice's direct queries, to which he would respond, "It's probably okay" or "It could work."*

*In subsequent meetings Larry even began to offer some construc-*
*tive ideas of his own but inevitably in his grumbling manner. The ef-*
*fect on the staff was notable: morale and initiative began to increase.*

## EXERCISES FOR SKILL DEVELOPMENT

### Individual Exercise

Review the case example of Sara, Jennifer, and Amanda provided in
the previous individual exercise. Although not all cases lend themselves to it, this case can be conceptualized as either a conflict management and negotiation case or a difficult employee case. For this
exercise, assume that Sara realizes that Amanda is a difficult employee, and that she needs to begin managing this situation now. This
will provide the experience of comparing the skills needed for dealing
with a difficult employee with those skills associated with conflict management and negotiation.

1. Address the case from the personality types perspective. Identify
   Amanda's personality type, and indicate how you would manage
   this situation. Indicate how you would tailor the guidelines for
   working with that personality type.

2. Now address this case from the solution-focused perspective. Specify the three steps, and detail the strategy you would use in Step 3.

### Alternative Exercise

Describe an actual experience with a difficult employee whom you know
personally. It does not matter whether this individual reports or reported
to you or to someone else. Specify how the situation was managed and
the eventual outcome. Then, using either the personality types or solution-focused perspective, suggest how the situation might have been
managed differently and its probable outcomes. Finally, indicate what
you learned by viewing this experience from a different perspective.

### Group Exercise

This exercise also utilizes the case example of Sara, Jennifer, and
Amanda noted in the previous individual exercise.

1. Divide into pairs in which one participant takes the role of Sara
   and the other the role of Amanda. Half of the pairs should role-

play the case from the personality-types perspective while the other half role-play it from the solution-focused perspective. Give at least 10 minutes for those playing the role of Sara to prepare. Allow about 20 minutes for the actual role plays.

2.  Return to the large group and discuss the role-play experience. Compare and contrast the experiences of using the two perspectives and approaches. Have the participants predict the outcome of their interventions. Finally, comment on how they might realistically follow up with Amanda.

The following case study utilizes the "unexpected" solution-focused strategy to resolve a situation involving a difficult employee.

*Jason Attavaro was the Director of Marketing Services for a large medical practice management group involving 150 physicians at 12 clinic sites and five hospitals. He was increasingly concerned about Willis, one of his most successful account executives, who had the unnerving habit of intimidating others in and outside of meetings. The more Jason attempted to get Willis to change, the more Willis seemed to badger and scream at other employees. Other account executives and support staff were angry and demoralized by Willis's behavior, and some threatened to quit if Jason didn't "fix" things. Not wanting to lose this talented performer to other practice management groups that were wooing Willis, and unwilling to fire him, Jason acknowledged that he had to do something different—even drastic. Jason analyzed the problem and his ineffective solutions and realized that neither his constant chiding that "you should treat others better" nor even quarterly performance standards to improve Willis' interpersonal behavior were making a difference. These strategies were clearly ineffective. Jason decided to do something very different: he used the "unexpected" strategy.*

*The following Monday, a memo went out to the marketing department. It announced that another account executive had been assigned to a highly treasured annual project that in the past had gone to Willis. Later that day, Willis stormed into Jason's office protesting the assignment. In a calm and collected manner, Jason said, "Because controlling your temper seemed to be too big a burden for you on this project, I assigned the project to someone else." Jason said nothing more and returned to the report he was writ-*

*ing. Stunned, Willis quietly and quickly left his office. The implication of this decision was clear: Jason didn't expect Willis to change ("too big a burden for you") and would simply work around Willis's temper in making assignments. The message and consequence were loud and clear: Control your temper if you want to be considered for special assignments. This approach rather quickly got Willis' attention, and his treatment of colleagues began to improve dramatically.*

# SELF-ASSESSMENT OF SKILL 5: NEGOTIATING AND MANAGING CONFLICT AND DIFFICULT EMPLOYEES

**Directions:** This assessment will help you evaluate your level of skill and attitudes toward negotiating conflict resolution and managing difficult people. Use the following statements to assess your attitudes and skills by circling the number that is closest to your experience: 1 = never, 2 = sometimes, 3 = often, and 4 = always. Respond in a way that reflects your skills today, rather than those you hope to have in the future. Answer as honestly as you can. Instructions on scoring and interpreting the results are provided in the analysis section at the end of the assessment.

1.  I try to understand the other party's situation before I enter into negotiations.   1   2   3   4

2.  I get as much background as I can before I devise my negotiation strategy.   1   2   3   4

3.  I'm clear about my basic objectives in a negotiation.   1   2   3   4

4.  I choose negotiating strategies that match my objectives.   1   2   3   4

5.  I take a flexible attitude toward negotiations.   1   2   3   4

6.  I believe that both parties can benefit in a negotiation.   1   2   3   4

7.  I begin negotiations determined to reach
    a satisfactory agreement.                          1   2   3   4

8.  I make my points using plain language.             1   2   3   4

9.  I make my points logically and clearly.            1   2   3   4

10. I avoid exposing the other party's
    weaknesses.                                        1   2   3   4

11. I am civil and courteous at all times
    during the negotiation.                            1   2   3   4

12. I set deadlines that are realistic and
    determined by the negotiation.                     1   2   3   4

13. I rely on intuition to help me understand
    the other party's tactics.                         1   2   3   4

14. I am sensitive to cultural differences in
    the negotiation process of the other party.        1   2   3   4

15. I am able to remain objective and put
    myself in the other party's frame of
    reference.                                         1   2   3   4

16. I know how to influence the other party
    into making an offer.                              1   2   3   4

17. I avoid making the first offer in a
    negotiation.                                       1   2   3   4

18. I make progress toward a negotiated
    agreement through a series of conditional
    offers.                                            1   2   3   4

19. I approach the negotiation process step
    by step.                                           1   2   3   4

20. I routinely summarize the progress made
    during negotiations.                               1   2   3   4

21. I take breaks tactically to give me time to
    think.                                    1    2    3    4

22. I consider using third parties when it
    appears negotiations are breaking down.   1    2    3    4

23. Using mediators is an effective way to
    break a stalemate.                        1    2    3    4

24. I make sure that a negotiated agreement
    is signed by each party.                  1    2    3    4

25. I attempt to negotiate a win–win situation
    whenever possible.                        1    2    3    4

### Self-Assessment Analysis

Add your circled scores together to arrive at your total score. Then refer to the scoring ranges below to identify your level of skill performance and attitudes toward negotiating conflict resolution and managing difficult people. You may want to refer back to sections of this chapter for suggestions on increasing and honing your negotiating skills.

76–100   You appear to have highly developed negotiating skills and attitudes that facilitate employee performance and professional development. Continue to enhance and maintain these skills.

51–75    You appear to have reasonably well-developed negotiating skills, but certain areas could be improved. By further developing these skills, you can become even more effective in increasing productivity and performance.

25–50    Your negotiating skills appear to need improvement. It may also be that some of your attitudes toward negotiating may hinder employee performance and professional development. You might focus on improving selected skills and attitudes (i.e., items that you scored as 1 or 2).

## REVIEW ACTIVITIES

1. Spell out and distinguish the difficult employee from the troubling employee and the troubled employee.

2.  Describe the five conflict resolution styles. Give the particular indication(s) for each one. Specify the expected benefits and "side effects" of each.
3.  List and describe the six steps or guidelines for negotiation.
4.  List the three steps of the solution-focused approach. Indicate the factors you would consider in choosing which strategy to employ in step 3.
5.  Specify the nature of the relationship between negotiation and conflict resolution.

## FOR FURTHER INFORMATION

Gill, L. (1999). *How to work with just about anyone: A 3-step solution for getting difficult people to change.* New York: Fireside/Simon & Schuster.

You will recognize Gill's three-step process as one of the two approaches highlighted in this chapter. If you found this approach interesting and useful, you owe it to yourself to read this example-packed book cover to cover.

Bramson, R. (1981). *Coping with difficult people in business and in life.* New York: Ballantine.

Bramson's book is a time-honored classic. For managers who find the personality types approach to be more accessible and applicable than Gill's three-step approach, this book provides a more detailed set of guidelines for working with difficult personalities.

Fisher, R., & Ury, W. (1988).*Getting to yes: Negotiating without giving in.* New York: Houghton-Mifflin.

In this award-winning book, the authors emphasize an easy-to-use, win-win strategy of negotiation. They emphasize being "soft on people and hard on principles" and focusing on the problem rather than attacking or blaming people. Their strategy of moving away from positions to finding the common ground of shared interests is useful in any situation, ranging from work situations to parent–child and husband–wife conflicts.

# Coaching for Maximum Performance and Development

The objectives of this chapter are to

- Explain the importance of the manager's coaching function

- Describe and distinguish three types of coaching

- Specify a format for providing coaching

- Define and illustrate the manager's use of coaching

- Explain and illustrate "coachable moments"

- Assess your attitudes and skills about coaching

- Provide skill development exercises and activities to develop or enhance coaching skills

## COACHING: A VITAL MANAGERIAL FUNCTION

Increasingly, health care organizations are looking to coaching as one of the key strategies for improving both productivity and job commitment. Many health care organizations expect all supervisors and managers to engage in coaching with those who report to them. Just as in other business sectors, an increasing number of health care organizations are specifying coaching as a written performance standard on which a manager's actual coaching behavior will be formally evaluated in performance appraisals. Why is coaching getting such attention? Because it clearly improves individual and team performance as well as job commitment and job satisfaction. High job commitment and job satisfaction mean low turnover rates. Turnover rates are so high in much of health care—averaging 20% or more annually in many hospitals—that it is no wonder that coaching by managers is of high interest to senior health care executives.

Three types of coaching activity are commonly expected of managers (Sperry, 2002): skill coaching, performance coaching, and developmental coaching. Table 1 provides a capsule summary of these three types. Although all three are described here, this chapter emphasizes performance coaching and developmental coaching.

## WHAT IS SKILL-BASED COACHING?

Skill-based coaching is what most people associate with the term *coaching*. Distinct from teaching, which relies on one-way instruction, coaching relies on observation, inquiry, dialogue, and discovery. The manager's recognition of a skill deficit is the beginning of the skill coaching process. Skill coaching addresses deficits in the basic job-related and relational skills. Until recently, job-related skills have been the main focus of skill coaching. Now, relational

**Table 1.** Three types of coaching

| Type of coaching | Purpose of coaching | Setting and time frame | Coaching strategy and tactic |
|---|---|---|---|
| Skill coaching | Reverse deficits of specific skills | Usually informal; one or more sessions | Assess, facilitate, and monitor skill development |
| Performance coaching | Increase overall performance and job effectiveness | Formal or informal; one or more sessions | Assess and intervene to remedy performance problems |
| Developmental coaching | Focus on future job responsibilities and/or career move | Brief, and usually during "coachable moments" | Assess and facilitate professional and career development |

skills—whether with other health care organization employees or with patients, their families, or other customers—are becoming a more common focus of skill coaching. Although skill coaching primarily involves a manager or supervisor working one-to-one with an employee, it can also involve some or all of the members of a work team. The primary purpose of skill-based coaching is to develop a skill that will facilitate an employee's or work team's efforts on a current project or task.

Typically, a manager will work collaboratively with an employee or team to achieve the following objectives (Sperry, 2002):

1.  An assessment of current skills
2.  The development of a skill-building plan
3.  Use of modeling, role playing, and other methods for employees to learn and practice the new skill or skills.
4.  Evaluation of skill-building results or skill acquisition

Coaching for skill acquisition typically occurs in a relatively short period of time, usually over a matter of days. It may be as short as a session or two.

*Jackie Miller-Simpson was recently promoted to night supervisor for medical laboratory services at Eastern Regional Medical Center. She had worked at Eastern as a senior lab tech for 6 years before her promotion. When she was promoted, Miller-Simpson's boss, William Alvarez, the Director of Laboratory Services, had told her that she would need more than technical know-how to succeed in this new job. After about 5 weeks, it became quite clear that, although Jackie had a high level of technical competence, she was unskilled in dealing with interpersonal issues that involved lab personnel. Jackie had adopted the motto, "It's my way or the highway." She came across to employees who were "underperforming" as demanding and confrontative. During this time, one of her employees had given notice of leaving, and two more were threatening to quit if Miller-Simpson wasn't replaced. Yesterday, a written complaint of "verbal harassment" had been filed.*

*Alvarez called in Miller-Simpson to discuss the written complaint. She offered no excuses and agreed that something had to be done, and she was willing "to do whatever it took." As they talked about the people skills needed by supervisors, it became clear that her listening and communication skills needed work. Even though Miller-Simpson had already gone through a 1-day communications workshop with the five other supervisors in her department, she realized it was just an introduction. She also needed feedback and advice on dealing with common situations she faced with her direct reports. Alvarez suggested that they meet for 30–45 minutes three times a week to discuss and role-play typical supervisor–lab staff issues. Alvarez monitored her progress both in their sessions and in observing her on the job, and this feedback influenced the coaching process itself. Soon after they began meeting, Miller-Simpson reported that she felt more confident and competent in listening and communicating. Noting the extent of her progress, at their fifth meeting Alvarez suggested spreading out their coaching sessions to once a week. Three weeks later things had improved sufficiently that both mutually decided that coaching sessions would now occur only on an as-needed basis.*

## WHAT IS PERFORMANCE COACHING?

"Performance" refers to the work outcomes specified in an individual's written job functions or performance standards. Performance coaching is a strategy for increasing, correcting, or re-calibrating an individual's overall performance and job effectiveness (Fournies, 2000). There are two reasons why performance coaching may be considered:

1. The employee's performance is *substandard* (i.e., low), in which case coaching is directed to achieving a standard level of performance.

2. The employee's performance is average or above average, but the expectation is for *peak performance*. In this instance, performance coaching is directed to achieving high-level performance.

In either instance, coaching to improve performance involves interventions to remedy problems that interfere with the expected level of job performance. In short, the primary purpose of performance coaching is to reduce or eliminate impediments to higher level job performance.

### Performance-Impacting Factors

Prior to proposing performance coaching to an employee, the effective manager analyzes the basis for the performance problem.

Several key factors can influence job performance. The following list is adapted from Salmon (1999):

- *Knowledge or skill deficit factors:* Determine if the employee lacks training or has skill deficits. If so, skill coaching may be indicated.
- *Job-related factors:* Determine if there are environmental or physical problems (i.e., temperatures that are too high or low), or if there are insufficient resources, priority conflicts, or time shortages. If so, the manager must address these matters first.
- *Inappropriate standards factor:* Determine if job standards or expectations are unclear, outdated, unrealistic, or inconsistent, and if the standards have been effectively communicated to employees. If not, address this factor more effectively.
- *Personnel factors:* Determine if there is a "willingness" problem (i.e., a lack of motivation or commitment, difficulty getting along with other employees) or some personal or family problem. If so, employee counseling may be indicated (see Counseling and Interviewing for Maximum Performance and Development, Skill 7).
- *Incentives factors:* Determine if incentives, particularly rewards and recognition, are insufficient to motivate high-level performance. Consider that it may be more rewarding for an employee to continue with sub-par performance because the incentives for higher performance are inequitable or not sufficient. If so, address the specific incentives issue.
- *Inappropriate feedback factors:* Determine if previous performance feedback has been accurate, timely, understandable, and useful to the employees. This, of course, is a management problem that needs to be squarely addressed.

Once these six performance-impacting factors are ruled out as explanations for lowered performance, the manager can proceed with introducing performance coaching.

## Introducing and Structuring Performance Coaching

Performance coaching has three phases: 1) preparation, 2) coaching, and 3) follow-up (Salmon, 1999).

In the *preparation phase*, the manager analyzes the situation for some plausible explanations for the low performance. This means ruling out the six performance-impacting factors previously described and speculating about other factors. The manager also focuses attention on data collection and planning activities in order to establish a direction and focus for coaching.

In the *coaching phase,* the manager typically will work collaboratively with an employee to achieve the following five objectives:

1.  *To assess the employee's overall performance and specific performance on given functions or duties.* Scaling is an easy and accurate way to establish an individual's or team's present level of performance and to compare it with the desired level. Simply ask the employee or team members to describe their ideas about past and present performance. Ask them to rate their current level of performance on a scale of 1–10, where 10 is the highest and 1 is the lowest. If the employee says 4, pose the question: "What has to happen for you to get to 5 on this scale?" Spend some time discussing and providing feedback on the answer to this question. Is it realistic? What support or resources might you need to provide for this to be accomplished? Record this self-rating and explanation for comparison when you monitor performance changes.

2.  *To set goals and clarify expectations—both the employee's and the manager's—for increasing performance level.* Goal setting is the key to successful performance coaching. Goal setting provides a structure for the coaching session itself and a clear focus for resulting action and outcomes. Many coaches use the mnemonic SMART to focus on achievable results. The *S* of SMART stands for *specific:* You must precisely define the aim. *M* stands for *measurement,* which means that there is an identifiable standard with which to assess achievement. *A* stands for *achievable,* which ensures that the employee or team has the resources needed to accomplish the goal. *R* stands for *relevant:* Make sure that the goal is worthwhile for the employee or team. *T* is for *time bound,* meaning it specifies the targeted completion date.

3.  *To establish a plan for continuing improvement.*

4.  *To implement the performance plan.*

5.  *To monitor progress, provide feedback, and encourage further progress.* The manager monitors performance on an ongoing basis. Scaling is also useful in monitoring progress. The manager should come up with his or her own assessment of the em-

ployee's or team's progress on the performance plan, again on a 1–10 scale, and record this rating as well as note other information about progress in writing. Coaching requires that the employee or team continually be stretched, or challenged, in order to improve on past levels of performance. For example, when the employee or team members indicate that they have reached "6" on the performance scale, challenge them to rescale their performance efforts by asking them what it will take to move to "7."

In the *follow-up phase*, the manager evaluates the overall outcomes of the coaching effort.

Coaching for performance improvement tends to be a process that can span one or two sessions or extend over a longer period of time. It may be episodic or ongoing, depending on the underlying factor or factors influencing the performance concern (Sperry, 2002).

## Some Guidelines for Performance Coaching

1. Before meeting with the individual or team, review written performance standards or expectations. Also review relevant policies, procedures, and guidelines to discuss the impact the problem is having on the employee, the team, and you as a manager. Have sufficient data necessary to describe the issue and work for a solution.

2. If the performance problem is having a negative impact on patients, staff, or other customers, you need to be prepared to provide specific information from conversations, memos, letters of complaint, telephone calls, and the like to highlight the seriousness of the matter.

3. Discuss the employee's performance in a nonpunitive, non-threatening manner. Avoid blaming and name calling. Rather, foster an atmosphere of concern and collaboration. Keep a problem-solving focus at all times, even if the employee becomes defensive or blaming.

4. Show that you understand and are concerned about the employee. Strive to achieve an atmosphere of respect, cooperation, and support. Communicate your intent to help the employee succeed rather than fail.

5. Review the concern about the performance issue for accuracy. Clarify that the stated problem is in fact the actual problem. Identify the causes of the performance issue before suggesting solutions. This means listening carefully to the employee's perspective on the problem. In other words, do not start off the meeting by saying that the employee needs performance coaching or personal counseling (Salmon, 1999).

*The director of the medical records department, Nicholas Anderson, had been on vacation and at a number of professional conferences for the past 6 weeks. Now that he was back in the office, he was eager to catch up with his departmental responsibilities. The first thing he noticed was that compliance was substandard on 6 of 10 quality indicators for patient medical files in the past quarter. Four months ago, he had brought in Alex Choy as his assistant director. Choy had an impressive record in his previous job, although he had had considerably more staff than line responsibility. Anderson was also concerned that Choy's monthly management reports were late. Anderson made an appointment to discuss the matter with Choy at 10 A.M. At 10:15 A.M., Anderson called Choy's secretary only to learn that he was not there. Apparently at about 9:45 A.M. a medical records supervisor had stopped in Choy's office to report that some staff members were coming late for their shift and taking extended coffee breaks. Choy had left his office to hold an impromptu pep talk with some medical records staff to remind them of their performance expectations. At 10:30, Choy appeared in Anderson's office.*

*Anderson focused the conversation on Choy's apparent performance problems. Anderson listened attentively and attempted to clarify the situation. It became clear that the recent impromptu meeting was not an isolated event but fit a recurring pattern. Both agreed that Choy was not allowing his subordinates to do their jobs. Rather than expecting the three supervisors under him to propose recommendations to solve problems, he was permitting them to bring problems for him to solve. By intervening directly, as he had that morning, he was accepting upward delegation, and as a result was becoming overburdened himself. Choy began to see that the more he tried to take on responsibility for all of the problems in the department, the more productivity suffered. What Choy needed was performance coaching focused on how to delegate responsibility and authority and avoid upward delegation. A coaching plan with that focus was proposed and mutually agreed on.*

## WHAT IS DEVELOPMENTAL COACHING?

Developmental coaching is an effective method for a manager to deal with an employee's future job responsibilities or even a career change. Although many managers would agree that employees are their most important resource, some managers insist that career issues are the responsibility of human resources specialists. They may believe that they have insufficient skills or are wary about raising expectations that they cannot meet, particularly involving promotions or raises.

Other managers who agree that an employee's developmental needs are part of their job responsibility are likely to postpone dealing with the developmental needs and career issues of their employees in favor of more pressing matters. They might like to sit down and discuss the employee's future in the corporation or overall career for an hour or two but feel that they have too many employees and too little time for such meetings. The result is that the average employee may receive very little developmental coaching over the course of his or her work life (Kaye, 2000).

## Developmental Coaching versus Career Counseling

Developmental coaching is not the same as career counseling and is not really the responsibility of human resources personnel rather than line managers. Developmental coaching is quite different from career counseling, which does require formal training and professional expertise. Career counseling is a process that typically involves scheduled sessions; a formal assessment of vocational interests, abilities, and personality needs; and focused discussion and inquiry for the purpose of maximizing person–career "fit." Although retirement counseling is a popular form of career counseling that is increasingly being offered in corporations today, unfortunately relatively little career and developmental counseling is being offered to early- and mid-career employees.

## Coachable Moments

Developmental coaching requires only limited training and can easily be done by most managers any time they have contact with an employee. Kaye (2000) contended that managers need only take advantage of "coachable moments"—those short, informal, spontaneous opportunities for career development—that occur throughout the course of a typical workday. Coachable moments occur in the context of ongoing work and provide managers a ready forum for addressing career development in the here and now in a matter of moments. To take advantage of coachable moments, managers who have made a commitment to developing their employees need only take three steps to act on that commitment.

## Three Phases of Developmental Coaching

There are three phases in development coaching: recognize, verbalize, and mobilize.

1.  *Recognize:* The manager first recognizes a coachable moment by picking up cues from an employee whose actions or words suggest an openness to developmental feedback. Coachable moments and opportunities tend to present themselves when an employee (Kaye, 2000)

    a.  demonstrates a new interest or skill
    b.  seeks feedback
    c.  is thinking about change in the organization
    d.  is experiencing a poor job fit
    e.  is searching for developmental opportunities

2.  *Verbalize:* Next, the manager verbalizes or talks to an employee in a way that helps the employee focus on developmental options.
3.  *Mobilize:* Finally, the manager needs to mobilize or suggest—on the spot—some immediate, specific steps the employee can take to develop his or her career.

This approach to developmental coaching is a skill that is easily learned and put into practice. Developing an awareness of coachable moments is more likely to occur in organizations that mean it when they say that "our employees are important" and where coaching is expected of all managers—and is one of their job standards. Whether this coaching skill becomes second nature to a manager depends on two things: first, the desire to develop personnel and, second, the effort to practice the skill. The following case example illustrates this approach.

*Tom Dorham, administrator of the pediatrics clinic, had two occasions yesterday to do developmental coaching. Early that morning he learned that one of his clinic supervisors, Jaime Castro, had been late in turning in his monthly activity report for the Women, Infants and Children program again. Because this was a federal subsidy program with strict reporting guidelines, Dorham was concerned. When he saw Castro later that morning, Dorham pulled him aside to discuss the late reports. Castro responded, "Yeah, I know the reports are late. There have been some errors. The only way to avoid them is to ride hard on those nurses and review their daily record keeping. But it's not my job, and I don't really want to do it." Dorham recalled that, when he talked to Castro about taking the clinic position a year ago, Castro reluctantly agreed, saying that his strengths were more in research and program evaluation rather than in line management. At the time, though, Dorham needed someone to take that position, and Castro was a loyal, steady player. However, it was becoming clearer that this supervisor was experiencing poor job fit. Dorham also recognized that this was a coachable moment. Rather than threaten or discipline Castro, Dorham said, "Jaime, you've really helped me out this past year. I know you have some valuable clinical program evaluation skills, but this job is not allowing you to use those skills and your interests as much as you probably could. Maybe there's a way to apply those skills more directly to our research efforts. Would you be willing to draft a proposal along those lines?"*

*When Dorham returned from lunch, Vanessa Evans, his administrative assistant, handed him a set of visuals that she had produced on her computer. They were as slick as anything the corporate graphic design department produced. She said, "I was getting this mock-up ready to send to graphics, but I thought I'd try out what I learned in the computer imaging course I'm taking at the university. That new color laser printer does everything." Dorham recognized this as a another coachable moment: His administrative assistant was demonstrating a new interest and skill. He acknowledged this valuable skill and interest. Then he added,*

*"You might want to ask Peter in graphic design if they have some new computer imaging programs that you could learn."*

When a manager picks up cues that an otherwise conscientious employee is not performing adequately or consistently, it may reflect poor job fit, as with Jaime Castro. Similarly, if a manager picks up cues about an employee's new skill or interest, it means the employee may be engaged in self-assessment about his or her career. Although this may not result in a different job or new career, it reflects the employee's self-directedness, a broadening of his or her skills, and increased job satisfaction, as in the example of Vanessa Evans. In either instance, a coachable moment is at hand.

## EXERCISES FOR SKILL DEVELOPMENT

### Individual Exercises

#### *Preparing for Performance Coaching*
Think about a situation in which you need to provide performance coaching to one of your employees. Use the three phases of performance coaching to structure your response. In the preparation stage, review the employee's performance problem with regard to the six performance-impacting factors and then speculate as to the most likely causative factors. In the coaching phase, anticipate how the five coaching objectives will play out. Consider how you might incorporate these objectives. Finally, in the follow-up phase, predict the likely outcomes. Alternatively, recall a past situation in which you attempted to provide performance coaching. Describe how you might handle that situation differently based on this approach to performance coaching.

#### *Recognizing Coachable Moments*
Review the recent past for examples of coachable moments that were missed or not recognized at the time. Maybe it was a time when an employee (perhaps even yourself) showed by his or her words or actions a new interest or skill, was experiencing a poor job fit, or was searching for a developmental opportunity. Take one of these examples and describe, in a few sentences, the particular circumstances. Then, following the three-step developmental coaching model (recognize, verbalize, and mobilize), describe how you might provide on-the-spot developmental coaching.

## Group Exercises

### *Practicing Performance Coaching*

This exercise involves role-playing the performance coaching case study of Alex Choy and Nicholas Anderson presented earlier in this chapter.

1.  Divide into pairs in which one participant takes the role of Alex Choy, the individual to receive performance coaching, and the other the role of Nicholas Anderson, the manager/coach. Reread and then role-play the case. Plan for at least 30 minutes to play out the first coaching session.

2.  Alternatively, role-play the case study utilizing skill coaching, focusing on the skill of delegation. You may want to refer back to the guidelines on developing the skill of delegation in the chapter on Delegating to Maximize Performance (Skill 3) and tailor them to this case example.

3.  Return to the large group to discuss your experience.

### *Developmental Coaching Role Plays*

Divide the group into pairs in which one participant takes the role of manager/coach and the other the role of employee.

1.  Both participants read the following scenario (the scenario is written from the perspective of the manager/coach). The person playing the manager/coach looks for developmental coaching opportunities and can make a few notes on how to respond to the developmental coaching theme in the scenario. Then begin the role play, which can last from 5 to 10 minutes.

    *Cynthia has been a clinic coordinator reporting to you for 2 months. She has drafted a proposal for reorganizing tasks in the purchasing unit, including a budget that demonstrates a large annual cost reduction. Three days later, she asks you if you have had a chance to review her proposal and the budget figures.*

2.  Switch roles, and then read and role-play the following scenario:

    *Wesley has been effectively auditing the hospital's pharmacy services for 3 years. One day he tells you "I'll probably be in this job forever. I thought I might be good at doing clinical outcome and quality improvement studies, but those people are always hired from the outside and have previous experience."*

3.  Return to the large group to discuss the coaching strategies used, the ease and difficulty of the coaching, and so forth.

## SELF-ASSESSMENT OF SKILL 6: COACHING FOR MAXIMUM PERFORMANCE AND DEVELOPMENT

**Directions:** This assessment will help you evaluate your level of skill and attitudes toward coaching. Use the following statements to assess your attitudes and skills by circling the number that is closest to your experience: 1 = never, 2 = sometimes, 3 = often, and 4 = always. Respond in a way that reflects your skills today, rather than those you hope to have in the future. Answer as honestly as you can. Instructions on scoring and interpreting the results are provided in the analysis section at the end of the assessment.

1. I presume that my staff are capable of doing their jobs well.    1   2   3   4

2. When coaching, my focus is on current performance and potential achievement.    1   2   3   4

3. I observe my people and target specific skills or behaviors for further development.    1   2   3   4

4. I create a work environment that fosters job performance and satisfaction.    1   2   3   4

5. I spend time with my employees to help them develop professionally and in their careers.    1   2   3   4

6. The first impression that those I coach have of me is openness and curiosity.    1   2   3   4

7. Being a manager means coaching employees.    1   2   3   4

8. I revise performance plans with the employee and provide additional coaching as needed.    1   2   3   4

9. My coaching sessions ensure privacy and are free of interruptions.    1   2   3   4

10. I make links between my staff's
    motivational needs and their goals.          1   2   3   4

11. I periodically review with employees their
    progress toward established performance
    goals.                                       1   2   3   4

12. I assume that everybody has
    underutilized strengths and capacities.      1   2   3   4

13. I assume that positive change is possible
    and achievable.                              1   2   3   4

14. I monitor an employee's use of a skill or
    behavior that was targeted for
    improvement.                                 1   2   3   4

15. I discuss with employees how they can
    perform to their maximum potential.          1   2   3   4

16. I communicate a positive attitude when
    coaching to convey my belief in
    employees' ability to achieve their goals.   1   2   3   4

17. When coaching, I assume that my staff
    can find their own solutions.                1   2   3   4

18. I actively identify performance
    improvement areas for specific
    employees.                                   1   2   3   4

19. I give feedback on poor performance that
    is constructive and specific.                1   2   3   4

20. I close coaching sessions by getting a
    specific commitment to a task.               1   2   3   4

21. I control coaching sessions by linking
    what has been said to the goal.              1   2   3   4

22. I follow up coaching by getting
    employees' feedback on their progress.       1   2   3   4

23. Coaching will succeed when staff are
able to take responsibility.          1    2    3    4

24. My superiors consider me to be an
effective coach.                      1    2    3    4

25. If asked for advice, I offer it in the form of
suggestions rather than directives.  1    2    3    4

## Self-Assessment Analysis

Add your circled scores together to arrive at your total score. Then refer to the scoring ranges below to identify your level of skill performance and attitudes toward coaching. You may want to refer back to sections of this chapter for suggestions on increasing and honing your coaching skills.

76–100   You appear to have highly developed coaching skills and attitudes that facilitate employee performance and professional development. Continue to enhance and maintain these skills.

51–75    You appear to have reasonably well-developed coaching skills, but certain areas could be improved. By further developing these skills, you can become even more effective in increasing productivity and performance.

25–50    Your coaching skills appear to need improvement. It may also be that some of your attitudes toward coaching may hinder employee performance and professional development. You might focus on improving selected skills and attitudes (i.e., items that you scored as 1 or 2).

# REVIEW ACTIVITIES

1. Briefly name and describe the three types of coaching that are expected of managers.
2. Which of these three types have you had experience providing?
3. Which one do you feel most comfortable with and competent to do? Least comfortable?

4. Briefly summarize the purpose, format, and strategy for each of the three types.
5. What are the main differences between developmental coaching and career counseling?
6. What is a "coachable moment?" Give an example of one from your work situation.
7. Compare the coaching formats and guidelines for each of the three types of coaching.
8. Make an outline that summarizes these comparisons.
9. Note three steps you can take to improve your skill of developmental coaching.

## FOR FURTHER INFORMATION

Fournies, F. (2000). *Coaching for improved work performance* (Rev. ed.). New York: McGraw-Hill.

In this revision of the classic book on performance coaching, the author provides a detailed description of the process of performance coaching that emphasizes behavior analysis. The interested reader will find detailed transcripts of actual coaching sessions.

# Counseling and Interviewing for Maximum Performance and Development

The objectives of this chapter are to

- Indicate the value of the manager's interviewing and counseling function
- Describe and distinguish the five types of interviews: employment, appraisal, exit, disciplinary, and counseling interviews
- Specify and demonstrate the six steps for effective employment interviews
- Specify guidelines for the effective use of counseling, disciplinary, appraisal, and exit interviews
- Assess your attitudes and skills regarding interviewing and counseling
- Provide skill development exercises and activities to develop or enhance interviewing and counseling skills

## INTERVIEWING

Formally talking with employees about their workplace behavior or performance or helping them deal with personal concerns they may have is called *interviewing.* Two points should be emphasized: *formal talking* and talking *with,* rather than *to,* employees. First, unlike everyday conversation between managers and employees, interviewing is a planned, formal activity with a particular objective involving specific techniques and skills. Second, interviewing involves talking with, rather than to, employees. Talking with people means that that the manager must listen as much as he or she talks. It implies that the employee has something to say and is encouraged to say it. Not surprisingly, interviewing is more likely to be effective when it involves active listening and two-way communication.

Managers routinely engage in various types of interviewing: employment, appraisal, exit, disciplinary, and counseling interviews. This chapter describes the process and core skills of interviewing and reviews specific skills and guidelines for each of the five types of interviewing. Because most managers find employment interviews and counseling interviews to be more challenging than the other types, the employment and counseling interviews are described in greater detail in this chapter.

## COUNSELING VERSUS COACHING

Of the various interview types, counseling is commonly confused with coaching. Both coaching and interviewing, particularly counseling interviews, focus on job performance. Whereas coaching focuses on job-related performance, counseling focuses on personal concerns and personality-related factors that have an impact on job performance. Although both share some similarities, counseling is quite different in its purpose and focus than coaching. More specifically, coaching is indicated when an employee lacks skill or knowledge about job responsibilities or work team or interpersonal behavior, whereas counseling is indicated for personal problems or organizational changes that affect an employee's job performance or motivation (Stephenson, 2000). Salters (1997) put it even more succinctly, stating that counseling is used primarily for "won't do" issues (i.e., issues reflecting character, motivation, or emotion), whereas coaching is used for "can't do" issues (i.e., issues reflecting lack of skill, capability, or knowledge).

Unlike coaching, which is an ongoing, daily managerial function, counseling is an intermittent function occurring when the need arises. Accordingly, whereas a manager typically engages in coaching with one or more employees every day, that same manager will only occasionally interview select employees for specific purposes. In fact, except for planned (performance) appraisal interviews, which may occupy several hours each week every 6 or 12 months, a typical manager may conduct only a few interviews in a week or a month. Although managers do not need to develop the level of interviewing skills expected of a human resources professional or a psychologist, they do need to become familiar with the basic process, techniques, and skills of interviewing.

## OBJECTIVES OF INTERVIEWING

Managers use interviewing to achieve three objectives:

1. To predict behavior
2. To change behavior
3. To establish or review expectations for behavior and performance

For example, a manager can utilize the employment interview to predict behavior, that is, to attempt to determine how an employee or potential employee will do in a specific job or with a particular work team. The appraisal and exit interviews are used to establish or review expectations for behavior and work performance. A manager utilizes the disciplinary and counseling interviews to change behavior that is substandard, such as tardiness or low productivity, or to address a negative attitude or a depressed mood that affects the employee's performance or the behavior of others. Table 1 offers an overview of these types of interviews.

## CORE AND SPECIALIZED INTERVIEWING SKILLS

Conducting effective interviews presupposes a reasonable level of competency and experience in the core interviewing skills. The core interviewing skills consist of engagement, active listening, and two-way communication. For the most part, disciplinary interviews, appraisal interviews, and exit interviews can be effectively conducted by managers who have mastered the core interviewing

**Table 1.**    Purposes of five types of managerial interviews

| Type | Purpose |
| --- | --- |
| Employment | To predict the candidate's likely job performance and "fit" with job, work team, organization, and manager |
| Counseling | To help an employee deal with personal or family issues that impact workplace behavior or job performance |
| Disciplinary | To improve attitudes and increase compliance with workplace rules and regulations |
| Appraisal | To review and possibly revise job expectations, productivity, and performance standards |
| Exit | To review "fit," job experience and expectations, workplace policies, and norms |

skills. These core skills are detailed in the chapter on Communicating Effectively and Strategically, Skill 4.

In addition to these core skills, specialized skills and strategies are essential in some interviews, particularly the employment interview and the counseling interview. These specialized skills and strategies are described and illustrated in some detail in the following two sections, which address employment and counseling interviews. The remaining sections of this chapter address disciplinary interviews, appraisal interviews, and exit interviews. A set of guidelines for conducting these three types of interviews is provided.

## EMPLOYMENT INTERVIEW

Interviewing new or prospective job candidates is a task that managers cannot afford to take lightly. Even though human resources personnel may conduct much of the screening and preemployment process, employment interviews provide the manager with a critical vantage point for assessing both the candidate's *capacity* to meet the job's performance standards and his or her *"fit"* with the job, work team, organization, and manager. Assuming the manager is charged with hiring and retaining highly productive and committed employees, it is incumbent on him or her to address the matter of assessment and prediction of both capacity and "fit" in a strategic manner.

Employment interviewing requires at least three sets of skills: 1) listening and communication skills; 2) planning and structuring an employment interview; and 3) planning, asking, and evaluating strategic questions (and situational scenarios). The first skill set, listening and communication skills, is covered in the chapter on Communicating Effectively and Strategically, Skill 4. The second and third skills are introduced in this section.

## Planning and Structuring an Employment Interview

Various ways of preparing for and conducting an employment interview should be explored. The following six-step process emphasizes the assessment of a candidate's capacity and "fit" for the job (adapted from Camp, Vielhaber, & Simonetti, 2001, p. 12):

1. Set realistic goals for the interview.
2 Define performance expectations necessary to perform the job successfully.
3. Ask questions and pose scenarios to predict the candidate's ability to meet the job expectations.
4. Decide what the preferred answers are before asking the questions.
5. Conduct the interview so as to maximize effective communication *and* accurate measurement.
6. Use behavioral decision making to predict the candidate's performance in the new job.

It may seem somewhat stilted and unnatural to think strategically about the employment interview process. However, this approach to planning the interview is obviously consistent with a screening and hiring philosophy that is strategic and performance based. Steps 2 and 3 are the heart of this approach. Assuming that the organizational unit already has developed performance standards for all job classifications, the manager need only operationalize performance expectations and prepare a list of questions and scenarios related to these expectations (Steps 2 and 3). If performance standards are lacking or are not well formulated, additional time will be needed to implement this approach. Readers will note that, although this approach is quantitatively focused, it cannot succeed unless the manager has developed effective communication skills (refer to Step 5).

An effective and strategically based employment interview consists of focused interview questions and situational scenarios that examine past or present job performance and predict the candidate's capacity to meet performance standards and his or her likely "fit" with the new job, work team, supervisor, and organization. There are key indicators that need to be elicited and considered. Of critical importance is the candidate's capacity to perform the new job based on past job performance. *Capacity* refers to the candidate's skills, competencies, and talents. As noted in the chapter on Becoming an Effective Leader in Health Care Management (Step I), unlike skills and experience, talents are innate and cannot be learned, although they can be honed.

*Strategic Questioning*    Managers typically indicate that questions such as

"What is your strength (or weakness)?"
"Why should I hire you?"
"What is your ideal job?"

are very sensitive questions, often learned from mentors, that they have used to separate effective from ineffective candidates. However, managerial experience and research increasingly are revealing that such generic questions in fact do not differentiate highly productive and effective employees from less productive and ineffective candidates.

In contrast, questions such as

"What were your key job objectives during the past year and how well did you perform against them?"
"If I asked your co-workers to rate your overall performance on a scale of 1–10 (1 = low, 5 = average, 10 = outstanding), how would they rate you?"
"What factors would they rate high (and low)? Why?"

have been shown to differentiate effective from ineffective candidates because they are performance-focused questions and are more likely to predict the candidate's capacity for meeting the performance requirements of a given job.

Framing effective questions is a polished skill that few managers master by trial and error. A number of excellent resources offer comprehensive lists of such targeted questions as well as situational scenarios. The For Further Information section at the end of this chapter lists references that the reader may want to explore.

*Situational Scenarios*    An effective interview also includes the use of situational scenarios, which involves posing situations to candidates in order to assess how they are likely to behave and function in job-relevant circumstances based on their responses to the scenarios. Three types of scenarios can be posed: 1) *real situations* that the candidate must deal with in the new job, 2) *hypothetical situations* that are designed to simulate real problems that the candidate is likely to encounter in the job, and 3) *actual situations* that the candidate has encountered in past jobs that resemble those that will be encountered in the new job (Beatty, 1994, pp. 56–57). An effective employment interview can incorporate at least one situational scenario for each key functional responsibility specified in the job description. Here are two examples of situational scenarios:

If you were a line supervisor in a small union shop and personally witnessed an employee deliberately sabotage a machine, what would you do? Assume there were no other witnesses to the sabotage.

You are the only one in a work team who understands how to program a specific device, but your manager has the habit of ridiculing you for your technical expertise in the front of your co-workers. How would you handle this matter?

*Federal Guidelines* So far the criterion for determining the line of inquiry in employment interviews has been to frame questions and pose situational scenarios that are performance focused. To this must be added an additional criterion: questions must follow federal guidelines as set out by the Equal Employment Opportunity Commission (EEOC) and the ADA. Any time a manager undertakes an employment interview, he or she must be certain about what can and cannot be asked and said in such preemployment interviews. Table 2 is a partial list of lines of inquiry that can and cannot be explored in such interviews.

## Providing Information in Interviews

Another purpose of the employment interview is to give information. Prospective employees need to know something about the organization, such as its policies, objectives, restrictions, and benefits that will most directly affect them and apply to them. Automatic increases, bonuses, and paid vacations probably mean much more to the young single person than do sickness benefits and retirement plans. Accomplishments of the organization, provisions for the

**Table 2.**   Lines of inquiry in employment interviewing

| Can ask/show | Cannot ask/show |
| --- | --- |
| About previous employment, including job performance | About marital status, race, ethnicity, religion, or sexual orientation |
| Whether the individual can meet the work schedule and attendance requirements | About the individual's partner, the partner's employment, or child care arrangement |
| For date of birth and proof of that age | Preference for younger people in hiring |
| About training and experience in the U.S. military | Reasons for military discharge or for copies of discharge papers |
| How long the applicant plans to stay on the job or about any expected absences | Direct questions about previous or possible future pregnancies |
| Names of job references | The origin of a name or anything about a name that would reveal its owner's marital status |
| Height or weight if it is a job requirement | Height or weight if there is no job requirement |
| If the individual can be cleared to work lawfully in this country and can provide proof of this after hiring | Proof of citizenship or about citizenship in another country |
| That a photograph be supplied for the employee's record after hiring | For a photograph before hiring |
| An address where the individual can be contacted | With whom the individual is living or whether the individual owns or rents his or her home |

family, and promotion opportunities mean much to the mature person looking for a career. However, the employment interview is not the primary forum for selling the candidate on the organization. That is the responsibility of the human resources department.

Part of the reason for giving out information is to let the interviewee know about the job that he or she will be doing. Again, honesty is the rule. If there is likely to be much overtime, the manager should say so. If the job is routine at times, that should be mentioned; at the same time, the more exciting features can be pointed out as well. If the applicant is not likely to understand the terminology, there is no need to spend a lot of time going into great detail about the job. The manager should let the applicant ask questions after he or she has given enough information to make those questions meaningful. It is even a good idea to help the applicant ask questions.

*Two months ago, Elena Dominguez had been hired as Director of Community Relations at Memorial Hospital. The consensus was that she didn't seem to be working out. Rather than getting out in the community and making contacts, she was seldom seen outside her office. She countered this by saying it was important to develop brochures and send out press releases highlighting the hospital's community outreach. This was problematic for many, particularly the marketing department and the hospital's publicist, who believed Elena was invading their turf. The vice president of human resources undertook a review of the selection process used in hiring Elena. It was quite instructive. All four of the interview ratings of Ms. Dominguez were in the excellent range, which is not surprising because she came across as confident, articulate, and savvy. However, it seemed that the interviews focused almost exclusively on probing her values and ideas about hospital–community relations rather than on strategy and previous job performance. It was interesting that, although her references were glowing, they were quite vague and did not allude to her previous accomplishments. Because this was the third recent hire that did not seem to be meeting expectations, it was decided that the hospital's selection and hiring policy needed revision.*

## EXERCISES FOR SKILL DEVELOPMENT

### Individual Exercise

1. Think about the employment interview involving your current position. Recall the type of questions that were asked and the issues or scenarios that were probed during your individual interviews (and group interview, if applicable). List those on the left side of a piece of paper. On the right side of the paper, place the letter *P* next to questions or items that were directly related to predicting "fit" and performance for that job. Then place the letter *C* next to those questions or items that probably found their way into the interview through custom or tradition. Next, place a *U* in front of those questions or items that are, for all practical purposes, unrelated to predicting "fit" and performance. Finally, place an *I* in front of any questions or items that probably should not have been asked because of EEOC and ADA guidelines. Tally the number of *C*, *U*, and *I* items and compare this with the number of *P* items. Presumably, items marked with *C*, *U*, and *I* probably had little place in the interview.

2.    Now specify the questions, issues, and scenarios that would have better served to predict your "fit" and performance potential for the job you were hired to perform. Use Steps 2–4 of the six-step interview process described above to structure your inquiry.

3.    As an alternative, select another employment interview, perhaps a recent or future interview that you conducted or will conduct, and plan and draft items for Steps 2–4.

### Group Exercise

Have each participant complete the first part of the previous individual exercise.

1.    Tally the number of *P*, *C*, *U*, and *I* items for all participants. Calculate the percentage of *C*, *U*, and *I* items and compare that with the percentage of *P* items. Discuss the implications of this finding.

2.    As a group, examine the questions and items for each participant that were designated as *I*. Discuss the reasons why these items would be construed as discriminatory or could lead to a charge of violating EEOC/ADA guidelines.

3.    Using the employment interview experience of one participant, construct a set of interview questions and scenarios that focus primarily on predicting "fit" and performance. Use Steps 2–4 of the six-step interview process to structure your response.

## COUNSELING INTERVIEW

The purpose of the counseling interviews is to help an employee deal with personal or non–work-related issues that have an impact on workplace behavior and job performance. In the other interview types, the manager typically initiates contact. In the counseling interview, the employee may approach the manager seeking advice. Accordingly, the manager's role is somewhat different. That is, the manager does not structure the time or duration of meetings or the agenda.

Typically, personal problems are not job related, yet they have an impact on job performance. For instance, because of family problems, an employee may be moody or irritable and as a result say and do things that create problems for co-workers. Financial problems may result in worry and difficulty concentrating on work tasks. Lack of concentration may create safety problems or have an impact on production schedules. Depression and substance abuse may have a similar impact. *Presenteeism*—the situation in which an employee is physically present in the workplace but is not adequately engaged in work—often reflects personal problems that result in the employee appearing to be distracted or unmotivated and consequently functioning below expectation. The counseling interview can be effective in addressing such concerns.

Because of the personal nature of these interviews and the fact that the employee has approached the manager for help, managers need to consider some unique features of this type of interview. These include the matters of referral and confidentiality.

## Referral

It is the rare manager who is a credentialed professional counselor or psychotherapist. Even if the manager were a professional therapist, it would be unethical to treat an employee who reported to him or her because of an ethical issue called *dual relations* or *agentry*. Most managers who conduct counseling interviews are aware of their limitations and know when they are in over their heads with severely troubled employees (i.e., those who are depressed or suicidal or both). Because of programs such as Depression Awareness and Recognition Training (DART), many managers can effectively recognize the signs and symptoms of depression in the workplace. Although recognition is a manager's responsibility, treatment is the responsibility of credentialed health care professionals.

Workplace protocols for treatment referral of employees with depression, drug and alcohol problems, and a host of personal problems and crises are common today. Employee assistance programs (EAPs) are probably the most common referral resources for managers. A useful rule of thumb for referral is: If a manager cannot help an employee deal with a personal problem or crisis in one or two counseling interviews, referral is probably indicated.

## Confidentiality

Among the various types of interviews, the counseling interview demands that employees' privacy be respected and that confidentiality be safeguarded. When at all possible, the manager should avoid documenting these problems in the employee's personnel record. If there was a discussion about performance, or the meeting resulted from a performance problem, then it may be necessary to put this in the files. However, because others have access to personnel records, the manager should use discretion in documenting the matter. Another caution is to avoid casually mentioning the problem to other managers. Not only can violating a confidence aggravate the problem, it virtually ensures that the employee will find it difficult, if not impossible, to trust and respect the manager's judgment again.

## Responding Skills

There are five common responding styles that are used in managerial interviews (Table 3). Each of these five responses has its place in the counseling interview, when used at the appropriate time. It is appropriate to use supportive and understanding responses at the outset to put the employee at ease and make him or her feel understood. Later on, when it is essential to elicit facts and details, the probing response is appropriate. Occasionally, interpretive and evaluative responses can be appropriate, but these are best used sparingly.

## The Understanding/Reflection Response

There are several advantages to utilizing the understanding or reflection response. When used early in the interview, this response style puts the employee at ease and facilitates talking and opening up without the fear of being judged or criticized. It promotes the feeling of being accepted and cared for. Furthermore, it builds and reinforces a bond of trust between employee and manager. Therefore, understanding or reflection is a preferred response style in counseling interviews, and an essential skill to learn, practice, and use.

The understanding response checks the accuracy of the listener's (manager's) understanding of the situation. This response says in essence: "Here's what I believe you are saying. Is this accurate?" An understanding response reflects back the employee's feelings. Reflecting feelings involves responding to the employee's

**Table 3.** Purpose and examples of five response styles

| Response style | Purpose | Impact | Examples |
|---|---|---|---|
| Probing | To elicit information by means of questioning | Moves conversation from feeling to facts or meaning | "Could you say more about how you arrived at that decision?" "How long have you been feeling distracted and anxious?" |
| Understanding/ Reflection | To "mirror" or reflect back the individual's feeling or concern in a non-judgmental, neutral fashion  Demonstrates the interviewer's understanding and empathy | Encourages self-disclosure and promotes trust | "What I hear you saying is that it has been very difficult for you and your family since you were assigned to rotating shifts." "You really feel disappointed and sad that the work team has not supported your efforts after you've tried so hard." |
| Supportive | To offer assurance and comfort (this expresses sympathy and differs from the empathy of the understanding response) | Reduces feeling of worry, aloneness, and so forth | "I can see that working the third shift is starting to take a toll on your health and your family." |
| Interpretive | To uncover the likely reason or motive behind a particular comment or concern | Moves conversation away from feelings to meanings | "It may well be that you're a bit more thinned-skin than you think you are." |
| Evaluative | To make a judgment about a particular employee concern based on the interviewer's own frame of reference | Moves conversation away from feelings to meanings | "Everyone has to choose which battles they're going to fight and which ones they're not. From my perspective, this one is not worth fighting." |

feelings but restating or "mirroring" them. The focus is not on the content of what was said but rather on the emotional tone underlying the content. Some specific guidelines for making such understanding/reflection responses are as follows:

- The usual format for a feeling reflection response is: "It sounds like you feel _____." Your response and tone of voice should be calm and neutral.
- If the employee responds with something like "Yeah, that's right," you know that your understanding response was accurate.
- When many feelings are expressed in a long statement, focus only on the last one.
- Because mixed feelings (i.e., fear and anger) are not uncommon, reflect both feelings when present ("What you're saying makes me think you're feeling sad but also angry that this has happened to you").
- Because understanding/reflection responses are meant to be neutral, avoid approval or disapproval when making these responses. In contrast, interpretive, evaluative, and supportive responses may be used to communicate approval or disapproval.

*Jack Wynn, a pharmacy tech, comes to you because he is upset with what has been happening lately at the outpatient pharmacy adjacent to the emergency room. He is bothered by his co-workers, who don't seem to accept his ideas and who don't want to help him when there are long lines of patients waiting to pick up prescriptions. He is particularly bitter that they seem to have excluded him from socializing with them on weekends. You hear his specific complaints but reflect back only his feelings: "You feel very strongly that your co-workers are not treating you fairly."*

## A Strategy for Conducting Counseling Interviews

A straightforward approach for conducting counseling interviews is the ERIC strategy (Sperry, 1987, 2002). Essentially, ERIC is a "mental map" that guides the manager's relationship with the employee in a counseling interview. ERIC is the acronym for four progressive steps of conducting a counseling interview. ERIC can be described as follows:

E—refers to three *E*s: engaging, exploring, and expectations. Begin the interview by *engaging* the employee in a relationship of respect and confidence. This is shown by the manager's use of active listening and by nonverbally attending to the employee (i.e., saying "uh-huh" and nodding the head to indicate attention and concern). During this process of engagement, the employee's problem or concern is *explored*. This exploration involves the antecedents and consequences of the problem along with the employee's beliefs about and *expectations* for resolving it.

R—refers to four *R*s: reformulation, reassurance, reframing, and renegotiation. By *reformulating* the employee's concern into a solvable entity, the employee is likely to feel less demoralized and more hopeful and empowered. Reformulation usually involves *reassurance* and *reframing*. It may require *renegotiation* when previous treatment plans did not account for the employee's understanding and expectations, which may have set the stage for noncompliance or for a negative set of treatment outcomes. The purpose here is to come up with a mutually developed treatment plan or contract.

I—refers to four *I*s: initial intervention, information, instruction, and interference. The *initial intervention* that follows from a mutually developed treatment plan usually involves *information* and permission giving. It also may involve *instructing* the employee in learning *interference* strategies to reverse, for example, anxious or dysphoric feelings or ruminative thoughts that significantly interfere with daily functioning. Such basic interference strategies as controlled breathing, affirmations, and thought stopping can be taught to an employee in a few minutes.

C—refers to four *C*s: continued intervention, compliance, consultation, and counseling interventions. *Continued intervention* is needed only when initial interventions have not been sufficient or when *compliance* with the plan is an issue. Outside *consultation* or referral may then be indicated. Otherwise, other *counseling interventions* can be implemented.

The rules for using ERIC are simple: 1) begin at the first (*E*) level of ERIC and move to subsequent levels only when the situation requires, and 2) in subsequent counseling interviews with the same employee, begin again at the first level, but expect to focus more time and effort at subsequent levels. As few as one or as many as all four levels of progression may be utilized in a single encounter, depending on employee need or circumstance.

The employee's concern may be adequately addressed at the first level with simple engagement skills or processes, such as when the manager's active listening allows the employee to "get something off his chest" so that he or she feels understood and encouraged to go on with life without further professional help. At other times, progression to the second level may be needed. For instance, the manager may need to reformulate the employee's perception of certain physical symptoms into a treatable illness such as depression or to reframe the employee's perceived "failure" as simply a correctable "lapse."

## DISCIPLINARY INTERVIEW

The disciplinary interview is usually scheduled to clarify and increase an employee's compliance with workplace rules and regulations. Usually this involves dealing with negative attitudes and problematic behaviors such as habitual tardiness, absenteeism, or damage or misappropriation of workplace property or resources. Managers may find disciplinary interviews to be difficult because these interviews have the potential to be very unpleasant. This type of interview is necessary because, when employees break rules or fail to comply with regulations and standards, the impact of such noncompliance can be significant. For example, if left untended, the habitual tardiness of one employee can quickly lower morale. Accordingly, the disciplinary interview can be an effective management skill in maintaining not only productivity but morale and job satisfaction.

## Guidelines for Conducting the Disciplinary Interview

1.  Take a positive and proactive stance toward the interview process. Regardless of how unpleasant the interview may appear, the likelihood of resolving the matter is greatly increased if you act quickly and directly.
2.  Avoid verbally attacking or belittling the employee. If you are angry and may lose your temper, postpone the interview until you have calmed down. Recall that your primary goal is to correct a situation that cannot be allowed to continue. From the moment you begin talking, the employee must know that you are trying to be fair. Being fair means listening to the employee's version of the situation.

3. More than any other kind of interview, the disciplinary interview requires that you be fully informed. This means having as much information as possible before the interview. Instead of a global statement such as "You have been tardy nearly every day this month," you can confidently and precisely state that "records show that you've been more than 15 minutes late on 8 of 10 days in the last pay period."

4. The employee should know from the start what the purpose of the interview is. Explain what the standard is and how the employee has failed to meet it, and that this behavior is unacceptable. Specify what corrections are expected and the time frame. Ensure that the employee has a chance to state his or her side of the issue. There is always the possibility that there may be some things in the employee's favor that you have not considered. For example, if you learn that "the second shift started doing this 2 months ago," you can consider the matter further.

5. Deal with the employee's specific disciplinary issue—not his or her overall job performance. It is better to handle performance matters in performance coaching or in an appraisal interview.

6. Terminate this interview as soon as the issue has been addressed. In other words, state the standard and the employee's noncompliance with it, indicate the acceptable behavior you expect from the employee, listen to all of the facts, answer pertinent questions, and ensure that the employee understands the consequences of continued noncompliance. Then, end the interview, if at all possible, on a positive note.

## APPRAISAL INTERVIEW

The formal performance appraisal process in most organizations concludes with a face-to-face meeting with the employee. Whether scheduled semiannually or annually, these interviews follow a specified protocol that focuses on reviewing employee job performance against previously agreed-on performance standards. The formal performance appraisal process does not and should not substitute for ongoing performance-based coaching. Rather, the two should complement one another. However, because some employees require considerably more coaching than others, and because some employees may not be particularly receptive to performance-based coaching, additional formal appraisal interviews—beyond those mandated by organizational policy—may be necessary. Additional appraisal interviews can be quite useful in reviewing the employee's overall performance. In short, the appraisal interview should not be considered an annual—or semiannual—ritual performed to satisfy an organizational policy. It should be scheduled as often as needed to discuss employee growth and development.

The primary purpose of the appraisal interview is to assess the employee's current and recent "fit" with his or her job, the work team, the organization, and the manager. A secondary purpose is to estimate the level of "fit" in the future. Appraisal interviews can be one of the most enjoyable of all interviews that managers have with employees—particularly for managers who view helping employees grow and develop as one of their primary leadership functions.

## Guidelines for Conducting the Appraisal Interview

1.  Set up appraisal interviews with employees with sufficient lead time and with the understanding that the focus is on the future as well as the past and that active participation is essential. Begin by letting employees report how they see themselves and their performance, noting how this compares with your perception of their performance. Review appropriate job performance data and 360-degree feedback, if such is available. 360-degree feedback is usually gathered by giving at least three different people the same inventory or checklist to rate their observations of your performance. One of these people should be your superior, another should be a peer, and a third should be someone who reports to you or someone whom you supervise or oversee. Keep employees actively involved throughout the entire interview. Project the honest impression that this is the employees' session, an opportunity to get the facts on how they are doing and where they are going.

2.  Focus on the future as much as possible. Even when you're talking about past performance, relate it to the employee's future performance. As much as possible, involve the employee in setting *performance* goals for the next period and deciding what actions will produce the best results, both personally and

for the organization. Similarly, employees need to participate in setting *personal* goals and selecting any corrective action that is indicated.

3. As in any interview, ensure that the employee accurately understands your message. As the interview draws to a close, you should begin to summarize and ask the employee to re-state, in his or her own words, what you have said. Clear up any misunderstandings that may have arisen. If you have de-cided on some specific training or corrective course of action, state it clearly and document it in writing. If a follow-up meet-ing is indicated, set the time and place.

4. Finally, note that some employees view appraisal efforts as fo-rums for criticizing them. They may find it difficult to accept criticism or have difficulty seeing themselves objectively. Rec-ognizing their sensitivity to criticism, some managers down-play or even avoid giving feedback. This is neither appropriate nor helpful. Rather, proceed with kindness as well as with firmness. In such an atmosphere, such employees usually be-come more receptive to feedback over time. Feedback that is accurate and presented in a nonjudgmental, nonthreatening manner is necessary for improving both the employee's and the organization's performance.

## EXIT INTERVIEW

The purpose of the exit interview is to review the exiting em-ployee's "fit," job expectations, and experience, as well as to receive feedback on workplace policies and norms. It is not intended to persuade the employee to change his or her mind about leaving. The manager's goal in this type of interview is to attempt to un-derstand the specific reason or reasons for this voluntary termina-tion as well as to review the organization's policies and working conditions, including whether policies, benefits, and wages are in line with those of competitors. This interview can also benefit the employee who is leaving. It can allow the individual to vent by de-scribing the decision to leave, to express any remorse, and to achieve some degree of emotional closure. Information gained from these interviews can be invaluable in preventing turnover. If a problematic workplace condition is identified, it needs to be rectified. If the information reveals that management has not been responsive, necessary steps should be taken to ensure that the matter is addressed.

## Guidelines for Conducting the Exit Interview

1.  Initiate exit interviews by putting employees at ease and expressing appreciation for taking the time to talk about their experience in the organization. Offer assurance that your purpose is not to convince them to stay or to make them reveal information about co-workers, but rather to find ways of improving the organization.
2.  Because poor "fit" or mismatch is a common reason for leaving a job, try to determine the degree of "fit" between the employee and the job, the work team, the organization's mission and values, and you as manager. If poor "fit" is a recurring theme in a number of exit interviews, hiring procedures may need to be reviewed.
3.  Listen and ask open-ended questions. Avoid interrupting and responding defensively, particularly about policy matters. If it becomes necessary to correct a misconception, you might say: "While it may have appeared that way, the policy actually reads. . . ."
4.  Focus on issues or concerns that you can do something about. Other circumstances may be impossible to discuss rationally, much less resolve. Thus, instead of continuing to discuss very emotionally charged situations or responding to very challenging and vengeful statements, you might simply say, "I can understand why you feel that way."

### EXERCISES FOR SKILL DEVELOPMENT

#### Individual Exercise

Complete the self-assessment at the end of this chapter. Then, analyze your overall results.

1.  Go through the 25 items and identify those that reflect the core interviewing skills: active listening, two-way communication, and engagement. Based on your response to these items, estimate

your level of competence for the core interviewing skills. Develop a plan for increasing your skills and your confidence in using these skills. This may include such things as participating in a workshop on active listening or communication.

2.  Go through the 25 items again and identify those that reflect specific counseling skills. Based on your response to these items, estimate your level of competency for the specific counseling skills. As mentioned earlier, conducting effective counseling interviews is a challenge for many managers. Consider ways in which you might increase your counseling skills and your confidence in using these skills: Talk with your mentor or other managers who are skilled in this area, take a course in counseling skills, seize every opportunity to practice these skills with your employees, and draft an action plan.

### Individual Understanding/Reflection Response Exercise

Using the following situations, practice writing out feeling reflection responses.

1.  I'm really concerned about Jim. I used to be his best friend. We did everything together, but I hardly see him anymore. He's been missing a lot of shifts and comes in late when he does show up. I think he may be on drugs. I'm afraid he's going to ruin his life and there's nothing I can do about it."

2.  "I don't know, Mrs. Smith, things aren't going very well for me. I'm not sure I have what it takes to cut it as a nurse here. I did well in school, but here things are different. There's a lot less structure. I feel lost much of the time."

3.  "I don't think I should be blamed because the cardiac bypass machine breaks down so often. After all, it's so old that we have a hard time getting spare parts for it. It should be replaced. I can't stop thinking that it will fail right in the middle of an operation and the patient will die and I'll be blamed for it. Why don't you just replace it now before something awful happens?"

4.  "I've been working here for 3 years now and I still don't feel like I fit in. I want to have friends and go out with the food service gang after our shift, but I'm just so nervous and afraid that when people get to know me, they won't like me. Or, they'll tease me and I won't be able to stand it."

## Group Exercise

This is a role-play exercise to develop counseling skills.

1.  Divide the group into subgroups of three participants. One participant plays the manager conducting the counseling interview, the second plays the employee, and the third plays the observer. Have each group pick one of the following scenarios:

    a.  A highly capable nursing supervisor has the potential to be in top management except for his abruptness and abrasiveness in dealing with subordinates. The director of nursing coached this supervisor on interpersonal skills, but it seems to have had little effect.

    b.  An administrative assistant in patient accounts appears to be increasingly distracted, has made a number of recording errors in the past 2 weeks, appears to be tired, and has lost considerable weight. Four weeks ago her mother died, and the assistant returned to work the following week.

    c.  An admissions clerk has used up much of her sick leave and vacation time in the past 2 months in order to care for her child, who has an inoperable brain tumor. When she is at work, she seems anxious, and she was observed crying in the ladies' room by a co-worker.

    This exercise requires 45 minutes. The manager and employee role-play a counseling interview based on the chosen scenario for approximately 25–30 minutes. The observer takes notes in the following areas: 1) core interviewing skills utilized, 2) specific interviewing skills utilized, and 3) what went well and what might be improved. Following the role-played interview, the observer provides feedback, and discussion follows in the remaining 15–20 minutes.

2.  Switch roles and repeat the same process with a different counseling scenario chosen from the examples provided or from your on-the-job experience.

## SELF-ASSESSMENT OF SKILL 7: COUNSELING AND INTERVIEWING FOR MAXIMUM PERFORMANCE AND DEVELOPMENT

**Directions:** This assessment will help you evaluate your level of skill and attitudes toward counseling and interviewing. Use the following statements to assess your attitudes and skills by circling the number that is closest to your experience: 1 = never, 2 = sometimes, 3 = often, and 4 = always. Respond in a way that reflects your skills today, rather than those you hope to have in the future. Answer as honestly as you can. Instructions on scoring and interpreting the results are provided in the analysis section at the end of the assessment.

1. I develop a strategy for the session based on the needs of the situation and the individual involved.    1   2   3   4

2. I arrange for a meeting room that is private and free of interruptions.    1   2   3   4

3. During interviews, I put the individual at ease and attempt to maintain a relaxed, friendly tone.    1   2   3   4

4. I attempt to act in a way that is candid, genuine, and nonmanipulative.    1   2   3   4

5. I start interviews by being direct and specific about my agenda or my concerns.    1   2   3   4

6. I try to listen actively and use good eye contact and positive body language to communicate my respect, interest, and concern.    1   2   3   4

7. I view the outcomes and success of counseling as dependent on the individual's involvement, so I encourage his or her full participation.    1   2   3   4

8. At the beginning of a counseling session, I try to show that I appreciate the individual's worth and value to the work team (or organization).    1   2   3   4

9. I listen carefully to understand the individual's frame of reference, way of

viewing things, values, attitudes, and
beliefs.                                             1    2    3    4

10.   I use understanding responses, such as
      "uh-huh" and appropriate body language,
      to support and encourage the individual
      to speak freely.                               1    2    3    4

11.   I attempt to restate, in my own words, the
      feelings and concerns underlying the
      individual's statements.                       1    2    3    4

12.   While I am reflecting the individual's
      feelings and concerns, I avoid any hint of
      approval or disapproval of them.               1    2    3    4

13.   I try to pace the interview so that it flows
      gradually rather than forcing or rushing it.   1    2    3    4

14.   I try to help individuals to better
      understand their values and attitudes as
      they relate to the concern at hand.            1    2    3    4

15.   In counseling sessions, I make certain
      that the individual understands that our
      discussion is confidential.                    1    2    3    4

16.   Because I recognize that my values,
      beliefs, and biases can influence the
      individual I am counseling, I try to keep
      them in check.                                 1    2    3    4

17.   In counseling sessions, I encourage the
      individual to consider alternative courses
      of action.                                     1    2    3    4

18.   I also encourage the individual to explore
      the various consequences of each
      alternative course of action.                  1    2    3    4

19.   When needed, I conduct follow-up
      counseling sessions to ensure that the
      problem or concern is fully resolved.          1    2    3    4

20. I try to end interviews and counseling
    sessions on a positive and encouraging
    note.                                         1   2   3   4

21. It is very important that individuals fully
    understand and take ownership for any
    decisions made in the session.                1   2   3   4

22. To avoid any possible misunderstanding
    on my part, I check my perceptions of the
    situation or concern with the individual.     1   2   3   4

23. Before beginning any interview or
    counseling session, I obtain and organize
    any necessary data and materials.             1   2   3   4

24. When there is improvement in job
    behavior or performance following a
    counseling session, I make sure to
    compliment the individual.                    1   2   3   4

25. If the individual is obviously upset or
    distracted, I try to deal with that matter
    before proceeding with the agenda.            1   2   3   4

## Self-Assessment Analysis

Add your circled scores together to arrive at your total score. Then refer to the scoring ranges below to identify your level of skill perform-ance and attitudes toward interviewing and counseling. You may want to refer back to sections of this chapter for suggestions on increasing and honing your interviewing and counseling skills.

76–100   You appear to have highly developed interviewing and coun-seling skills and attitudes that facilitate employee perform-ance and professional development. Continue to enhance and maintain these skills.

51–75    You appear to have reasonably well-developed interviewing and counseling skills, but certain areas could be improved. By further developing your interviewing and counseling skills, you can become even more effective in increasing pro-ductivity and performance.

25–50    Your interviewing and counseling skills appear to need improvement. It may also be that some of your attitudes toward counseling may hinder employee performance and professional development. You might focus on improving selected skills and attitudes (i.e., items that you scored as 1 or 2).

## REVIEW ACTIVITIES

1.    Briefly name and describe the five types and purposes of managerial interview.
2.    Which type have you had the most experience with? The least?
3.    Which one(s) do you feel most competent and comfortable doing? Least competent and comfortable doing?
4.    What are the major advantages of strategic employment interviewing over traditional employment interviewing?
5.    Specify three concrete steps you can take to improve your strategic interviewing skills.
6.    Make a chart of the five types of interviews, and list at least four guidelines for the effective use of each interview. Try to do as much of this exercise from memory before referring back to the text.

## FOR FURTHER INFORMATION

Camp, R., Vielhaber, M., & Simonetti, J. (2001). *Strategic interviewing: How to hire good people.* San Francisco: Jossey-Bass.

An excellent resource for information on conducting employment interviews, this text provides a list of strategically focused questions that are developed based on the six-step model described in this chapter.

Beatty, R. (1994). *Interviewing and selecting high performers: Every manager's guide to effective interviewing techniques.* New York: John Wiley & Sons.

Beatty's book provides a list of more than 500 focused interview questions covering 32 topic areas such as job performance, interpersonal skills, teamwork, willingness to take risks, and drive and motivation.

# Thinking and Deciding Strategically

The objectives of this chapter are to

- Describe the value and necessity of strategic thinking and decision making in health care organizations

- Define strategic thinking and contrast it with strategic planning

- Describe the strategic thinking process and its six steps

- Describe the strategic planning process and its seven steps

- Describe the role of strategic thinking in strategic planning

- Describe and illustrate the six steps of the decision-making process

- Assess your attitudes and skills regarding strategic thinking and decision making

- Provide skill development exercises and activities to develop or enhance strategic thinking and decision-making skills

## STRATEGIC THINKING IN HEALTH CARE SETTINGS

It is fashionable today to use the words *strategic thinking* in the titles of articles, books, and workshops. These publications or workshops are often about strategic planning and learning to develop mission statements. Unfortunately, individuals can engage in the so-called strategic planning process without ever engaging in strategic thinking. Why is this? Because strategic thinking

> is not about some cumbersome planning process to emerge with a big document. It is about maintaining an acute sensitivity to changing conditions, an active mind, a willingness to think in a variety of ways, an avoidance of traps formed by what you know, and an ability to decide. (Wells, 1998, p. ix)

Strategic thinking is a mental discipline consisting of broad-ranging, flexible, and creative thinking. It requires the ability to conceive the future, see and create possibilities, and focus on choosing the more appropriate direction.

Stated another way, thinking strategically involves finding connections in apparently unrelated events or circumstances as well as understanding how various trends and occurrences interrelate to affect a specific organization. In short, it is a way of thinking "outside the box" and about the future while being mindful of the limitations of the here-and-now.

Although thinking strategically is typically specified in the job descriptions of CEOs, presidents, and senior vice presidents and thereby expected of them, strategic thinking should not be limited to top management. Every manager should think strategically every day and encourage all of his or her employees to do the same. In learning the strategic planning process described in this chapter, strategic thinking is the core skill that will be developed.

## THE PROCESS OF STRATEGIC THINKING

Strategic thinking can be summed up in three simple questions: What seems to be happening? What possibilities do we face? What are we going to do about it? These questions reflect the natural flow that is characteristic of strategic thinking. In *Choosing the Future: The Power of Strategic Thinking*, Stuart Wells (1998) described what he calls the cycle of strategic thinking based on these three questions. It is important to note that this cycle of strategic thinking lays the groundwork for taking action, although the processes of both data gathering (i.e., a situational or strengths, weaknesses, opportunities, and threats [SWOT] analysis) and implementing the strategy are outside the cycle.

The cycle consists of three phases: perceiving, understanding, and reasoning. Each of these phases is related to the one of the three questions noted. There are two steps for each phase, for a total of six steps:

1. Acquiring insight
2. Developing foresight
3. Identifying strategic levers for competitive advantage
4. Matching levers with capabilities
5. Choosing a core strategy
6. Making the strategy work

In the following description of the process of strategic thinking, the reader will note that the three phases of the strategic thinking process—perceiving, understanding, and reasoning—represent different forms of thought processing. All three forms are distinct but interconnected, and all three are essential for effective strategic thinking to ensue.

## Perceiving Phase: What Seems to Be Happening?

The question "What seems to be happening?" characterizes the perceiving phase of the strategic thinking process. This phase expands the often restricted view most managers have of their organizations, and facilitates visualizing the organization in its larger context. In this phase, the manager distinguishes the details of what has happened and what is currently happening (Step 1: *acquiring insight*) from what could potentially happen (Step 2: *developing foresight*). In this phase, the manager looks in depth at the various forces, circumstances, and individuals and casts them together into a focused picture that provides some alternative views of the future. The purpose of this phase is not to collect data, as so often happens in traditional strategic planning, but rather to build the necessary knowledge base for the other phases of this process of thinking strategically.

## Understanding Phase: What Possibilities Do We Face?

The question "What possibilities do we face?" characterizes the understanding phase of the strategic thinking process. This phase identifies.strategic possibilities. Step 3 (*identifying strategic levers for competitive advantage*) is a tactic for determining the most advantageous possibilities and opportunities for both perceiving or taking in information and influencing the organization's external environment. Step 4 (*matching levers with capabilities*) takes these opportunities and matches them with the organization's existing and possible strengths. This step involves looking at the interplay of the weaknesses of the organization against the threats posed by the environment. It also articulates how the organization can focus on a limited number of its strengths in order to form the base of a strategy.

## Reasoning Phase: What Are We Going to Do About It?

The question "What are we going to do about it?" characterizes the reasoning phase of the strategic thinking process. This phase narrows and refines the strategy and begins the process of enacting it. Step 5 (*choosing a core strategy*) involves making a decision about the best fitting strategy from among all of the generated strategic possibilities. Step 6 (*making the strategy work*) focuses on thinking about various ways and means of implementing the strategy.

## STRATEGIC PLANNING PROCESS

Although similar in some respects to strategic thinking, the strategic planning process typically involves the following seven steps:

**Step 1: Decision to plan and allocate resources.** The decision to plan and allocate resources is the first step in strategic planning. Assuming that corporate leaders recognize the value of and need for strategic planning and can dedicate the resources of people, place, time, and money, the process can begin in earnest.

**Step 2: Situational analysis.** The second step is also called an environmental scan and internal review by some (Birnbaum, 1990). The basic question to be considered in this second step is, "Where are we today?" By reviewing the threats and opportunities from the suprasystem or environment and the strengths and weaknesses of the subsystems, this question can be answered.

**Step 3: Mission statement.** The third step is the specification of the vision, or mission statement. A mission statement is a brief, clear statement of objectives that crystallizes the organization's vision and serves as a guidepost for present and future decisions about structure, power, and resources. An effective mission statement succinctly specifies, in 20 words or less, what functions the organization will perform for whom. The questions to be answered are, "What should our business be?" and "Who are our customers?"

**Step 4: Goal setting.** This step addresses the question of goals: "Where do we wish to arrive, and when?" Goal statements that articulate the mission statement and are focused, feasible, and prioritized are a necessary prerequisite for the preparation of a strategy.

**Step 5: Developing strategy.** The fifth step addresses the question, "How do we get from here to there?" This step involves the development of a game plan for achieving the corporate mission.

**Step 6: Implementing strategy.** This important step involves revising other subsystems, particularly structure, to maximize the probability that the strategy can be achieved. It also involves developing an operational plan and tactics. The *operational plan* is the game plan for implementing the strategy. The *tactics* of the operational plan are the action steps: the how-to-do-it, the who-does-it-and-when, and the what-are-the-resources-required steps. The operational plan is developed by those closest to the "action." Whereas strategic plans may have a 3- to 5-year time span, an operational plan has a time span of 1 year or less.

**Step 7: Evaluation.** This step involves assessing and monitoring the effectiveness of implementing the strategy. Comparing strategy implementation with the mission statement provides crucial feedback for course correction and revision. (Sperry, 1993, pp. 33–37)

So how does the process of strategic thinking differ from the strategic planning process? Table 1 offers a comparison of the two processes. The steps that are in bold type represent strategic thinking. The reader will note that only Step 5—developing a strategy— of the strategic planning process actually involves the process of strategic thinking. As noted earlier in this section, a situational analysis (Step 2 in the strategic planning process), often called a SWOT analysis, is often a data-gathering exercise rather than an occasion for thinking strategically about the data gathered. Strategic thinking transforms data collection into knowledge that is a basis for further strategic thinking.

## DECISION MAKING IN HEALTH CARE SETTINGS

Health care managers are currently faced with making more and tougher decisions that were unheard of even 10 years ago. Of all the decisions a manager faces, personnel decisions are probably the

**Table 1.**   The strategic thinking and the strategic planning processes

| Strategic thinking process | Strategic planning process |
| --- | --- |
| 1. Acquiring insight | 1. Decision to plan and allocate resources |
| 2. Developing foresight |  |
| 3. Identifying strategic levers for competitive advantage | 2. Situational analysis |
|  | 3. Mission statement |
| 4. Matching levers with capabilities | 4. Goal setting |
| 5. Choosing a core strategy | 5. Developing a strategy |
| 6. Making the strategy work | 6. Implementing strategy |
|  | 7. Evaluations |

most challenging. Everyday decisions about employee reassignment, cross-training, and replacing employees with less qualified personnel point up the intensity and complexity of decisions that managers must make today in the face of shrinking time and available resources. Critical shortages in certain professions, such as nurses and nursing assistants, demand that quick hiring decisions be made before a candidate is lost to competing health care systems.

Even more challenging are personnel decisions involving involuntary terminations, discrimination, harassment issues, and the like, which can result in legal nightmares. Next to communication skills, decision making and problem solving are the skills that a manager utilizes most throughout the course of a given day. Not surprisingly, the ability to make solid, informed decisions has been, and remains, the mark of the effective manager.

## Decision-Making Styles

Every manager brings to the decision-making process a particular way of thinking and style of approaching problems that influence the type of decision made. Three styles of decision making can be described. The first is the *decisional avoidance* style, wherein the manager attempts to maintain the status quo by avoiding or smoothing over problems. The second can be called the *reactive decisional* style, which is probably the most common of the three styles. Here a manager confronts a problem directly, although reactively, and initiates the changes necessary to solve it. The third style, called *proactive decisional,* is more preventive in focus. This manager anticipates possible problems so that decisions for corrective action can be made that prevent the spread of the problem or concern.

## Levels and Types of Decision Making

The three levels of decision making in a health care organization—strategic, administrative, and operational—are closely related to the three levels of organizational planning: strategic, long range, and operational planning. There are also two major types of decisions. *Programmatic decisions* involve routine and recurrent matters and are usually easily addressed with "standard operating procedures." *Nonprogrammatic decisions* involve circumstances that are sufficiently unique or unusual to fall outside the purview of an organization's policies and procedures. This type of decision requires the manager's careful consideration and usually involves a formal, multistep decision-making methodology. Both the levels and types are described together in this section.

*1. Strategic Decision Making* Decisions at this level apply to the entire organization, are conceptual in nature, and usually have long-term consequences for organizations and, in the case of health care, for the community. These decisions, which involve the organization's basic goals and strategy and its relationship with the external environment, are made largely by senior management. This is the main province of nonprogrammatic decisions.

*2. Administrative Decision Making* Decisions at this level, also called *tactical decision making,* are made by middle management and apply primarily to one unit or several related units in an organization. These decisions can have long-term or medium-term consequences. Nonprogrammatic decisions are also made at this level, along with some programmatic decisions.

*3. Operational Decision Making* Decisions at this level are made and carried out by supervisors or lower level managers. These decisions involve day-to-day operations and apply primarily to a single unit. These decisions typically have short-term consequences. This is the main province of programmatic decisions, although supervisors occasionally deal with nonprogrammatic decisions.

## Six-Step Decision-Making Process

Decision making is one very practical application of strategic thinking. The manager's responsibility when faced with a nonprogrammatic decision is to think through the situation, utilize good judgment in making a decision, and act decisively in implementing the decision. There are six steps in the decision-making process. The reader will note that these steps are similar to those of strategic planning.

**Step 1: Identify the problem.** Problems keep an organization from achieving its mission and goals. The decision-making process begins by determining the underlying cause of a problematic situation. Questions to answer are: How serious is it? How does it impact our mission? What is the cause? How has it been handled in the past? This step requires collecting pertinent information in order to accurately identify the basic underlying problem, not simply its symptomatic, surface manifestations. Therefore, it is a time-intensive step and should not be short circuited. Preparing a problem statement formalizes this step.

**Step 2: Determine possible solutions.** Once the problem is identified, the manager then considers possible solutions and specifies standards to evaluate them. Information should be collected, factors related to these solutions should be analyzed, and priorities should be set.

**Step 3: Specify alternative courses of action.** Once the problem and its possible solutions have been identified, the manager develops several alternatives to accomplish the solutions. Each alternative should be developed and analyzed before any alternative is evaluated and dismissed.

**Step 4: Evaluate the alternatives and decide on a course of action.** Each alternative is then reviewed in terms of specified criteria such as its utility, viability, and cost with regard to the mission and resources of the organization; its anticipated effectiveness in solving the problem; and its consequences for the unit and the rest of the organization. The alternative that best fits the criteria is usually selected.

**Step 5: Implement the decision.** Once a course of action is selected, an action plan is developed. This plan serves as the basis for implementing the decision.

**Step 6: Follow up on the implementation.** The manager assesses the results of the enacted decision, using the set of standards specified in the second step in order to determine the effectiveness of the decision and course of action taken.

*Claremont General is a 340-bed community hospital that, along with two smaller hospitals, serves a medium-size metropolitan area. Although its medical and surgical services and staff have grown over the past 5 years, admissions and bed occupancy rates have been declining—from 78% to 64%—in the past 2 years. Because overhead costs have increased by 11% during that period, the hospital is seriously financially stressed for the first time in several years. The hospital's executive committee assigned Fred*

Williamson, the Director of Planning, to come up with a proposal and recommendation for dealing with the decline.

Williamson initiated the decision-making process by attempting to identify the problem (Step 1). He began by collecting information, which included a demographic projection of the community—anticipated to grow by 2%–3% for the next 5 years—and data on each nearby hospital's occupancy rates (the two other hospitals serving the community had admission and bed occupancy rates in the range of 68%–70% and had experienced a growth rate of 3%–4% in the past 2 years). He interviewed several program directors and found contrasting views of the declining rates at Claremont General. The chief of medicine, a cardiac surgeon, believed it was because the hospital had not approved his plan for a heart transplant program. The director of nursing was convinced the problems were low salaries and morale resulting in poor quality of care, which deterred patient admissions. Survey data on hospital employees seemed to bear out the nursing director's point: Low salaries and high turnover rates were increasing stress and decreasing morale. However, there was no indication that these factors could explain the precipitous drop in admissions. Probably the most telling finding was that two orthopedic surgeons with large surgical practices had left the medical staff 18 months previously over a dispute about office space in the hospital's professional building. They were now practicing out of the two smaller hospitals, where they were admitting their surgical patients. Fred concluded that, for all practical purposes, the decline in occupancy rates could be attributed to losing the patients admitted by the two orthopedic surgeons. The problem statement thus was "decreased occupancy levels primarily attributed to surgical patients being admitted elsewhere."

Williamson next focused on possible solutions (Step 2). Increasing staff salaries, especially for nurses, and establishing a heart transplant program were not seriously considered; instead, Williamson focused on luring the orthopedists back to the hospital. Accordingly, he considered some alternative courses of action (Step 3). The first was offering to increase the office space as the two surgeons had originally proposed. The second was offering to establish an orthopedic ambulatory care center at Claremont General. The surgeons were currently negotiating with one of the other area hospitals for such a center. The third alternative was suggested by the hospital CEO: Appoint one of the orthopedists to the hospital's board of directors and the other as assistant chief of medicine. In evaluating the alternatives (Step 4), it became clear rather quickly that the third alternative was unrealistic, given the chief of medicine's professional jealousy. The first alternative was realistic but not viable because the orthopedists were given nearly double the space at the two other hospitals that they had requested at Claremont. Although it was almost certain that the state would approve a certificate of need for the ambulatory orthopedic center, a cost-benefit analysis suggested that financing the construction of a center with such a limited focus would be very difficult. A variation of the proposal, however, in which Claremont would develop a general ambulatory surgical center that would emphasize orthopedic care, was a very viable and realistic alternative.

Preliminary discussion with the orthopedists indicated their high interest in being involved with such a center. The proposed plan was unanimously approved by the executive committee and the board. Implementation of the plan (Step 5) began immediately. A generous office agreement was reached with the orthopedists and the request for a certificate of need was submitted, while architects worked with a committee, co-chaired by one of the orthopedists, on planning the surgical center. Rather soon, occupancy figures began to rise as increasing numbers of orthopedic surgery patients were admitted (Step 6).

## EXERCISES FOR SKILL DEVELOPMENT

### Individual Exercise

Consider the following case example:

You are the director of pharmacy services for an academic medical center that has four pharmacies, including three that provide 24-hour service. The pharmacy providing 24-hour service to the emergency room (ER) has been particularly difficult to staff on the second and third shifts for the past 6 months. The pharmacy supervisor for the second shift has complained to you that she regularly spends 2–3 hours a night, at least three times a week, backing up the ER pharmacy staff. Besides the fact that this work is not in her job description, she is concerned that she is not able to provide pharmacy consultation to medical and surgical resi-

*dents who are on call, or to comply with the hospital's risk management protocol for all the hospital's pharmacy services, because of her "disrupted schedule." She confronted you as you arrived at the medical center at 7:00 A.M. today, angrily announcing that she is tired of waiting for more staff and tired of being overworked and abused: "If something isn't done by Friday night's shift, you can find yourself another pharmacy supervisor." Today is Tuesday.*

1. Utilize the first four steps of the six-step decision-making process to address this matter. Use your imagination to fill in details on the data collection for Step 1, and write a succinct problem statement.

2. Prepare a detailed outline of Steps 2–4. Include at least three alternative courses of action and three standards and criteria for evaluating each alternative. This exercise is completed at this point. Thus, you would not decide on a specific course of action.

### Group Exercise

Divide into groups of four and continue working with the case exercise provided in the preceding Individual Exercise.

1. Begin by reviewing the detailed outlines that were prepared in the Individual Exercise. Choose an outline that reflects the group's consensus about the alternative courses of action.

2. As a group, analyze each of the proposed courses of actions in terms of the specified standards and criteria and arrive at a decision about the best course of action.

3. Develop a detailed plan for Steps 5 and 6. Then role-play a meeting between the pharmacy director and the night supervisor.

### Alternative Group Exercise

Taking the Claremont General case example, have one small group member play the role of Fred Williamson, with the other three playing members of the hospital's executive committee. Suggested time for this exercise is 45 minutes: 30 minutes for the role play and 10–15 minutes for discussion.

1. Role-play a meeting in which Mr. Williamson presents his proposal and recommended course of action to the executive committee, followed by a discussion during which the committee comes up with its decision—which may or may not match the decisions offered in the case example.

2. Discuss the role play with particular attention to the impact of group dynamics on the decision-making process.

## SELF-ASSESSMENT OF SKILL 8: THINKING AND DECIDING STRATEGICALLY

**Directions:** This assessment will help you evaluate your level of skill and attitudes regarding strategic thinking and decision making. Use the following statements to assess your attitudes and skills by circling the number that is closest to your experience: 1 = never, 2 = sometimes, 3 = often, and 4 = always. Respond in a way that reflects your skills today, rather than those you hope to have in the future. Answer as honestly as you can. Instructions on scoring and interpreting the results are provided in the analysis section at the end of the assessment.

1. I follow a multistep decision-making model to ensure a sound decision.      1   2   3   4

2. I discuss my strategy with all individuals involved.      1   2   3   4

3. I make my decisions in a timely fashion and ensure that they are implemented.      1   2   3   4

4. I use my understanding of the organization's culture to get support for my decisions.      1   2   3   4

5. I consider the actions and reactions that have an impact on and follow from my decisions.      1   2   3   4

6. I weigh all probabilities when considering forecasts and planned outcomes.      1   2   3   4

7.  I explain my decisions clearly and ask for feedback about them.    1    2    3    4

8.  My superiors consider me a strategic thinker.    1    2    3    4

9.  I put monitoring systems in place in order to check progress.    1    2    3    4

10. I make an effort to enlist support for my decisions throughout the decision-making process.    1    2    3    4

11. I utilize different scenarios to test the viability of proposed actions and to improve forecasts.    1    2    3    4

12. In order to arrive at the best possible decision, I encourage my team to express divergent views.    1    2    3    4

13. I consult with all appropriate stakeholders to get their input before making a decision.    1    2    3    4

14. I use the 80/20 rule (20% of effort contributes to 80% of the results) in prioritizing significant factors.    1    2    3    4

15. I conduct SWOT analyses on our operation as well as on those of our competitors.    1    2    3    4

16. I develop a strong case to support all of my strategic decisions.    1    2    3    4

17. I combine analytical methods and creative approaches in making decisions.    1    2    3    4

18. I consider the type of decision I will make before beginning the process.    1    2    3    4

19. I make sure that I have the necessary background information before making a decision.    1    2    3    4

20. I constantly check to ensure that my team
    operates within the strategy.                    1    2    3    4

21. It is important for my strategy to "fit" with
    my colleagues' strategies.                       1    2    3    4

22. I avoid delaying decisions that have to be
    made.                                            1    2    3    4

23. I understand the role of intuition in
    making decisions and use it when
    analytical methods are insufficient.             1    2    3    4

24. I strive to make my decisions on a cost-
    effective basis.                                 1    2    3    4

25. I consider the underlying values—mine
    and others—before making a decision.             1    2    3    4

## Self-Assessment Analysis

Add your circled scores together to arrive at your total score. Then, refer to the scoring ranges below to identify your level of skill performance and attitudes toward strategic thinking and decision making. You may want to refer back to sections of this chapter for suggestions on increasing and honing your strategic thinking and decision-making skills.

76–100  You appear to have highly developed strategic thinking and decision-making skills and attitudes that facilitate your ability to effectively and efficiently manage your areas of responsibility. Continue to enhance and maintain these skills.

51–75   You appear to have reasonably well-developed strategic thinking and decision-making skills, but certain areas could be improved. By further developing these skills, you can become even more effective in increasing the productivity and performance of your department.

25–50   Your strategic thinking and decision-making skills appear to need improvement. It appears that you may not fully understand the importance of this skill and its overall relation to the successful operation of your department. You might focus on improving selected skills and attitudes (i.e., items that you scored as 1 or 2).

## REVIEW ACTIVITIES

1.  In your own words, briefly define strategic thinking and strategic planning. Indicate at least two ways in which they differ.
2.  Estimate the extent to which strategic thinking is valued and practiced in your health care organization. At what levels of the organization is it practiced? If it is absent or only occasionally practiced, suggest some possible explanations for this finding.
3.  How could strategic thinking be implemented in your health care organization? In your unit?
4.  Describe your dominant style of decision making. Indicate the type and level of decision making that is expected of you in your current position.
5.  Describe a recent decision-making situation that involved you. Use the six-step decision-making process to review your decision process.
6.  Based on the results of the self-assessment and ideas gleaned from this chapter, devise a plan for enhancing your strategic thinking and decision-making skills.

## FOR FURTHER INFORMATION

Wells, S. (1998). *Choosing the future: The power of strategic thinking.* Boston: Butterworth–Heinemann.

This one-of-a-kind book can really stimulate a manager's strategic thought processes. The strategy Wells proposes helps you know when to focus on questions instead of answers, delay a decision pending further information, balance contrasting models of thinking, and transform ideas into actions.

# Mastering the Budgeting Process

*with Alan Whiteman, Ph.D.*[1]

The objectives of this chapter are to

- Describe budgets as a management tool
- Explain the relationship between planning and budgeting
- Review the preparation and analysis of budgets
- Specify the steps in performing variance analysis
- Assess your attitudes and skills toward the budgeting process
- Provide skill development exercises to develop or enhance budgeting skills

## BUDGETS AS A MANAGEMENT TOOL

One of the most commonly utilized management tools for financial planning is the budget. This tool is critical to efficient and effective

---

[1]Alan Whiteman, Ph.D., is Associate Professor and Director of the Health Services Administration program at Barry University, Miami Shores, Florida.

management of health care organizations because these organizations must cope with declining revenues and scarce resources. A well-orchestrated budgeting process focuses the organization's management team on the actions that must be taken for the organization to remain viable and succeed.

Budgets provide managers with an excellent tool to strategically manage their area of responsibility. The budget process forces managers to review their operations, devise plans for the next fiscal year, and quantify these plans by budgeting funds for all aspects of their plans. Once the budget is approved, managers then monitor their operational and planning successes by determining the effectiveness of their decisions.

This chapter concentrates on the components of the budgeting process. It also discusses six types of budgets and the steps that must be taken to analyze these budgets. After completing this chapter, managers should be able to understand the importance and use of budgeting, plan the steps that they must take in completing their segment of the budget, and analyze variances in the budget for their area of responsibility.

## WHAT IS BUDGETING?

Budgeting has been defined as the formulation of plans for a given period in numerical terms (Herkimer, 1988). This simply means that, once the written segment of the planning process is completed, the next step is to apply a monetary value to each part of the plan, thus translating the plan into a comprehensive financial projection of the coming period.

Budgeting is a proactive portion of the organizational management process. Budgets provide health care managers with a means to develop plans, set goals, and measure actual performance. Businesses, health care or otherwise, that do not have a budget keep managers guessing as to what they will earn and what they will spend.

Budgets provide a 1-year snapshot of an organization's planned income and spending. If the budgeting process is properly implemented, managers at all levels, from supervisors to senior executives, will have a vested interest in the accuracy and success of the budgeting process. In general, the budgeting process is seen as an onerous burden by most employees because it can be a tedious and time-consuming exercise. The manager's job is to create a feeling of ownership in the final product among those employees that he or she supervises.

The budgeting process allows health care managers to meet the basic requirements of their jobs. These requirements include planning, communicating, organizing, staffing, directing, evaluating, controlling quality, innovating, and marketing (Allen, 1997). Budgets provide managers with a tool to measure the effectiveness of their management skills in meeting departmental and corporate objectives.

## TYPES OF BUDGETS

The budgeting process is focused not on a single type of budget but rather on a series of budgets that, when combined, produce a master budget that guides the operation of a health care facility. Budgets are designed to meet the needs of the organization. There are no required or standard formats, such as those that exist for financial statements.

Gapenski (1999) identified the following types of budgets:

1. *Statistics budget:* The department manager identifies the volume of services to be provided and the units of resources required to provide services. The process of developing statistics depends on the collection of data, including historical data about services provided to patients in previous periods, area demographics, and plans for increasing market share. This is the basis for forecasting future volumes.

2. *Revenue budget:* This budget provides the key element of the operating budget. Revenue is key because expense projections, and to some extent capital expenditure projections, all depend on the projection of operating revenue (Ross, Williams, & Pavlock, 1998). The volumes from the statistics budget, when combined with price information, allow the organization to project revenues. Developing a revenue budget requires the manager to look at the various fees paid by federal and state programs, managed care, and private-pay patients.

3. *Expense budget:* The expense budget uses data from the statistics budget and focuses on the cost of providing services. This budget is usually divided into labor and nonlabor components, and must take into account fixed and variable costs. Variable costs

change in relation to changes in volume. As more services are provided, variable costs will increase proportionally. Fixed costs remain the same as more services are provided to patients. It is important to identify fixed and variable costs prior to beginning the budgeting process. Some organizations utilize more sophisticated approaches and identify blended categories of fixed and variable costs.

4.  *Operating budget:* This budget is a combination of the revenue and expense budgets. In smaller organizations, the statistics budget is also incorporated into this document. This budget is usually prepared at the departmental level because of its importance to department managers.

5.  *Cash budget:* This budget focuses on cash flow and is used for short-term cash management. It represents the major instrument for planning the use of cash during the year. The cash budget also indicates whether capital expenditures are being financed in such a way as to create a chronic cash drain and thus a need for long-term financing. In addition, the cash budget shows when and if a short-term loan is needed and when it can be repaid (Ross et al., 1998).

6.  *Capital budget:* This budget accounts for the acquisition of new or replacement of old capital items. These items include land, land improvement, buildings (including construction), fixed equipment, major moveable equipment, and major repairs. It is a means to review and justify why such resources are needed (Nowicki, 2001).

Health care managers most frequently work with operating budgets. Operating budgets are a consolidation of the revenue budget and the expense budget. The data used to create an operating budget consist of assumptions about volume of service, revenue per service unit, the breakdown of fee-for-service and capitated revenue, and variable and fixed costs. These assumptions are based on historical data, projected volumes, and anticipated changes in reimbursement and expenses.

## THE BUDGETING PROCESS

The budgeting process is a complex series of events that eventually flow together to create a management tool to guide the health care facility's operations for the year. The process itself involves multiple steps requiring the critical input of all levels of management, from the board of directors to supervisors, and all of the organization's departments. A general description of these steps follows, although the process will vary by organization (Herkimer, 1988):

1. A budget kick-off meeting is held to review the organization's mission, goals, and objectives and some basic assumptions for the budget year. During the kick-off meeting, the budget manual, budget calendar, historical and current financial and statistical data, and any other relevant information are circulated among all department managers. A budget committee, usually comprising various senior managers, is empowered to oversee the budgeting process. The budget director in most instances is the chief financial officer.

2. Each department manager is required to establish and document a department mission and departmental goals and objectives.

3. Each department manager is required to negotiate with the budget director as to which expenses are fixed and which are variable, and to develop standard rates for each variable expense item.

4. Department managers are required to generate a 3-year capital expenditure plan.

5. The budget committee reviews all proposed capital expenditures and advises the department managers of their decisions.

6. Each department manager, in conjunction with the budget director, develops the department's projected volume forecast.

7. Each department manager, in conjunction with the budget director, identifies each service or product generated for sale by the department and registers the current price as the basis for projecting the preliminary revenue budget.

8. The budget director collects all department budgets and generates the preliminary budget.

9. The budget director analyzes the preliminary budget in order to identify any department(s) not generating the desired revenue contribution.

10. The budget director meets with the appropriate department manager(s) to review all budgets that are not generating the desired contribution to readjust the expenses and possibly the pricing of certain items.

11. The budget director consolidates all of the department budgets and creates a master budget.
12. Using the master budget and the capital expenditure budget, the budget director develops a monthly cash flow forecast.
13. The budget director consolidates and packages the master budget and all supporting documentation.
14. The budget committee and administration review the package and make appropriate changes.
15. The final master budget is submitted to the finance committee of the board of directors for approval.
16. After approving the final budget, the finance committee presents it to the governing board and recommends its acceptance. The budget, after approval, is ready for presentation to the department managers.
17. The board-approved budget is distributed to all department heads at a meeting. It is reviewed and officially implemented at this time.
18. After operating for a short period, the budget is analyzed through variance analysis techniques. This is an ongoing process throughout the budget period. Department managers are required to meet with the appropriate financial officer on an ongoing basis to review and explain positive and negative variances.

The key aspect of budgeting that has an impact on department managers is the translation of product-line decisions into precise and specific sets of resource expectations. Product lines are a consolidation of patients along lines that make sense to the organization, such as all patients having diagnostic imaging studies being assigned to the radiology department. The primary input from the department (Cleverley, 1997) can be to

1. Define the volumes by patients and by case type to be treated in the budget period
2. Define the standard treatment protocol by case type
3 Define the required departmental or activity center volumes
4. Define the standard cost profiles for departmental or activity center outputs
5. Define the prices to be paid for resources

The final output of this process is a set of standards that can be used by management as guidelines for operations. Variance analysis allows the manager to identify areas for financial performance improvement and to implement the appropriate changes to modify the performance.

## OTHER BUDGETING TECHNIQUES

### Zero-Based Budgeting

The budgeting process usually begins with an in-depth analysis of the previous year's budgeted and actual data, in order to make adjustments for the coming year. Zero-based budgeting, as its name indicates, begins each year with a budget of zero. Department heads must justify each line item entry on their budget. In some cases, department heads must create budgets for various alternate models of operation, taking into consideration several different funding and expense relationships that might occur (Gapenski, 2002). Zero-based budgeting is a very labor intensive and costly process. Thus, most health care managers have not found the benefit worth the cost of preparation.

### Flexible Budget

The budgeting process discussed in this chapter can be prepared in either a fixed format, where volumes are assumed not to change, or in a flexible format, which adjusts for different levels of volume activity. A flexible budget enables management to analyze and adjust costs based on a series of different volume forecasts. A flexible budget provides a means to modify a budget by compensating for the two most common types of budgeting errors: 1) inaccurate volume estimates and 2) underestimation of patient demand for services (Ross et al., 1998).

## VARIANCE ANALYSIS

A variance is the difference between the budgeted amount and the actual amount. Variance analysis is an examination and interpretation of differences between what actually happened and what was planned (Gapenski, 1999).

Variance analysis is critical to the managerial control process. Actions taken in response to variance analysis often have the potential to dramatically improve the operations and financial performance of the organization (Gapenski, 1999). The purpose of variance analysis is to find areas in which operations need to be fine-tuned, and to make the necessary operational corrections to correct the variance. In addition, if the actual amount and the budgeted amount are very close, then management is assured that the planning process was effective.

The data in Table 1 demonstrate the use of variances. This revenue example shows that the health care organization projected higher earnings than it actually received. The manager's role is to determine why this revenue has varied significantly. The health care organization may have been overly optimistic in projecting either the number of anticipated patient services, or the revenue per service used to calculate the budget. The expense budget may have been higher than the actual as a result of the reduction in patient services. This simple example focuses attention on the type of questions that should be asked in variance analysis.

*Drs. Smith, Johnson, and Lopez, all board-certified diagnostic radiologists trained in magnetic resonance imaging (MRI), have decided to open a new health care business venture, the Downtown MRI Center. The doctors and a team of professional advisors have conducted extensive market research and strongly believe that they can be successful in the current reimbursement environment. They ask Mary Buck, C.P.A., to assist them in preparing an operating budget that is presented in a pro forma profit and loss statement (Figure 1). They plan to use this budget as both an operating tool to manage the business and a document that can be presented to various lenders when they apply for loans and/or leases.*

*Mary meets with the doctors and guides them in preparing a set of assumptions she can use in the construction of the operating*

**Table 1.**   Sample data illustrating the importance of variance analysis

|  | Budget | Actual | Variance |
|---|---|---|---|
| Revenue | $1,200,000 | $900,000 | $300,000 |
| Expenses | 750,000 | 600,000 | 150,000 |

Downtown MRI Center
Projected Revenues and Expenses
for the Period August 1, 2001–July 31, 2002

| REVENUES | AUG | SEPT | OCT | NOV | DEC | JAN | FEB | MAR | APR | MAY | JUN | JUL | TOTAL |
|---|---|---|---|---|---|---|---|---|---|---|---|---|---|
| Scans/mo | 100 | 130 | 160 | 190 | 220 | 220 | 220 | 220 | 220 | 220 | 220 | 190 | 2,310 |
| Gross Revenue @ 550 | 55,000 | 71,500 | 88,000 | 104,500 | 121,000 | 121,000 | 121,000 | 121,000 | 121,000 | 121,000 | 121,000 | 104,500 | 1,270,500 |
| Bad Debt −10% | 5,500 | 7,150 | 8,800 | 10,450 | 12,100 | 12,100 | 12,100 | 12,100 | 12,100 | 12,100 | 12,100 | 10,450 | 127,050 |
| Adjusted Gross Revenue | 49,500 | 64,350 | 79,200 | 94,050 | 108,900 | 108,900 | 108,900 | 108,900 | 108,900 | 108,900 | 108,900 | 94,050 | 1,143,450 |
| **EXPENSES** | | | | | | | | | | | | | |
| Manager 1 | 4,000 | 4,000 | 4,000 | 4,000 | 4,000 | 4,000 | 4,000 | 4,000 | 4,000 | 4,000 | 4,000 | 4,000 | 48,000 |
| Technologist 1 | 3,600 | 3,600 | 3,600 | 3,600 | 3,600 | 3,600 | 3,600 | 3,600 | 3,600 | 3,600 | 3,600 | 3,600 | 43,200 |
| Receptionist 1 | 1,800 | 1,800 | 1,800 | 1,800 | 1,800 | 1,800 | 1,800 | 1,800 | 1,800 | 1,800 | 1,800 | 1,800 | 21,600 |
| Runner | — | — | — | 1,600 | 1,600 | 1,600 | 1,600 | 1,600 | 1,600 | 1,600 | 1,600 | 1,600 | 14,400 |
| Marketing Rep | 3,500 | 3,500 | 3,500 | 3,500 | 3,500 | 3,500 | 3,500 | 3,500 | 3,500 | 3,500 | 3,500 | 3,500 | 42,000 |
| Management Fee @ 7.50% | — | 4,125 | 5,363 | 6,600 | 7,838 | 9,075 | 9,075 | 9,075 | 9,075 | 9,075 | 9,075 | 9,075 | 87,450 |
| Prof Comp @ 15% | — | 8,250 | 10,725 | 13,200 | 15,675 | 18,150 | 18,150 | 18,150 | 18,150 | 18,150 | 18,150 | 18,150 | 174,900 |
| Staff Benefits @ 22% | 2,838 | 2,838 | 2,838 | 3,190 | 3,190 | 3,190 | 3,190 | 3,190 | 3,190 | 3,190 | 3,190 | 3,190 | 37,224 |
| Rent | — | 4,206 | 4,206 | 4,206 | 4,206 | 4,206 | 4,206 | 4,206 | 4,206 | 4,206 | 4,206 | 4,206 | 46,266 |
| Equipment Lease | — | — | — | — | — | — | 20,000 | 20,000 | 20,000 | 20,000 | 20,000 | 20,000 | 120,000 |
| Contrast Dye | 2,000 | 2,600 | 3,200 | 3,800 | 4,400 | 4,400 | 4,400 | 4,400 | 4,400 | 4,400 | 4,400 | 4,400 | 46,800 |

**Figure 1.** Downtown MRI Center projected revenues and expenses. (Note: Figures are in dollars.)

*(continued)*

Figure 1. *(continued)*

| | | | | | | | | | | | | | Total |
|---|---|---|---|---|---|---|---|---|---|---|---|---|---|
| Medical Supplies | 165 | 165 | 165 | 165 | 165 | 165 | 165 | 165 | 165 | 165 | 165 | 165 | 1,980 |
| Film | 1,200 | 1,560 | 1,920 | 2,280 | 2,640 | 2,640 | 2,640 | 2,640 | 2,640 | 2,640 | 2,640 | 2,640 | 28,080 |
| Infectious Waste Control | 40 | 40 | 40 | 40 | 40 | 40 | 40 | 40 | 40 | 40 | 40 | 40 | 480 |
| Laundry | 200 | 260 | 290 | 320 | 350 | 350 | 350 | 350 | 350 | 350 | 350 | 350 | 3,870 |
| Telephone | 325 | 325 | 325 | 325 | 325 | 325 | 325 | 325 | 325 | 325 | 325 | 325 | 3,900 |
| Security | 52 | 52 | 52 | 52 | 52 | 52 | 52 | 52 | 52 | 52 | 52 | 52 | 624 |
| Contingency | 3,000 | 3,000 | 3,000 | 3,000 | 3,000 | 3,000 | 3,000 | 3,000 | 3,000 | 3,000 | 3,000 | 3,000 | 36,000 |
| Insurance—Liability | 150 | 150 | 150 | 150 | 150 | 150 | 150 | 150 | 150 | 150 | 150 | 150 | 1,800 |
| Insurance—Magnet | 6,500 | 500 | 500 | 500 | 500 | 500 | 500 | 500 | 500 | 500 | 500 | 500 | 12,000 |
| Billing—4% | — | 2,200 | 2,860 | 3,520 | 4,180 | 4,840 | 4,840 | 4,840 | 4,840 | 4,840 | 4,840 | 4,840 | 46,640 |
| Marketing/Advertising Exp | 2,200 | 2,200 | 2,200 | 2,200 | 2,200 | 2,200 | 2,200 | 2,200 | 2,200 | 2,200 | 2,200 | 2,200 | 26,400 |
| Accounting | 11,500 | 500 | 500 | 500 | 500 | 500 | 500 | 500 | 500 | 500 | 500 | 500 | 17,000 |
| Utilities | 2,100 | 2,100 | 2,100 | 2,100 | 2,100 | 2,100 | 2,100 | 2,100 | 2,100 | 2,100 | 2,100 | 2,100 | 25,200 |
| Postage | 150 | 150 | 150 | 150 | 150 | 150 | 150 | 150 | 150 | 150 | 150 | 150 | 1,800 |
| Cryogens & Service Contracts | — | — | — | — | — | — | 8,500 | 8,500 | 8,500 | 8,500 | 8,500 | 8,500 | 51,000 |
| Janitorial | 115 | 115 | 115 | 115 | 115 | 115 | 115 | 115 | 115 | 115 | 115 | 115 | 1,380 |
| Patient Transport | — | — | 510 | 510 | 510 | 510 | 510 | 510 | 510 | 510 | 510 | 510 | 5,100 |
| Development Fee | — | — | — | — | — | — | — | — | — | — | — | — | — |
| Total Monthly Expenses | 45,435 | 48,236 | 54,109 | 61,423 | 66,786 | 71,158 | 99,658 | 99,658 | 99,658 | 99,658 | 99,658 | 99,658 | 945,094 |
| Excess Revenues over Expenses | 4,065 | 16,114 | 25,092 | 32,627 | 42,115 | 37,742 | 9,242 | 9,242 | 9,242 | 9,242 | 9,242 | (5,608) | 198,356 |
| Return on Investment—5% | 203.25 | 805.70 | 1,254.58 | 1,631.35 | 2,105.73 | 1,887.10 | 462.10 | 462.10 | 462.10 | 462.10 | 462.10 | (280.40) | 9,917.80 |

*budget. Because Downtown MRI Center is new, there are no historical data on which to base the projections. The projections will be based on data provided by vendors, the doctors' experience, and Mary's knowledge. The assumptions used to create the operating budget are as follows:*

- *The center will immediately become Medicare and Medicaid providers.*

- *The center will apply for all managed care plans in the area.*

- *Average reimbursement per scan is $550.00.*

- *Allowance for bad debt will be 10%.*

- *Equipment lease payments will begin after 6 months of operation.*

- *Rent payments will begin in the second month of operation.*

- *Management fees (consisting of 7.5% of gross revenue) will be paid beginning in the second month of operation. The business has elected to hire a firm that specializes in managing MRI centers.*

- *Radiologist compensation (consisting of 15% of gross revenue) will be paid beginning with the second month of operation.*

- *Billing fees (consisting of 4% of gross revenue) will be paid beginning in the second month of operation.*

- *The business has elected to utilize an outside agency for billing.*

- *Cryogen supply and equipment service contracts will commence after 6 months of operation because of a 6-month warranty period.*

- *The business plans, if it meets projected performance, to pay a return on investment to shareholders at the end of the first year, and quarterly each subsequent year.*

- *The business assumes, based on market research, that it will perform scans per month as listed at the top of the projected revenues and expenses.*

- *The business does not plan to solicit any other investors at this time. The founding doctors have the financial strength to obtain the necessary financing.*

*Based on the documents prepared by Mary, the doctors obtain the financing, build the center, and enter into operation. The doctors have hired Ray Francis of Medical Managers, Inc., to operate the business. Dr. Lopez meets with Ray and reviews a copy of the budget with him. He explains to Ray that he and his company expect to meet the revenue and expense projections in the budget. He further states that the doctors expect to meet with Ray monthly to review operations and need Ray to provide them with a variance report on the monthly budget. The Medical Managers, Inc., management contract has a performance clause that links the contract's longevity and future fee increases to meeting budget projections.*

| Think of the budgeting process in your organization. Fill in the blanks to get you started in preparing for your unit's next annual budget. |
|---|
| Describe your budgeting needs based on your plan, mission, objectives, and goals. |
| What is the "focal question" to start the budgeting process with your staff? |
| Which staff members are needed at the meeting? |
| How would you explain the need for developing an accurate budget for your unit? |
| What are some ground rules for this group and situation? |

**Figure 2.**　Budget inventory tool.

## EXERCISES FOR SKILL DEVELOPMENT

### Individual Exercise

The best place to begin practicing budget development is with your own personal finances. Using your knowledge of your personal expenditures/income and your prior years' tax returns, create a personal or family budget for the next 12 months. If possible, use a spreadsheet computer program to develop a document that is similar to the budget inventory tool in Figure 2.

### Group Exercise

You are part of the management team of the new Bedrock Clinic, scheduled to open later this year. Bedrock Clinic projects a patient volume of 225 patients the first month, and a steady growth of 20% per month for the remainder of the first year. The average patient revenue per visit is $63.50. You do not have all of the data necessary to create a detailed expense budget. It is safe to assume that expenses will average 57% of operating revenue per month, excluding the doctor's salaries. Your job is to develop an operating budget for the next year. Prepare a budget that is a 12-month projection, with separate budget calculations for each month presented in a spreadsheet format. This exercise requires that you project the total revenue and expenses for each month, based on the data included in the exercise.

# SELF-ASSESSMENT OF SKILL 9: MASTERING THE BUDGETING PROCESS

**Directions:** This assessment will help you evaluate your level of skill and attitudes toward preparing, using, and analyzing budgets. Use the following statements to assess your attitudes and skills by circling the number closest to your experience: 1 = never, 2 = sometimes, 3 = often, and 4 = always. Respond in a way that reflects your skills today, rather than those you hope to have in the future. Answer as honestly as you can. Instructions on scoring and interpreting the results are provided in the analysis section at the end of the assessment.

1. I know the budgeting process that my
   organization uses.                           1   2   3   4

2. I develop my goals and objectives for the coming year before I prepare my budget.    1    2    3    4

3. I work closely with my fellow managers and use their expertise during budgeting.    1    2    3    4

4. I have learned the role of the budget committee and my relationship to this committee.    1    2    3    4

5. I communicate budget issues directly with my staff and get their input.    1    2    3    4

6. I fully understand the mission, vision, and goals of my organization.    1    2    3    4

7. I know the benefits and shortcomings of the budgeting process.    1    2    3    4

8 I estimate revenues by looking at their source, volume, and timing.    1    2    3    4

9. I budget revenue for new products or services.    1    2    3    4

10. I budget expenses by reviewing the previous period's actual expenses.    1    2    3    4

11. I adjust my budget periodically to correct for changes in projections.    1    2    3    4

12. I regularly analyze my budget and actual performance variances.    1    2    3    4

13. I find that regular budget reviews help me fine tune my department's performance.    1    2    3    4

14. I follow a standardized format for reviewing my budget performance.    1    2    3    4

15. I study the budget manual and follow it closely in preparing my budget.    1    2    3    4

16. I carefully analyze the potential impact of
    capital expenditures on my department.          1    2    3    4

17. I prefer a flexible budget so that my
    projections can be corrected for changes.       1    2    3    4

18. I stay current on community, industry, and
    national changes that may have an
    impact on my department's budget.               1    2    3    4

19. I actively participate in budget committee
    meetings.                                        1    2    3    4

20. I carefully review the previous budget
    before preparing the new budget in order
    to improve my budgeting skills.                 1    2    3    4

21. I always look for ways to improve my
    department's financial performance.             1    2    3    4

22. I carefully review my budget performance
    before any purchases are made.                  1    2    3    4

23. I collect data and develop strategies
    before the budgeting process begins.            1    2    3    4

24. I plan my departmental activities in great
    detail prior to budget preparation.             1    2    3    4

25. I analyze my department's strengths,
    weaknesses, opportunities, and threats
    before I prepare my budget.                     1    2    3    4

## Self-Assessment Analysis

Add your circled scores together to arrive at your total score. Next, refer to the scoring ranges below to identify your level of skill performance and attitudes toward the budgeting process. You may want to refer back to sections of this chapter for suggestions on increasing and honing your budgeting skills.

76–100   You appear to have highly developed budgeting skills and attitudes that facilitate your ability to effectively and efficiently manage your areas of responsibility. Continue to enhance and maintain these skills.

51–75    You appear to have reasonably well-developed budgeting skills, but certain areas could use improvement. By further developing these skills, you can become even more effective in increasing the productivity and performance of your department.

25–50    Your budgeting skills and your attitude toward the budgeting process appear to need improvement. It appears that you may not fully understand the importance of this skill and its overall relation to the successful operation of your department. You might focus on improving selected skills and attitudes (i.e., items that you scored as 1 or 2).

## REVIEW QUESTIONS

1.  What is the significance of developing a budget as a management tool?
2.  What basic information do you need to perform a variance analysis?
3.  Explain how an operating budget is developed.
4.  Why is it important to develop a written plan prior to developing a budget?

## FOR FURTHER INFORMATION

Gapenski, L. (1999). *Healthcare finance: An introduction to accounting and financial management.* Chicago: Health Administration Press.

This book provides a balance of information on accounting and financial management as it relates to the health care industry. The text provides an excellent resource for both novice and more experienced managers.

# Mastering and Monitoring Financial and Human Resources

*with Alan Whiteman, Ph.D.*[1]

The objectives of this chapter are to

- Specify the basic components of a financial system

- Identify a revenue stream and recognize expenses

- Analyze balance sheets and other financial accounting statements

- Explain the significance of financial data and its uses

- Review the analysis of financial accounting statements

- Review the basics of computing full-time equivalents (FTEs) when filling positions

- Recognize the difference between productive and nonproductive time

- Assess your attitudes and skills in using, interpreting, and analyzing financial data

- Provide skill development exercises and activities to develop or enhance strategic thinking and decision-making skills

---

[1]Alan Whiteman, Ph.D., is Associate Professor and Director of the Health Services Administration program at Barry University, Miami Shores, Florida.

## FINANCIAL MANAGEMENT
## IN HEALTH CARE SETTINGS

In order to properly manage their assigned areas of responsibility, managers must have an understanding of the various financial management concepts and tools that are available to them to successfully accomplish their assigned tasks. They must be able to identify the sources of revenue and recognize the expenses that have an impact on their area(s) of responsibility, and master the techniques associated with managing this information. Decisions involving financial and human resources must be based on managers' overall understanding of the organization's mission, goals, and objectives. Good managers work diligently to coordinate their areas of responsibility with their peers, who are managing other diverse areas of the organization.

Managers in health care organizations must work with two distinct types of accounting. The first is financial accounting, which involves identifying, measuring, recording, and communicating the economic events and status of the organization to interested parties that are both internal and external to the organization (Gapenski, 1999). Financial accounting produces three standardized financial statements: the balance sheet, statement of income and expenses, and statement of cash flows. Financial accounting statements are produced under generally accepted accounting principles (GAAP). This activity is regulated by the Securities and Exchange Commission, which delegates the responsibilities for establishing standards to the Financial Accounting Standards Board (FASB). This chapter concentrates on explaining these basic financial accounting statements and leads the reader through the use of these critically important tools.

The second type of accounting is managerial accounting. Managerial accounting focuses mostly on subunit (e.g., departmental) data used internally for managerial decision making (Gapenski, 2002). Managerial accounting reports are designed by management, at all levels, to provide the necessary data to effectively and efficiently manage their area(s) of responsibility. This chapter focuses on utilizing financial data for effective and efficient management, and provides guidance in the use of managerial accounting information.

Finally, this chapter provides managers with a methodology for monitoring human resources. It will assist managers in understanding and carefully monitoring staffing within their departments. After completing this chapter, the reader should be able to understand the importance and use of financial data, the analysis of these data, and the utilization of information gained through analysis.

## BASICS OF A FINANCIAL SYSTEM

The reports and other materials that a manager receives in an organization are, generally, only a part of the total data package that is used to operate the entity. To understand financial management, it is essential to recognize the overall system in which an organization operates. The four segments that make a health care financial system work are 1) the original records, 2) the information system, 3) the accounting system, and 4) the reporting system. The original records provide evidence that some event has occurred, the information system gathers this evidence, the accounting system records the evidence, and the reporting system produces reports of the effect (Baker & Baker, 2000).

The role of the manager is to understand the flow of the system, his or her specific area of operations, and the reports or information that he or she will need to effectively manage. Every manager, regardless of the type of operational responsibilities held, will need to constantly monitor various types of data to fine-tune performance.

The type and quantity of information that is available to managers is dependent on the information system used by the organization. Some organizations use a combination of manual and computer systems, whereas other organizations operate highly sophisticated management information systems. The role of a manager is to determine the specific financial information needs of the organization and request or design reports that meet these needs.

*Lucy Pratt-Jones has been hired recently as the Director of Medical Records for Smallville General Hospital. Her responsibilities include managing the medical records department, transcription services, and the medical staff library. Lucy's predecessor, Cindy Nomuri, was at Smallville for 30 years. Cindy focused her efforts on keeping the medical staff happy by providing excellent service and pampering the doctors through significant expenditures. When Cindy retired, she left the hospital with a tremendous financial deficit in her areas of responsibility. Leroy Green, Chief Executive Officer, has given Lucy the responsibility of immediately analyzing the financial situation, including the staffing, and providing him with a plan to resolve the situation. Lucy has 30 days to complete this assignment. She begins by reviewing her old finance textbooks to refresh her memory on the approaches she may use for analysis.*

## WHAT IS MEANT BY REVENUE STREAM?

Revenue is the income that is received by a health care entity. This revenue may represent the funds generated by the provision of patient care services. It may be derived from normal day-to-day operations that are not directly related to patient care, such as educational programs, research grants, and space rental. Revenues also may be attributed to nonoperating gains, for example, interest on investments, donations, or numerous other sources (Cleverley, 1997).

Revenue flows into an organization are sometimes referred to as the *revenue stream*. This phrase can also be used more specifically to identify a particular source of revenue. For example, in a hospital that provides a women's health center for relaxation, this center is a unique service that provides a new revenue stream for the hospital. The role of the manager may include monitoring the current revenue stream, identifying other potential revenue streams, or making recommendations on the direction to take in managing a specific income stream.

## EXPENSES

Expenses are the costs that relate to the earning of revenues. In other words, expense is the cost of doing business. Revenue represents the inflow of funds into the organization and expenses represent the outflow of funds from the organization (Baker & Baker, 2000).

Health care organizations are unique in that many management areas of responsibility focus on critical functions that are not

directly responsible for producing revenue. These departments—
for example, a medical records department or a billing and collec-
tions department—are referred to as cost centers. These cost centers may be organized into groups that make up a particular
management unit. By organizing these cost centers into a central-
ized functional unit, the manager may be able to receive his or her
own management reports. This will provide the manager with a
meaningful set of tools that can be used to monitor and effectively
manage operating expenses (Baker & Baker, 2000).

Expenses can be grouped by various factors depending on the
specific needs of a manager. They may be categorized as inpatient
versus outpatient, by product line, or in any other fashion that creates valid information by which to manage the appropriate areas of
responsibility.

## USING FINANCIAL DATA FOR MONITORING

The information contained in financial accounting statements provides the basic tools that are used for monitoring financial performance. Depending on the specific area(s) of responsibility, managers may be held accountable for maintaining and/or increasing
revenues, and they will always be responsible for planning and
managing expenses.

The keys to successful financial management are the abilities
to carefully plan revenue and expenses, monitor revenue and expenses, and respond to unexpected changes in the environment by
having a contingency plan prepared in advance. In addition to financial accounting reports, it is critical that each manager develop
managerial accounting reports that provide critical data about the
operation of his or her units. These managerial accounting reports
and their development are discussed later in this chapter.

Another critical tool for monitoring financial performance is
the use of benchmarks. Benchmarks are standards that can be used
as a point of reference in measuring an operation. There are three
sources of benchmarks:

- Internally developed historical standards
- Engineered standards
- Comparative group standards

Internally developed standards based on historical performance are the easiest, least costly, and most commonly used method of benchmark development. These historical data can be utilized in the development of the annual operating budget (Cleverley, 1997). For example, a hospital chief financial officer (CFO) wants to review clerical staffing in the emergency room because of high labor costs. All that this individual needs to do to develop benchmarks is to obtain historical data from various sources and compare these data with the current situation. Of course, the chief financial officer must ensure that the current emergency room operations are the same as those represented by historical data.

Engineered standards can be developed internally or by using external consultants. The key component of developing standards in this manner is the extensive studies that are conducted to define benchmarks (Cleverely, 1997). The problems that arise with engineered standards are the cost of producing the standards and the time involved to conduct the necessary studies and prepare the standards.

Comparative group standards are available throughout the health care industry. A significant number of professional associations conduct annual surveys of their member organizations and compile the survey results in some meaningful fashion. An example of this benchmarking effort is the Medical Group Management Association's Annual Cost and Production Surveys. Other groups, such as the American Hospital Association, gather similar data.

Before a manager compares benchmark data against his or her organization, he or she must understand the method used to gather the data as well as the definitions used in the surveys. The data collected in the surveys may not be directly comparable with his or her organization's data. It is also important to understand the geographic disparities that may be present in the data.

*Dr. Bashir, a family practitioner, is concerned that his operating expenses, based on his monthly financial statements, are too high compared with those of his peers in the local community. The doctor is in solo practice, and has 6.3 full-time employees working in the office. The national average, based on data provided by a professional association, is 4.7 full-time employees per full-time family practitioner. Therefore, this particular practice may be overstaffed, and a complete operational analysis must be conducted by an outside expert.*

## EXERCISES FOR SKILL DEVELOPMENT

### Individual Exercises

1. Identify expenses associated with operating your home. Identify if these are expenses or costs and if any of the items are related to staffing human resources (e.g., domestic help, lawn service).

2. Using financial information to effectively and efficiently manage is a critical skill that must be developed and continuously refined. It is best to approach financial management by first identifying your specific needs for information in your current position. Figure 1 lists just a few typical opportunities to use financial information. Check off the boxes in the left column that identify your needs for information. In the right column, add your own specific ideas on meeting these needs by obtaining the appropriate financial data.

### Group Exercise

Consider the following case example:

*The Accounts Payable Supervisor at Greenville Hospital is working on her budget for next year. She wants to annualize her staffing portion of the budget. She has three full-time and two part-time (equal to one full-time) accounting clerks under her supervision. Each of her full-time employees is entitled to 15 days' paid vacation, 5 sick days, 8 holidays, and 2 personal days.*

Now analyze the case in terms of the following issues:

1. Calculate the amount of productive and nonproductive time for the department.

2. Does she have enough employees to keep the department fully staffed at all times?

## Review Questions

1. From what sources does your organization receive its revenue?
2. Identify any unique revenue streams for your organization.
3. Identify at least three cost centers in your organization.

| Opportunities for using financial information | What you will do to maximize these opportunities |
|---|---|
| Finalizing action plans | |
| Analyzing issues | |
| Solving problems | |
| Prioritizing items | |
| Assessing financial risks associated with new projects | |
| Identifying financial data for problem solving or decision making | |
| Budgeting | |

**Figure 1.**  Financial information management worksheet.

## UNDERSTANDING BALANCE SHEETS AND OTHER FINANCIAL DATA

### Key Concepts in Financial Accounting

In order to use financial accounting statements effectively, it is important to master some key concepts. Financial statements are prepared for a specific period of time, generally referred to as the *accounting period*. These statements usually represent a 1-year time period, or some segment of it. Most managers of health care organizations receive financial statements on a monthly basis to give them an ongoing snapshot of how their organization is performing. In hospitals and other larger organizations, the financial statements generally are prepared in house and are directed to the senior executives of the entity. In smaller organizations, such as medical practices, the financial statements are prepared by the entities' accounting firms and provided to the physician(s), the practice manager, or both.

Financial accounting statements are prepared using one of two methods. They may be prepared on a cash basis of accounting or on an accrual basis of accounting. Smaller businesses tend to use the cash basis method, and larger, more complex organizations use the accrual method.

*Cash basis accounting* is very simple to understand and use. This method accounts for cash when it is actually collected and expenses when they are actually paid. The easiest way to think of this process is to remember how we manage our personal finances. When a paycheck is received, the amount deposited is recorded in the individual's checkbook. Next, checks are written to various vendors for unpaid bills that are owed. This is the cash basis method of accounting.

*Accrual accounting* differs significantly because it accounts for revenues when the money is actually earned, regardless of whether it has been collected or not. Accrual accounting records expenses when the expense is incurred, not when it is paid. For example, if a patient has a chest X-ray in January, the health care organization may not receive payment until April. Under the accrual system, the revenue for that chest X-ray would appear in the January financial statement as an account receivable (receivables are revenues earned but not collected as of the reporting date). If the revenue ultimately is not collected, an adjustment is made at a later date for bad debt. Expenses work the same way. If the organization received a shipment of X-ray film in March and paid the invoice in April, the expense would be reported on the March financial statements.

All financial accounting statements prepared or audited by an accountant will have an auditor's report attached to them, which will tell how the audit was conducted and the outcome of the audit. Financial statements that are not audited will have a compilation report attached. This report will make a general statement about how the information was compiled and whether it meets GAAP. This information is crucial in assessing the validity and value of the data contained in the reports.

Financial accounting statements also may have explanatory notes attached to them. Reading these notes is crucial because the note will explain the referenced specific entry on the financial statement. For example, a balance sheet entry under current liabilities reads "notes payable $38,000." This entry has a symbol, number, or letter next to it identifying a note. The reviewer can turn to the note with the same identifying character and find that "notes payable" represents two term loans, one of $23,000 with a 3-year term and another of $15,000 with a 5-year term. This entry now provides the reader with a significant piece of information about the business operations. (An example of explanatory notes appears on the balance sheet in Figure 2.)

## Information Contained in Financial Statements

Business entities prepare an annual report that includes the balance sheet, statement of revenues and expenses, and statement of cash flows. Larger health care organizations and those required to do so by federal or state law prepare audited financial statements, which comprise the majority of an annual report for the organization.

Publicly traded companies mail annual reports to all shareholders. Privately held organizations distribute their annual reports to owners, senior managers, or both. Not-for-profit organizations file these annual reports with various agencies, and these reports may be available to the public under various legislative acts.

*Balance Sheet*    The balance sheet is a snapshot of the health care organization. It is a convenient means of organizing and summarizing what a firm *owns* (its assets), what the firm *owes* (its liabilities), and the difference between the two (the organization's equity) at a given point in time (Ross, Williams, & Pavlock, 1998). The balance sheet represents the basic accounting equation:

$$\text{Assets} = \text{liabilities} + \text{shareholders' equity}$$

Assets are classified as either current or fixed. A *fixed asset* is one that has a relatively long life, such as a truck or a computer. Fixed assets are either tangible (e.g., a computer) or intangible, such as a trademark or a patent. A *current asset* has a life of less than 1 year (Ross et al., 1998).

Liabilities are classified as either current or long term. *Current liabilities,* just as current assets, have a life of less than 1 year. Accounts payable is an example of a current liability. *Long-term liabilities* are debts not due in the coming year. A loan that is paid off over 5 years is an example of long-term debt (Ross et al., 1998). *Equity* is the difference between the total value of the assets and the total value of the liabilities. This may appear on the balance sheet as shareholders' equity or owners' equity (Ross, 1996).

A key concept to remember in reviewing a balance sheet is that the more liquid an organization, the more likely the organization is to remain viable. *Liquidity* is the ability of an organization to meet its short-term maturing obligations (Cleverley, 1999). To determine liquidity at a quick glance, the reviewer should look at current assets. Current assets will be listed, as are all assets, in a declining order of liquidity. *The assets listed first will be those that can most readily be turned into cash.* This is an extremely important concept to remember.

*Sunshine Diagnostic Imaging Center is located in Greenville, Florida. The center has been in operation for 1 full year. During the past year, Sunshine has suffered from competition from the local hospital as well as from decreases in reimbursement from various insurance plans and has been unable to obtain managed care contracts with the key plans in the area. Doug Kinnear, the administrator, has been trying to obtain additional capital by inviting potential investors to buy an interest in the center. Doug has presented several potential investors with Sunshine Diagnostic Imaging Center's balance sheet (see Figure 2) for the first year of operation ending December 31, 2002. This balance sheet has not attracted any new investors, and Doug is thinking of other information to share with the potential investors.*

*Statement of Revenues and Expenses* The statement of revenues and expenses summarizes the operation of the health care organization. It focuses on income, expenses, and profitability. The statement is broken into two distinct sections: revenue collected and operating expenses.

Sunshine Diagnostic Center
Statement of Assets, Liabilities, and Stockholder's Equity (deficit)
Income Tax Basis December 31, 2002

## Assets
Current Assets

| | | |
|---|---|---|
| | Cash in Bank | $ 467.00 |
| | Total Current Assets | 467.00 |

Property and Equipment

| | | |
|---|---|---|
| | Building Improvements | 185,000.00 |
| | | 185,000.00 |
| | Less: Accumulated Depreciation | (6,794.00) |
| | Property and Equipment—Net | 178,206.00 |
| | Recoverable Deposits | 675.00 |
| | *Total Assets* | 179,348.00 |

## Liabilities and Owner's Equity
Current Liabilities

| | | |
|---|---|---|
| | Cash Overdraft | (20,037.00) |
| | Advances | (1,691.00) (A) |
| | Payroll Taxes Payable | 31,644.00 |
| | Notes Payable | 210,930.00 |
| | Total Current Liabilities | 260,920.00 |

Long-Term  Liabilities

| | | |
|---|---|---|
| | Notes Payable | 221,559.00 (B) |
| | Total Long-Term Liabilities | 221,559.00 |
| | Total Liabilities | 482,479.00 |

Owner's Equity

| | | |
|---|---|---|
| | Capital | (289,959.00) |
| | Capital—other | 48,663.00 |
| | Suspense | 1,132.00 |
| | Current Period Income (Loss) | (60,703.00) |
| | Total Owner's Equity | (303,132.00) |
| | *Total Liabilities and Owner's Equity* | 179,348.00 |

## Notes
Note A—A $1,691 payroll advance was made to Mary Jay.
Note B—A signed note with a repayment schedule is on file with the bookkeeping office.

**Figure 2.**　Balance sheet for Sunshine Diagnostic Imaging Center.

The statement of revenues and expenses may have variations depending on the organization and the individual preparing the document. Some entities will break down the revenue section into various categories by payer or even by business division. The operating expenses will vary by organization and may be presented in varying degrees of detail, based on the criteria stated for revenue.

In addition to the basic data presented on a statement of revenues and expenses, other information may appear. It is very common to find a column to the right of the expense amount indicating the percentage of the total revenue or the total operating expense represented by that item. This is extremely useful information when analyzing the financial statement.

Another variation on the statement of revenue and expenses is the appearance of additional columns of data that represent a comparison of the same period from the prior year. This may be followed by more columns that represent year-to-date for the current year and year-to-date for the prior year. These data can be very helpful in the analytical process.

*Doug Kinnear is still diligently trying to come up with a solution to the problem of attracting additional investors. He decides that he needs to share more information with the potential investors, so he prepares a statement of revenues and expenses (Figure 3) and forwards this to the potential investors with a cover letter explaining all of the positive events that are happening at the center.*

In reviewing financial statements, it is very important to understand the relationship between costs and changes in the operational activities of health care organizations. For example, a medical office that normally operates from 9:00 A.M. to 5:00 P.M., Monday through Friday, sees exactly 100 patients per week, or 20 patients per day. If the office decides to offer extended hours until 8:00 P.M. on Tuesday and Thursday evenings, during this additional 6 hours of operation the office will see 12 additional patients. This change in operations will increase labor costs, utilities, and supplies, to name a few categories. It will most likely also increase revenue over a period of time. All of these changes should be apparent in a close review of the statement of income and expenses for each month.

## Sunshine Diagnostic Imaging Center
### Statement of Revenues and Expenses—Income Tax Basis
### for the 12 months ending December 31, 2002

| | | |
|---|---:|---:|
| **Revenues Collected** | | |
| Fee Income | $570,243.00 | 67.8% |
| Other Income | 270,500.00 | 32.2 |
| Total Revenue Collected | 840,743.00 | 100.0 |
| **Operating Expenses Paid** | | |
| Advertising and Promotion | 13,965.00 | 1.7 |
| Alarm Expense | 381.00 | |
| Auto Expense | 10,559.00 | 1.3 |
| Bank Charges | 1,904.00 | .2 |
| Contributions | 195.00 | |
| Credit Card Processing | 422.00 | .1 |
| Drugs/Medical Supplies | 117,011.00 | 13.9 |
| Dues and Subscriptions | 212.00 | |
| Entertainment and Promotion | 3,922.00 | .5 |
| Equipment Lease | 171,677.00 | 20.4 |
| Insurance—General | 17,270.00 | 2.1 |
| Insurance—Group | 13,613.00 | 1.6 |
| Insurance—Malpractice | 5,590.00 | .7 |
| Legal and Accounting | 4,345.00 | .5 |
| Licenses and Taxes | 24,247.00 | 2.9 |
| Linens, Laundry, and Uniforms | 1,484.00 | .2 |
| Meetings and Seminars | 66.00 | |
| Office Supplies | 18,091.00 | 2.2 |
| Outside Services | 5,663.00 | .7 |
| Medical Director Fees | 9,000.00 | 1.1 |
| Payroll—Office | 260,775.00 | 31.0 |
| Payroll Taxes | 24,702.00 | 2.9 |
| Postage | 14,922.00 | 1.8 |
| Professional Fees | 18,832.00 | 2.2 |
| Rent | 67,186.00 | 8.0 |
| Repairs and Maintenance | 8,565.00 | 1.0 |
| Repairs and Maintenance–MRI | 42,778.00 | 5.1 |
| Telephone | 11,373.00 | |
| Transcriptions | 3,228.00 | .4 |
| Utilities | 14,039.00 | 1.7 |
| Total Operating Expenses Paid | 886,016.00 | 105.4 |
| Income (Loss) From Operations | ($45,273.00) | (5.4)% |
| **Other Income and Expenses Paid** | | |
| Interest Paid | 15,430.00 | 1.8 |
| Total Other Income and Expenses paid | 15,430.00 | 1.8 |
| Revenues (Losses) Collected in Excess of Expenses Paid | ($60,703.00) | (7.2)% |

**Figure 3.** Statement of revenue and expenses for Sunshine Diagnostic Imaging Center.

*Statement of Cash Flows*    The statement of cash flows is designed to give additional information on the flow of funds within an entity. It summarizes the sources that make funds available and the uses of those funds during a given period. This statement is included in the annual reports of health care organizations.

## Analyzing Financial Statements

There are several approaches that can be used in reviewing the financial performance of a health care organization. Any one or a combination of these approaches may best serve a particular situation.

*Trend Analysis*    One method that should be used on a regular basis is a trend analysis, comparing a particular health care organization's performance with its performance for a comparable prior period. This will allow the reviewer to identify differences that may have implications for the operation of the entity. This can be accomplished by having the financial accounting statements prepared, as previously described, with columns containing comparative data.

*Benchmark Data*    Another method is to compare one health care organization with other comparable health care organizations by using benchmark data. Many professional associations compile detailed operational information about their member organizations. These data can be obtained and used to review a given organization against its peers. For example, the Medical Group Management Association annually collects data from its member medical group practices and compiles these data into revenue and expense reports. A family medical practice that wanted to know if its staffing pattern was appropriate could obtain their report and compare its staffing pattern with the national averages.

*Ratio Analysis*    An excellent tool that is used in all other industries to monitor financial operations is ratio analysis. Ratio analysis combines data from the balance sheet and the statement of income and expenses that have easily interpreted financial significance (i.e., numbers that measure various aspects of financial performance) (Gapenski, 1999).

Ratios are used as a guide to review trends and modify operational activities to improve performance. Ratio analysis provides a better "snapshot" of operations if a somewhat larger time frame is used. For example, it is possible to calculate ratios monthly, but a better analysis is achieved if the calculations are performed quarterly and compared with other calendar quarters. Combining these data with the operational knowledge of the manager provides an excellent set of tools for continuous monitoring of operational performance.

Unfortunately, an almost unlimited number of financial ratios can be constructed, and the choice of ratios depends, in large part, on the nature of the business being analyzed, the purpose of the analysis, and the availability of comparative data. Generally, ratios are grouped into categories to make them easier to interpret (Gapenski, 1999). Almost all health care or non–health care financial management textbooks or accounting textbooks provide a significant number of ratios that can be used. For our purposes, the following ratios are a sampling of those that can be applied in the analysis of financial data for a health care organization.

*Liquidity Ratios*　Liquidity is the ability of a firm to meet its short-term obligations by paying its bills and meeting all financial obligations. The more liquid the firm, the better it is able to meet its current liabilities (Cleverley, 1997). Liquidity is measured by the following ratios:

*Current ratio:* indicates the ability of the business to meet its obligations; the higher the value the better (the industry standard is 2)

$$\frac{\text{Current assets}}{\text{Current liabilities}}$$

*Days in patient accounts receivable ratio:* indicates how effectively accounts receivables are being collected; lower is better (45–60 days is the industry standard)

$$\frac{\text{Net patient accounts receivable} + \text{due from third parties} - \text{due to third parties}}{\text{Net patient revenue}/365}$$

*Days cash on hand ratio:* indicates the number of days' cash on hand available to the entity, or the number of days the entity has the ability to operate its business; higher is better (the industry average is 30.6 days)

$$\frac{\text{Cash} + \text{marketable securities}}{(\text{Expenses} - \text{depreciation} - \text{provision for bad debt})/365}$$

*Profitability Ratio*    *Total profit margin ratio:* indicates the profit margin above the operating overhead; the higher the better (the industry average is 5.0%)

$$\frac{\text{Net income}}{\text{Total revenue}}$$

## EXERCISES FOR SKILL DEVELOPMENT

### Individual Exercises

Obtain a copy of an annual report for a health care organization that interests you. These may be obtained from the Internet, a brokerage firm, or a local health care organization. Carefully read and review the document, looking at each of the financial statements along with the notes, the auditor's report, and any other descriptive materials that are provided. Draw your own conclusions about this organization.

As a second exercise, answer the following questions to determine if you are meeting the specific goals you are presently working to achieve in understanding financial statements. In addition to challenging you to think through your existing financial analysis process, this exercise will help you hone your skills for working with future goals and analysis processes.

1. List one or two goals that you plan to attain over the next few months regarding the understanding and use of financial data.

2. What are the one or two key reasons you intend to attain these goals?

3. List one or two additional goals that you will set for yourself, once you have mastered a basic understanding of financial data. *Note:* Once you have listed the goals you intend to stick with, those you intend to reassess, and your reasons for each, test your decisions by running these by a trusted colleague, a coach, or your work group.

4. What do you want to accomplish next in this area?

### Group Exercise

Carefully review the materials related to Sunshine Diagnostic Imaging Center, including the Statement of Assets, Liabilities and Stockholder's

Equity (Deficit), and the Statement of Revenues and Expenses, that appear in Figures 2 and 3. Discuss this material with the members of your group and answer the following questions:

1.  What do current liabilities represent on the balance sheet?

2.  Did Sunshine make or lose money in 2002?

3.  Identify three expense categories that you would investigate if you were the manager of Sunshine and explain the significance of each.

4.  Perform a ratio analysis of Sunshine using the ratios that appear on pages 210–211 of this chapter and the financial statements that appear in Figures 2 and 3.

## Review Questions

1.  What is the difference between cash and accrual accounting?
2.  Define the terms *revenue* and *expense.*
3.  What is ratio analysis? Why is it an important concept?
4.  Explain the terms *assets* and *liabilities.*
5.  What is meant by the term *cash flow?*

## MONITORING HUMAN RESOURCES FROM A FINANCIAL PERSPECTIVE

The health care industry is a people business. The industry's purpose is to provide health care services to the population by offering both preventive medicine and treatment for the multitude of illnesses that face us as humans. In order to provide services to the population, the industry must employ the appropriate tools to deliver the care. This delivery mechanism is almost totally dependent on human beings to diagnose, treat, and follow up on care that is provided. American medicine may utilize advanced technology to deliver the latest and best in care, but the technology is managed and operated by people.

The single most important commodity in health care is people. It is also one of the largest expenditures. Many health care organizations expend more than 40%–70% of their total budget on human resources. It is critical that this costly resource is carefully monitored and managed. This is a step in the overall financial management process that is reviewed in this chapter.

Health care entities create other unique situations for managing human resources. Most businesses operate for a specific period of time each day for 5–7 days per week. In the health care industry, many of the entities operate 7 days per week and 24 hours per day, year round. Thus these facilities must be staffed with all levels of personnel during all hours of operation. The manager is responsible for seeing that each position is staffed and that the appropriate number of personnel is available for every shift.

## Staffing Measurements

The staffing measurement that is most commonly used for monitoring is the full-time equivalent (FTE). One FTE is the equivalent of one full-time employee paid for 1 year. For the purposes of this discussion, one FTE is equivalent to 2,080 work hours per year, including productive and nonproductive time (Baker & Baker, 2000). Productive time is equal to the employee's net hours on duty when performing the functions in his or her job description. Nonproductive time is paid time when the employee is not on duty performing job-related functions (e.g., vacation, sick time).

FTEs are almost always calculated on an annualized basis. This method is necessary because each employee who is eligible for benefits will not be on duty for the full number of hours paid for by the organization (Baker & Baker, 2000). Information on FTEs is vital in determining the staffing needs for a manager's area(s) of responsibility, a critical step in operational planning and control.

## Monitoring Scheduled Work Hours

Managers must review employee work hours on a regular basis. It is important to monitor the employees' work patterns (e.g., time they arrived at work, time they left work, absenteeism). Employees may only be working their assigned shifts and not creating a problem with overtime, but they may not be working 100% of the time that they are being paid to be productive at work.

## Monitoring Overtime Work Hours

One of the most critical areas in monitoring human resources is maintaining control over the use of overtime. Overtime, if not properly managed, can drive operating costs up significantly. During the course of normal operations, it may become necessary to utilize overtime to complete special projects, service an unusually high patient volume, or cover for unexpected emergencies. However, overtime should never be used as a means of meeting normal operational objectives. Use of overtime on a regular basis is an indication that the department is not properly staffed, employees are not functioning efficiently, or employees are using overtime as a regular means to increase their salaries.

Labor, as mentioned previously, is one of the largest segments of any health care budget. Therefore, it is imperative for all managers to carefully review their operational plans and decide on staffing needs prior to completing their annual budget. Changes in staffing patterns or increased use of overtime should occur only when operations change or emergencies arise.

## MANAGERIAL ACCOUNTING: USING INFORMATION

The task facing managers, once they understand the basic concepts of financial management, is obtaining and properly utilizing the information available to them to meet their management responsibilities. A good example is to look at Lucy Pratt-Jones in the earlier case example. Lucy has been given a complex assignment by her immediate supervisor. Her first task is to identify the information she will need to analyze her areas of responsibility. Second, she will have to find the sources of information she needs. Finally, she will have to design managerial reports that will "massage" all of the appropriate information into a format that is usable.

This leads us to the next topic, managerial accounting. Whereas financial accounting, as has been previously discussed, focuses on organization-level data for presentation in a business's financial statements, managerial accounting focuses mostly on subunit (e.g., departmental) data used internally for managerial decision making. The focus of managerial accounting is to develop information to meet the needs of managers in the organization.

Managerial accounting reports are focused on the future, and, thus, play an important role in the planning of future strategies. The information is used for development of budgets. In addition, this type of report may be used as an analytical tool to determine the effects of potential changes in a department or line of business.

*The Serene Outpatient Surgery Center is developing its marketing plan for the coming year. Yousef Haddad, the Administrator, thinks that he would like to entice more plastic surgeons to the center but is unsure if this will be a profitable strategy. Yousef assigns Betty Lou Czymanski, the Chief Financial Officer, the task of evaluating revenues and costs associated with plastic surgery cases. He asks her to prepare financial projections for adding one or two plastic surgeons to the staff. Yousef is focused on determining the value that is added to the center's operations by modifying its revenue stream with a different mix of physician providers.*

Managerial accounting focuses on analyzing costs and projecting revenues for various business unit operations. Managerial accounting reports are used for the purpose of effectively billing, collecting, and managing the funds owed to the health care business. These reports are examples of valuable analytical tools used for identifying potential problems in collecting accounts receivable, thereby affording managers the opportunity to analyze the situation and devise strategies that will facilitate the collection of revenues, allowing for their organizations to remain viable and financially healthy.

Another grouping of commonly used managerial accounting reports is accounts receivable reports obtained from the facility's billing system. These reports provide a detailed picture of the health care facility's accounts receivable management process. Using these tools effectively affords managers the opportunity to restructure their strategies and processes to improve their organizations' financial performance. Managers can use standardized reports that are provided as a part of their system or they can design custom reports to meet their management needs.

Health care businesses today utilize computer-based accounts receivable management systems that may be freestanding or a part of an overall facility-wide information system. These systems all contain a standard set of accounts receivable management reports (managerial accounting reports), and many have the capability of producing custom-designed managerial accounting reports.

The budget that was developed for the Downtown MRI Center in Skill 9, Mastering the Budgeting Process, is an example of the development and use of a managerial accounting report. The accounts receivable reports presented in Figures 4–7 are examples of commonly produced standardized reports, with each software manufacturer utilizing its own format. These reports include a practice analysis (Figure 4) that details the types and number of procedures and revenue information for studies performed at Downtown MRI Center. A sample insurance analysis (Figure 5) is included in these reports that details the financial activity of patient claims billed to various insurance carriers. A sample insurance aging report (Figure 6) is also included, demonstrating how a manager would review the length of time that an insurance company takes in paying claims. Finally, a sample of a patient accounts receivable aging report summary page appears (Figure 7). This report summarizes outstanding accounts receivable by how old the claims are from the date of original billing. The older the claim, the less likely an organization is to collect it.

Managerial accounting has a significant advantage over financial accounting in that it is not structured and it is not regulated by GAAP. Thus, managers are free to think "outside the box" and utilize their creative abilities in designing reports and analytical tools. Creativity of this nature can lead to some very innovative strategies. Caution must be exercised, however, by managers who are excited about letting their creative energies flow and who rush to develop new tools. Even though managerial accounting lends itself to creativity, managers must base their analysis, projections, and reports on data that are valid, consistent, and therefore reliable. The basis for managerial accounting flows from financial accounting reports.

## EXERCISES FOR SKILL DEVELOPMENT

### Individual Exercise

Identify managerial accounting reports that you presently use. Review these reports and determine what additional information you would like to have as a management tool. Next, design a managerial accounting report that would assist you in completing your work assignments.

## Practice Analysis

| Code | Description | Amount | Quantity | Average | Cost | Net |
|------|-------------|--------|----------|---------|------|-----|
| 70540 | MRI ORBIT, NECK, FACE | 1,500.00 | 1 | 1,500.00 | 0.00 | 1,500.00 |
| 70551 | MRI BRAIN | 4,500.00 | 3 | 1,500.00 | 0.00 | 4,500.00 |
| 70553 | MRI BRAIN WITH AND WITHOUT | 36,750.00 | 21 | 1,750.00 | 0.00 | 36,750.00 |
| 72141 | MRI CERVICAL | 73,500.00 | 49 | 1,500.00 | 0.00 | 73,500.00 |
| 72146 | MRI THORACIC | 6,000.00 | 4 | 1,500.00 | 0.00 | 6,000.00 |
| 72148 | MRI LUMBAR | 94,500.00 | 63 | 1,500.00 | 0.00 | 94,500.00 |
| 72156 | MRI CERVICAL WITH AND WITHOUT | 3,500.00 | 2 | 1,750.00 | 0.00 | 3,500.00 |
| 72158 | MRI LUMBAR WITH AND WITHOUT | 15,750.00 | 9 | 1,750.00 | 0.00 | 15,750.00 |
| 72196 | MRI PELVIS | 9,000.00 | 6 | 1,500.00 | 0.00 | 9,000.00 |
| 72220 | SACRUM AND COCCYX | 1,500.00 | 1 | 1,500.00 | 0.00 | 1,500.00 |
| 73220 | MRI UPPER EXTREMITY OTHER | 4,500.00 | 3 | 1,500.00 | 0.00 | 4,500.00 |
| 73221 | MRI JOINT OF UPPER EXTREMITY | 61,500.00 | 41 | 1,500.00 | 0.00 | 61,500.00 |
| 73720 | MRI LOWER EXTREMITY OTHER | 9,000.00 | 6 | 1,500.00 | 0.00 | 9,000.00 |
| 73721 | MRI JOINT OF LOWER EXTREMITY | 127,500.00 | 85 | 1,500.00 | 0.00 | 127,500.00 |
| 76499 | UNLISTED DIAGNOSTIC RADIOLOGY | 250.00 | 1 | 250.00 | 0.00 | 250.00 |
| ATTORNEY | ATTORNEY PAYMENT | -5,095.58 | 10 | -509.56 | 0.00 | -5,095.58 |
| INS ADJ | WRITE OFF DISALLOWED | -222,090.18 | 208 | -1,067.74 | 0.00 | -222,090.18 |
| INS PAY | INSURANCE PAYMENT | -155,705.99 | 271 | -574.56 | 0.00 | -155,705.99 |
| LEASE | LEASE PAYMENT | 40,000.00 | 1 | 40,000.00 | 0.00 | 40,000.00 |
| PT CK | PATIENT PAYMENT | -1,488.44 | 22 | -67.66 | 0.00 | -1,488.44 |
| WRITE OFF | WRITE OFF | -9,854.03 | 21 | -469.24 | 0.00 | -9,854.03 |

*(continued)*

**Figure 4.** Practice analysis for Downtown MRI Center.

**Figure 4.** *(continued)*

Practice Analysis
As of March 12, 2002

| | |
|---|---:|
| Total Procedure Charges | $489,250.00 |
| Total Product Charges | $0.00 |
| Total Inside Lab Charges | $0.00 |
| Total Outside Lab Charges | $0.00 |
| Total Billing Charges | $0.00 |
| Total Insurance Payments | -$160,801.57 |
| Total Cash Copayments | $0.00 |
| Total Check Copayments | $0.00 |
| Total Credit Card Copayments | $0.00 |
| Total Patient Cash Payments | $0.00 |
| Total Patient Check Payments | -$1,488.44 |
| Total Credit Card Payments | $0.00 |
| Total Debit Adjustments | $0.00 |
| Total Credit Adjustments | -$231,944.21 |
| Total Insurance Debit Adjustments | $0.00 |
| Total Insurance Credit Adjustments | $0.00 |
| Net Effect on Accounts Receivable | $95,015.78 |

## Group Exercise

Have each member of the group carefully review the reports that appear in Figures 4–7. The members of the group can then discuss these reports and draw conclusions about Downtown MRI Center's financial operations. After completing the review and discussion, have the group answer the following questions:

1.  What is the significance of the information presented in these reports?

2.  Do these reports present enough information to properly manage the business activities of this entity? Explain why or why not.

3.  Are the accounts receivable of this entity being properly managed?

4.  Identify the four most commonly performed accounting procedures.

5.  Which insurance plan owes the most money?

## Insurance Analysis
### As of 3/12/2002

| Insurance Carrier | -- Claims -- | | -- Charges -- | | -- Payments -- | | |
|---|---|---|---|---|---|---|---|
| | # | % | Amount | % | Amount | % | |
| UN104 INSURANCE CO. 1 Secondary | 2 | 5.0 | $3,250.00 | 9.0 | -$353.49 | 13.8 Balance | $2,896.51 |
| UN105 INSURANCE CO. 2 Primary | 2 | 0.6 | 3,000.00 | 0.7 | -631.61 | 0.4 Balance | 2,368.39 |
| UN106 INSURANCE CO. 3 Primary | 5 | 1.4 | 3,250.00 | 0.7 | -1,367.60 | 0.9 Balance | 1,882.40 |
| UN108 INSURANCE CO. 4 Primary | 1 | 0.3 | 1,500.00 | 0.3 | -418.42 | 0.3 Balance | 1,081.58 |
| UN109 INSURANCE CO. 5 Primary | 1 | 0.3 | 1,500.00 | 0.3 | -290.00 | 0.2 Balance | 1,210.00 |
| USA00 INSURANCE CO. 6 Primary | 3 | 0.8 | 4,500.00 | 1.0 | -3,033.29 | 2.0 Balance | 1,466.71 |
| USA01 INSURANCE CO. 7 Secondary | 1 | 2.5 | 0.00 | 0.0 | 0.00 | 0.0 Balance | 0.00 |

| | Primary | Secondary | Tertiary |
|---|---|---|---|
| Total Charges | $447,750.00 | $36,000.00 | $0.00 |
| Total Number of Claims | 353 | 40 | 0 |
| Average Charge / Claim | $1,268.41 | $900.00 | $0.00 |

Unapplied insurance payments are not reflected on this report.

**Figure 5.** Insurance analysis for Downtown MRI Center.

Primary Insurance Aging
As of 3/30/02

| Date of Service | Procedure | --Past-- 0–30 | --Past-- 31–60 | --Past-- 61–90 | --Past-- 91–120 | --Past-- ≥21 | Total Balance |
|---|---|---|---|---|---|---|---|
| **INSURANCE CO. A (INSOA)** | | | | | | | |
| COMMAR | MARY | | *Policy: 095549487-01 Group:0024718* | | | | |
| 9/10/2001 | 70553 | | | | $1,750.00 | | |
| Claim: 337 | Billed: 11/21/2001 | $0.00 | $0.00 | $0.00 | $1,750.00 | $0.00 | |
| | Insurance Totals | $0.00 | $0.00 | $0.00 | $1,750.00 | | $1,750.00 |
| GRUDON | DONALEE | | *Policy: 261334201-01  Group: 3097360* | | | | |
| 11/7/2001 | 73721 | | | | $1,500.00 | | |
| Claim: 357 | Billed: 11/27/2001 | $0.00 | $0.00 | $0.00 | $1,500.00 | $0.00 | |
| | Insurance Totals | $0.00 | $0.00 | $0.00 | $1,500.00 | | $1,500.00 |
| **INSURANCE CO. B (INSOB)** | | | | | | | |
| DYER | RALPH | | | *Policy: 072324712   Group: 3097360* | | | |
| 6/29/2001 | 72141 | | | | | $1,500.00 | $1,500.00 |
| Claim: 287 | Billed: 8/26/2001 | $0.00 | $0.00 | $0.00 | $0.00 | $1,500.00 | $1,500.00 |
| | Insurance Totals | $0.00 | $0.00 | $0.00 | $0.00 | $1,500.00 | $1,500.00 |
| DAVRON | DAVID | | *Policy: 115-40-3870* | | | | |
| 7/3/2001 | 72148 | | | | | $1,500.00 | $1,500.00 |
| Claim: 291 | Billed: 9/27/2001 | $0.00 | $0.00 | $0.00 | $0.00 | $1,500.00 | $1,500.00 |
| | Insurance Totals | $0.00 | $0.00 | $0.00 | $0.00 | $1,500.00 | $1,500.00 |
| **INSURANCE CO. C (INSOC)** | | | | | | | |
| SHAMAR | MARSHA | | *Policy: 0103468350104035* | | | | |
| 2/27/2001 | 72141 | | | | | $1,500.00 | $1,500.00 |
| 2/27/2001 | 72148 | | | | | $1,500.00 | $1,500.00 |
| Claim: 116 | Billed: 4/3/2001 | $0.00 | $0.00 | $0.00 | $0.00 | $3,000.00 | $3,000.00 |

**Figure 6.** Primary insurance aging report for Downtown MRI Center.

| | ---Current---<br>0–30 | ---Past---<br>31–60 | ---Past---<br>61–90 | ---Past---<br>91+ | Total<br>balance |
|---|---|---|---|---|---|
| | | | | 60.00 | $60.00 |
| Reports<br>Aging Totals | $0.00 | $0.00 | $0.00 | $95,015.78 | $95,015.78 |
| Percent of<br>Aging Total | 0% | 0% | 0% | 100% | 100% |

**Figure 7.** Patient accounts receivable aging report summary for Downtown MRI Center.

## Review Questions

1. Explain the concept of managerial accounting.
2. How are managerial accounting reports designed?
3. What is the purpose of benchmarking?
4. Why would ratio analysis be used?
5. What is meant by the term *liquidity*?

## SELF-ASSESSMENT OF SKILL 9: MASTERING AND MONITORING FINANCIAL AND HUMAN RESOURCES

**Directions:** This assessment will help you evaluate your level of skill and attitudes toward using, interpreting, and analyzing financial data. Use the following statements to assess your attitudes and skills by circling the number closest to your experience: 1 = never, 2 = sometimes, 3 = often, and 4 = always. Respond in a way that reflects your skills today, rather than those you hope to have in the future. Answer as honestly as you can. Instructions for scoring and interpreting the results are provided in the analysis section at the end of the assessment.

1. I can read and analyze my organization's
   financial statements.                          1   2   3   4

2. I know the purpose of the balance sheet,
   statement of revenue and expenses, and
   statement of cash flows.                        1   2   3   4

3.  I use managerial accounting reports to manage my unit.                     1   2   3   4

4.  I understand the difference between profit and cash flow.                   1   2   3   4

5.  I use accounting ratios to analyze financial information.                   1   2   3   4

6.  I select ratios that will provide me with the specific information I need.  1   2   3   4

7.  I seek accounting professionals to assist me in understanding complex issues.   1   2   3   4

8.  I review my income and expenses along with my budget to monitor performance.    1   2   3   4

9.  I closely monitor employee overtime.                                        1   2   3   4

10. I learn from and continually improve on my financial analysis skills.       1   2   3   4

11. I read all of the reports, notes, and additional information that accompany my organization's financial statements.   1   2   3   4

12. I always look for ways to improve the quality and quantity of financial information I receive within my organization.   1   2   3   4

13. I know the concept of liquidity and consider this concept in my management of funds.   1   2   3   4

14. I use the concept of working capital in managing my organization's funds.   1   2   3   4

15. I know how my organization's mission and goals relate to its overall financial management.   1   2   3   4

16. I am aware of the impact that my
    department has on the overall financial
    performance of the organization.　　　1　2　3　4

17. I analyze the impact that capital
    expenditures may have on the
    organization before I make major
    requests.　　　　　　　　　　　　　1　2　3　4

18. I use benchmarks in monitoring
    performance.　　　　　　　　　　　　1　2　3　4

19. I use comparative data when reviewing
    financial statements.　　　　　　　　　1　2　3　4

20. I analyze the cash flows that my
    organization generates.　　　　　　　　1　2　3　4

21. I know the difference between current
    and long-term liabilities.　　　　　　　　1　2　3　4

22. I know whether my organization uses the
    accrual method of accounting or the cash
    basis.　　　　　　　　　　　　　　　　1　2　3　4

23. I utilize accounting ratios to analyze
    financial data.　　　　　　　　　　　　1　2　3　4

24. I compare my department with industry
    norms.　　　　　　　　　　　　　　　　1　2　3　4

25. Strong financial management skills are
    important in my assigned duties.　　　　1　2　3　4

## Self-Assessment Analysis

Add your circled scores together to arrive at your total score. Then refer to the scoring ranges below to identify your level of skill performance and attitudes toward financial management. You may want to refer back to sections of this chapter for suggestions on increasing and honing your financial management skills.

76–100     You appear to have highly developed financial monitoring and management skills that facilitate your ability to effectively and efficiently manage your areas of responsibility. Continue to enhance and maintain these skills.

51–75     You appear to have reasonably well-developed financial monitoring and management skills, but certain areas could be improved. By further developing these skills, you can become even more effective in increasing the productivity and performance of your department.

25–50     Your financial monitoring and management skills appear to need improvement. It appears that you may not fully understand the importance of this skill and its overall relation to the successful operation of your department. You might focus on improving selected skills and attitudes (i.e., items that you scored as 1 or 2).

## FOR FURTHER INFORMATION

Gapenski, L. (2002). *Healthcare finance: An introduction to accounting and financial management* (2nd ed.). Chicago: Health Administration Press.

This book provides a balance of information on accounting and financial management as it relates to the health care industry. The author provides an excellent resource for both novice and more experienced managers.

# Evaluating Organizational and Personal Resources and "Fit"

The objectives of this chapter are to

- Discuss the value of assessing organizational and personal resources and evaluating "fit" for health care managers

- Identify and describe the dimensional perspective

- Define and describe the basic types of "fit"

- Assess your personal and organizational resources

- Evaluate your "fit" with job, organization, and family

- Assess your attitudes and skills regarding organization and personal resources and "fit"

- Provide skill development exercises and activities to develop or enhance the skill of evaluating organizational and personal resources and "fit"

## ASSESSING ORGANIZATIONAL
## AND PERSONAL RESOURCES

The section on Becoming an Effective Leader in Health Care Management, Step I, indicated that there were two critical ingredients in becoming an effective manager. The first ingredient is that effective managers are successful at what they do because they have developed a wide variety of leadership skills. This chapter also suggested a second ingredient—that it is easier to be an effective manager if one is in the right place at the right time and with the right managers and co-workers. In other words, although skills are a necessary condition for effectiveness, having an adequate "fit" or match with a job and an organization that prizes such skills is the sufficient condition. Truly effective managers are able to develop, enhance, and maintain their leadership skills because their work environment not only "permits" managers to use these skills but requires and rewards their utilization.

For example, two managers may have developed exactly the same level of competence for the same technical, operational, relational, and analytic skills. One manager takes a new position with health care organization A, which is convinced that skillful leaders effect high productivity and employee commitment and supports and rewards its managers for utilizing those skills. The other manager takes a new position with health care organization B, a rather traditional organization that encourages and rewards technical skills and competence but not the other sets of skills. Even though the second manager has the capacity for and prior experience in delegating, coaching, managing conflict, thinking strategically, and working with teams, his superiors are not likely to reward such skills, or even support the manager's use of these skills. In short, degree of fit is critically important.

## DIMENSIONAL PERSPECTIVE

So what are the organizational and personal factors or resources that have an impact on fit? Eight factors or dimensions seem to be operative. They provide a useful perspective for thinking about fit. This chapter provides the manager with the knowledge and skills necessary to assess both organizational and personal resources and to evaluate the degree of fit between health care managers and their jobs, their organizations, and their family and career. These eight dimensional perspectives are listed in Table 1. There are aspects or indicators of each dimensional perspective that lend themselves to assessment. These indicators are listed in Table 2, and questions for assessment of these indicators are provided in the following text.

## Vision, Mission, Strategy, and Values

- What is the organization's vision, mission, and strategy?
- What are the organization's stated core values? How were they derived? What are the organization's actual core values? What modification in core values is needed for the organization to realize its vision?
- Who is responsible for developing the mission and strategy? Articulating it?
- How many employees know the mission and strategy? Follow it?
- Does each unit have its own strategy derived from the overall strategy? Do employees in your unit know it and use it to inform their work decisions and actions?
- What value does the organization place on strategic thinking— as distinct from strategic planning? Is strategic thinking actually practiced in the organization? By whom and at what level(s) of the organization is it practiced?
- Do you practice strategic thinking? Does your superior expect it of you? Reward you for it?
- Do you expect your employees to think strategically in their work in the unit?

**Table 1.** An eight-dimensional perspective

| |
| --- |
| Vision, mission, strategy, and values |
| Structure, communication, and rewards |
| Leadership |
| Culture |
| Employee competency, health, and commitment |
| Financial and capital resources |
| External environment |
| Personal resources |

**Table 2.** Indicators of organizational and personal resources

| Dimension | Representative indicators |
|---|---|
| Vision, mission, strategy, and values | Vision, mission, strategy and core values |
| | Extent to which mission/strategy affects employee actions |
| | Attitudes toward and and practice of strategic thinking among managers and employees |
| Structure, communication, and rewards | Organizational chart |
| | Match between actual reporting relationships and organizational chart |
| | Informal leaders and opinion makers |
| | Reward and sanction system |
| | Dominant communication patterns |
| Leadership | Dominant leadership style in the organization |
| | Corporate attitude and practice of coaching |
| | Corporate attitude and practice of delegation |
| | Corporate attitude and use of teams and team building |
| Culture | Cultural influence on quality, quantity, patient satisfaction, and so forth |
| | Match with core values and mission |
| | Extent to which it fosters or impedes giving input and risk-taking |
| Employee competency, health, and commitment | Hiring process and selection criteria |
| | Match of employee competence and values to organization need and values |
| | Employee health, psychological well-being, and job satisfaction |
| | Stress levels/job strain and job re-design to increase decisional control over high-demand jobs |
| | Level of commitment and rates of turnover, absenteeism, days off, and presenteeism |

Financial and capital resources

Cash flow and reserves
Corporate reputation and comparative ranking
Space, equipment, and supplies
Adequacy of technology, especially clinical and management information systems

External environment

Competition and market share
Impact of local, state, and federal rules, laws, and regulations
Community attitude and organization's value to community

Personal resources

Personal core values
Personal and professional priorities
Talents, skills, competencies
Career aspirations and dream job
Family and social support
Health status
Stress and time management strategies

## Structure, Communication, and Rewards

- Sketch out the corporate organizational chart. How well does it reflect the way the organization actually works?
- Describe the informal organization. Who are the opinion makers in the organization? In your unit?
- Who really runs the organization? Your unit?
- Describe reporting relationships and communication patterns in the overall organization. What type of communication pattern predominates: top-down, one-way versus two-way, or another?
- How is your unit organized and structured? What is the predominant communication pattern?
- What is the work flow in your unit? What facilitates it? What impedes it?
- What is the nature of the reward and sanction system in the organization? What behaviors and attitudes are rewarded? Sanctioned? What type of rewards are used most often? How do they affect performance and productivity?
- What rewards and sanctions are utilized in your unit? What behaviors and attitudes are rewarded? Sanctioned? What type of rewards are used most often? How do they affect performance and productivity?

## Leadership

- What is the overall dominant leadership style of the organization? In top management? How is delegation viewed? How common is delegation? How is it primarily used—to reduce a superior's busy work or to develop employees or both?
- Who is your immediate superior? What is his or her dominant leadership style? Generally, how much input do you have in the decisions that your superior makes?
- What is your leadership style? What is your attitude toward delegation? How do you utilize delegation in your unit?
- What is the organization's attitude toward coaching? Is coaching required; that is, is it written into managers' performance standards? How many managers regularly engage in skill, performance-based, and developmental coaching? What kind of training in coaching skills is offered?

- Does your immediate supervisor coach you or mentor you? If not, why not?
- What place do teams have in the organizations? What kinds are used? What is the organization's attitude toward teams and team building? What kind of team-building training exists?
- What is the impact of teams on productivity and job commitment and satisfaction?
- How is a manager's performance evaluated? What weight is placed on overall employee productivity? Skills and use of coaching? Teams? Delegation?

## Culture

- What aspects of work are most emphasized in your organization: precision, speed, quantity, quality, patient or customer satisfaction, innovation, employee safety, or others?
- If you were to tell an acquaintance or relative about what it is like to work in your organization, how would you describe the corporate atmosphere? Your unit's atmosphere?
- To what degree are corporate values reflected in the culture?
- Does the culture encourage employees to make suggestions, take risks, and offer feedback?

## Employee Competency, Health, and Commitment

- Generally speaking, how do employees feel about working for the organization? For your unit?
- What are employees' main concerns regarding the overall organization? In your unit?
- Describe the hiring process in terms of how prospective employees are recruited, interviewed, and offered jobs. Are there selection standards? Is the recruitment and selection program set up to recruit the best qualified candidates? If not, why?
- To what extent does the hiring process seek to match a prospective employee's basic values and skills and talents with the organization's core values and employment needs? Is the process more deliberate, proactive, and strategic or more reactive and hit-or-miss? What is the real cost of hiring unqualified employees, in terms of mistakes they make and lost productivity to supervisors and trainees alike?

- Has your unit analyzed its human resources needs? Are employees working overtime, taking work home, and missing deadlines? Do employees complain or joke about the work load?
- How committed are employees to the organization? What is the absenteeism rate? The presenteeism rate (i.e., employees are physically present but perform at less than 80% of expected productivity and performance)?
- Does the organization retain its talent and experience, or is there constant turnover resulting in the ongoing need to recruit and train new staff? What is the impact of turnover on productivity, stress levels, and morale?
- Does the organization assess job strain (i.e., demand–control model)? How effectively are work stressors (i.e., redesigning jobs to increase decisional control over high-demand, high-stress jobs, and so forth) addressed?

## Financial and Capital Resources

- What are the organization's financial and capital resources? Is there money to do the job? Do decreases in reimbursement rates strangle cash flow and throw the organization into a crisis mode? Occasionally or often?
- What is the extent of the organization's reserves?
- What is the organization's reputation among its peers? Are there centers of excellence? Has it received state or national recognition? In terms of benchmarking and best practices, how does it compare?
- How open is the organization in discussing financial concerns, rate hikes, and its financial forecast?
- Is access to the budget made available to employees or employee groups?
- Are sufficient space, equipment, and supplies available to allow staff to provide competent, quality care?
- Is existing technology compatible with current needs and demands? Will it be for the future?
- Is the organization reactive or proactive in future planning regarding the need for capital resources, particularly clinical information and management systems?
- Who is primarily involved in planning capital improvements and equipment? What is the role of unit managers and supervisors?

## External Environment

- What is the competition for your health care services or products? What is your organization's current market share? Anticipated market share?
- What are the growth opportunities?
- What are the community's overall attitude toward and expectations for the organization?
- How do you imagine the organization changing within the next 5 years?
- What local, state, and federal regulations, laws, or legislation have recently had an impact on the organization's viability? How will pending or proposed regulations have an impact on it?

## Personal Resources

- What are your own core values? Personal and professional priorities?
- What are your unique talents and abilities? How would you assess your current level of technical skills; operational skills (i.e., team leading, delegation, time management, and so forth); interpersonal or relational skills (i.e., communication, coaching, and so forth); and analytical skills (i.e., strategic thinking, budgeting, and so forth)?
- What are your career aspirations? At what stage of career development are you currently? What is your dream job? What training or promotions or relocation will it require to achieve such a job?
- What is the type and extent of your family and social support?
- What is your current health status? What are your health beliefs and behaviors?
- What is your current level of job-related stress and your capacity to cope with it?

## EVALUATING LEVEL OF "FIT"

Now that a careful assessment of organizational and personal resources has been completed, it is possible to evaluate various types of fit between and among the various dimensions. Several dimensions of a manager's job, career, organizational, family, and personal needs, demands, and values have an impact on his or her performance and effectiveness. A number of these are highlighted in this section. Because fit, or *synchronism,* is central to this evaluation strategy, a brief discussion of fit is in order.

## Types of Fit

The various dimensions of an organizational system are interrelated and influence one another. For instance, the organizations' structure and culture affect employee behavior (i.e., productivity, satisfaction, and health), but their behavior also has an impact on structure and culture. Similarly, a reasonable degree of relatedness should exist between the stage of an organization's development and the subsystems.

Managers have found it quite revealing to assess and evaluate the relationship and degree of fit between and among these dimensions. Using the eight-dimensional perspective presented earlier, managers should be able to anticipate the impact of a change in one or more dimensions on themselves and their organizations as well as their fit between and among themselves and these dimensions.

An organization's success and viability depend largely on the fit among various organizational dimensions, including the fit with managers' skills. The better the fit, the higher the productivity, job satisfaction, and overall health; decreased productivity, lowered satisfaction, and higher job stress are associated with poor fit (Beer, 1980; Muchinsky, 1993).

Some of the more useful dimensions of fit that a manager should assess include the following. Strategy–culture fit is the degree to which shared norms, beliefs, values, symbols, and rituals positively support and reflect the organization's vision, mission, and strategy. Strategy–leader fit is the degree to which the executives' behaviors responsibly support and facilitate the accomplishment of the organization's strategy. Strategy–member fit is the degree to which members are aware of, are committed to, and actually achieve the organization's mission and strategy. Strategy–environment fit is the degree to which the organization interfaces with its internal and external environment in accomplishing its strategy.

The degree of strategy–structure fit can be very revealing because strategy involves the organization's long-term goals and objectives, while structure is the way the organization is put together to administer the strategy. Chandler (1962) was one of the first to insist that structure must follow strategy. By this he meant that an organization must establish its strategic plan prior to forming its organizational structures and that, whenever corporate strategy changes, structural changes must also take place. The assumption is that a good match between strategy and structure will result in increased organizational performance and decreased problems, whereas a mismatch results in more problems and less productivity. Such a mismatch is called an incompatible organizational design. Certain strategies lend themselves to certain structural designs. For example, a health information systems corporation in a fast-changing market would fare better with a more flexible, organic structural design than with a hierarchical bureaucratic structural design.

However important the degree of fit between these organization subsystems and dimensions, there are four types of fit that are particularly important for managers: self–job fit, self–organization fit, self–family–career fit, and self–family–job/organization fit.

*Self–Job Fit*   The presence of high executive–organization fit is no guarantee that there will be a high level of executive–job fit, and vice versa. However, generally speaking, the better the match between employee talents, competencies, skills, and experience and the job's requirement, the more likely the executive will be productive and satisfied (Lowman, 1993). The poorer the fit, the greater the likelihood of distress, role ambiguity, role conflicts, and derailment. Several job-related factors can have a negative or positive impact on the degree of fit.

Work schedules can have an impact on job productivity, commitment, and job satisfaction as well as employee health. For some employees, flexible work hours offer an alternative to the traditional fixed working schedule and provide employees some choice in arrival and departure times. For other employees, work scheduling might require second shift, night shift, or rotating shift assignment. Research indicates that many shift workers experience problems with health and social adjustment. Because of an interruption in circadian rhythms, shift workers often complain of lack of sleep, fatigue, appetite loss, and constipation. They also experience family and marital difficulties (Muchinsky, 1993). In short, such job-related factors not only can affect employee productivity, health, and interpersonal relationships, they can have an impact on family relations.

*Self–Organization Fit*　　Levinson (1981) considered manager–organization fit as critical to a manager's professional effectiveness and personal well-being. Essentially, the better the fit between the manager's values and beliefs and the organization's values and mission, the greater the likelihood of high job performance, commitment, satisfaction, and personal self-esteem. Conversely, the poorer the fit, the higher the likelihood of disillusion, distress, and derailment (Muchinsky, 1993).

*Self–Family–Career Fit*　　This type of fit focuses both on the relationship of the manager to his or her family—both nuclear family and family of origin—and the manager's career path as it has an impact on the family and as the family has an impact on it. Individuals choose specific career paths for many reasons, including personal reasons and family influence. Pleasing a parent or carrying on a family tradition may have a significant impact on career path, as witnessed by the number of physicians who are the sons or daughters of a physician or one of several generations of physicians in a family. Also, salary, benefits, or status can significantly influence career choice, as when an individual forgoes his or her passion to paint or sculpt in favor of a high-salary position in order to send a child to a private school or maintain a certain lifestyle. The converse is also true, as was noted when managed care was perceived as reducing physician income levels. As a result, some individuals with the aptitude for medicine chose to pursue careers in finance or computers instead. The price one pays for a poor fit (e.g., appeasing family rather than following one's dream) can be high (e.g., unhappiness, a sense of unfulfillment).

The other way in which fit may be low or poor is when job demands interfere with family life or an intimate relationship, or there is spillover of stress from job to family or spouse. Organizations that strive to be family friendly, with flex time, work–life programs, and the like, can increase self–family–career fit.

*Self–Family–Job/Organization Fit*　　Despite the potential for a good or high fit among the executive, the job, and the organization,

family dynamics or social support network can have a negative—
or positive—impact on the executive's job performance, satisfaction, and overall sense of well-being. For this reason, the degree of
fit with family dynamics and social support networks needs to be
considered. McCubbin and Thompson (1989, 1999) have presented
convincing data that family factors (i.e., illness, conflicts, and other
problems) can have a significant impact on an employee's productivity and health. These outcomes are more likely with female employees. Similarly, this and other research confirms that high satisfaction with marriage, relationship with a significant other, family
members, or social network can effectively buffer job-related stress.
In short, this dimension of fit should be assessed or evaluated.

*Edward Linus had been recruited to head up the medical center's
integrated medical information system, which would connect the
three affiliated hospitals on the medical center campus. He had
been a project team leader in charge of 5 researchers, and now he
would be managing a group of 19 technicians, programmers, and
network engineers. Although he had some misgivings about moving from a research and development center position to a senior
management position, the search committee assured him that he
"would make the transition with flying colors." Among other
things, the position required him to move his family across the
country from a major metropolitan area to a smaller community.
It meant his wife, a social worker, would have to find a new job
and their two teenage sons would have to acclimate to a new high
school.*

    *In addition to the difficulties with the relocation, Edward's dif-
ficulties on the job were increasing by the day. Before, he had spent
85% of his time in the lab "doing science," which was his passion,
and the rest on managing his team. Now he was spending 90% or
more of his time trying to manage what seemed like an unman-
ageable department. He had been used to a smooth-functioning research team in which collaboration and delegation characterized
his leadership style. Here, the organization of his department was
elusive, and those reporting to him gave him verbal feedback on
project progress but seldom provided written documentation.
Getting commitments seemed impossible. As a result, he felt ma-
nipulated and powerless. When Edward described his management woes to his superior, all he got was a smile and a terse "What*

*did you expect? This isn't an R&D lab." After 1 month, with an unhappy wife and kids, Edward was ready to move back. Unfortunately, his old job was now filled.*

## EXERCISES FOR SKILL DEVELOPMENT

### Individual Exercise

This exercise involves your own personal and professional life.

1.  Assess your current job situation in light of the eight sets of indicators of the dimensional perspective. Use the questions provided in the text to guide your assessment. It may take an hour or longer to compile this information.

2.  Then, evaluate the level of fit for each of the four types involving your professional life.

### Group Exercise

Divide into groups of four, individually re-read the case example presented earlier, and compare Edward's current position with his previous job situation in light of the eight sets of indicators—and related questions—of the dimensional perspective.

1.  Working individually, use Table 2 to assess the actual and presumed indicators. Note which indicators in the list are operative.

2.  Next, specify the levels of fit for all four types of fit.

3.  Now have each individual describe his or her operative indicators list. Come to a group consensus on the indicators that are operative.

4.  Discuss and come to a group consensus on the four types of fit in the case of Edward.

## SELF-ASSESSMENT OF SKILL 11: EVALUATING ORGANIZATIONAL AND PERSONAL RESOURCES AND "FIT"

**Directions:** This assessment will help you evaluate the level of fit among yourself and your job, organization, and family. Use the following statements to assess your level of fit by circling the number that is closest to your experience: 1 = never, 2 = sometimes, 3 = often, and 4 = always. Respond in a way that reflects your level of fit today, rather than the level you hope to have in the future. Answer as honestly as you can. Instructions on scoring and interpreting the results are provided in the analysis section at the end of the assessment.

1. I feel energetic, healthy, and happy.    1    2    3    4

2. I have made the most of my talents and abilities.    1    2    3    4

3. I have an inner sense of balance that allows me to move through the day with serenity.    1    2    3    4

4. I am comfortable with who I am.    1    2    3    4

5. I am seldom anxious, angry, or depressed without knowing why.    1    2    3    4

6. My job performance is consistently the best I can do.    1    2    3    4

7. My job is an extension of my personal value system.    1    2    3    4

8. I can arrange my work life so it doesn't spill over into my personal life.    1    2    3    4

9. I am satisfied with my job performance.    1    2    3    4

10. My talents and skills are a good fit with this job.    1    2    3    4

11. My values match the organization's core values.    1    2    3    4

12. I am committed to my organization's mission of high performance and quality.    1    2    3    4

13.  The culture of this organization is healthy and employee friendly.

1    2    3    4

14.  My organization's policies, salaries, and expectations of employees are fair and reasonable.

1    2    3    4

15.  I like working in this organization and have no plans to leave.

1    2    3    4

16.  My family is always there for me when I need support and encouragement.

1    2    3    4

17.  I am deeply committed to my significant other.

1    2    3    4

18.  My job has sufficient flexibility so I can attend to my family's needs.

1    2    3    4

19.  My work life does not take priority over my family life.

1    2    3    4

20.  I recognize my own interpersonal needs when it comes to forming relationships with others.

1    2    3    4

21.  There is a good fit between me and this organization.

1    2    3    4

22.  There is a good fit among me and my job, family, and organization.

1    2    3    4

23.  There is a good fit between my talents and skills and my job.

1    2    3    4

24.  I maintain balance in my personal and professional life by pursuing hobbies and interests.

1    2    3    4

25.  The job I have and the place I work do not disrupt my relationships with family or friends.

1    2    3    4

## Self-Assessment Analysis

### *Section I*

Add your circled scores together to arrive at your total score. Now that you have computed your total score, refer to the scoring ranges below to identify your overall level of fit among yourself and your job, organization, and family. You may want to refer back to sections of this chapter for suggestions on increasing your level of fit.

76–100    You appear to have a high level of fit among yourself and your job, organization, and family. A high level of fit is usually associated with high productivity, job satisfaction, and personal well-being.

51–75    You appear to have a moderate level of fit among yourself and your job, organization, and family. Efforts to increase the level of fit can increase your job satisfaction and overall sense of well-being.

25–50    You appear to have a relatively low level of fit among yourself and your job, organization, and family. You might review those items that you scored as 1 or 2, as well as the five subscales in Section II, to formulate a plan for increasing your level of fit.

### *Section II*

In Section I you determined your overall level of fit. Here you can determine specific levels of fit. Sum up your scores for each of the following item sets:

Items 1–5    _____    Self items

Items 6–10    _____    Self–job fit items

Items 11–15 _____    Self–organization fit items

Items 16–20 _____    Self–family fit items

Items 21–25 _____    Self–family–job/organization fit items

## REVIEW ACTIVITIES

1.    Discuss the value of assessing organizational and personal resources and evaluating the level of fit among the various

dimensions. What practical consequences, if any, might there be as a result of this process?

2. Give a one-sentence description of the eight-dimensional perspective. Then indicate how the results of assessing these dimensions (as was done in the Individual Exercise) had or could have an impact on your current personal life.

3. Describe how your evaluation of the four types of fit can have a positive impact on your own career development and planning.

4. Indicate how your assessment of the various dimensions and your evaluation of the types of fit will or can have an impact on your own work unit, and possibly the entire organization.

## FOR FURTHER INFORMATION

Betof, E., & Harwood, F. (1992). *Just promoted! How to survive and thrive in your first 12 months as a manager.* New York: McGraw-Hill.

A useful guide for any manager to better understand his or her work environment. Recommended chapters include Chapter 6 ("Assessing Your Organization's Health"), Chapter 10 ("Up Close and Personal: The Impact of Moving Up on Your Family, Health and Time"), and Chapter 11 ("Achieving a New Life Balance").

Sperry, L. (1996). *Corporate therapy and consulting.* New York: Brunner/Mazel.

Recommended chapters include Chapter 3 ("Organizational Dynamics") and Chapter 4 ("Organizational Diagnosis"), which contain an extended discussion of organizational subsystems and stages of development as well as an assessment approach to analyzing various organizational dimensions.

# Managing Stress and Time Effectively

The objectives of this chapter are to

- Describe the value and necessity of the skills of stress management in health care organizations

- Define structural, relational, and time stressors

- Differentiate long-term stress management strategies from short-term or immediate stress management strategies

- Discuss the demand–control model of job strain and workplace stress

- Describe and illustrate strategies for effectively managing structural and time stressors

- Assess your attitudes and skills regarding stress and time management

- Provide skill development exercises and activities to develop or enhance skills in managing stress and time

## STRESS AND STRESSORS IN
## HEALTH CARE ORGANIZATIONS

### Stress

Stress seems to be increasing in today's fast-paced health care environment. It tends to affect individuals more than they realize, largely because of the increasing influence that work exerts on life today. In mainstream American culture, we typically identify ourselves with what we do (e.g., "I'm a hospital administrator"). Typically, individuals in health care settings spend more hours involved in their work than in any other activity, including sleep. Furthermore, many of our friendships may be at work. Finally, nearly 80% of all couples are dual-earner or dual-career families.

Stress arises in the health care organization in a variety of ways, such as work backlogs that continually increase, demanding superiors who exert pressure by adding assignments, and changing priorities and tightening deadlines. Troubling, troubled, and difficult employees can be particularly stressful for health care managers. There is also stress unique to health care settings, that is, working in an environment of illness, emergencies, trauma, and death.

### Stressors

The word *stressor* typically brings to mind life events such as financial pressures, death of a close relative, family conflicts, or work deadlines. Actually, a stressor may be almost anything that adversely affects us: exposure to high or low temperatures; environmental toxins; caffeine, alcohol, or drug use; certain foods; lack of exercise; conflicted relationships; and strong emotional reactions. Stressors can compel individuals to smoke, drink, take drugs, and overeat. They can induce back problems, skin disorders, respiratory infections, and circulation problems. Research increasingly demonstrates that stress lowers resistance to illness and weakens the immune system. Three types of stressors have an impact on those who work in health care settings: environmental, relational, and time stressors.

**Environmental stressors:** Stressors that arise from the organizational environment and situation in which an individual works are referred to as environmental stressors. Such stressors include unfavorable working conditions and job design that results in a sense of loss of control over one's job. Employees who feel they have lost control of their jobs inevitably feel helpless to do more than simply remain afloat amid the torrents of rising demands, conflict, and uncertainties. Ultimately, they become susceptible to the physical and psychological conditions that prolonged stress can cause and aggravate (Karasek & Theorell, 1990).

**Time stressors:** This type of stressor typically results from work overload, which simply means having too to much to do in too short a period of time. This stressor may be the most common and pervasive source of stress faced by health care employees and managers. Both feel increasingly compelled to accomplish more tasks in shorter time frames and are often not in control of the time needed to complete these tasks. Although an occasional time stressor may actually energize some individuals in completing a task, such as filing their income tax return before April 15, a constant state of time pressure is nearly always harmful and deleterious for all individuals.

**Relational stressors:** This type of stressor results from interpersonal conflicts in the workplace. Three kinds of conflict are commonly faced by managers: role, issue, and interaction conflicts. Role conflict involves conflict resulting from role expectations that are incompatible. Issue conflicts involve disagreement over defining or solving a problem. Interaction conflicts involve mutual antagonism among employees in a work team or unit. This section does not focus on relational stressors because they are addressed in the chapters titled Negotiating and Managing Conflict and Difficult Employees (Skill 5) and Counseling and Interviewing for Maximum Performance and Development (Skill 7).

This section addresses both organizational stressors, such as environmental and time stressors, and personal stressors. It assists managers in recognizing these two common stressors. It provides long-term stress management strategies, which principally address environmental and time stressors, and short-term or immediate stress management strategies, which are useful in addressing the so-called personal stressors. It emphasizes and illustrates skills and strategies for dealing with such stressors and provides the reader with skill development exercises and activities to enhance his or her understanding of and skills in managing them.

## TWO VIEWS OF STRESS

Our response to stress is as individualized as our fingerprints. For some individuals, a constant stream of minor hassles—traffic tie-ups, spilled coffee, or misunderstandings with co-workers—take their toll. Others can ignore these little things but are incapacitated by major stressors such as the breakup of a relationship or the onset of a medical illness. Most of us have special symptoms—tensed neck muscles, headaches, or a wave of anxiety—that signal us to slow down and destress. Unfortunately, too few recognize the signal or heed it.

Many books and workshops on stress management focus entirely on making a personal change such as learning a skill (e.g., relaxation) or changing one's self-talk. These approaches assume that stress is strictly a matter of personal perception and attitude, and is unrelated to environmental influences. This "personal view" of stress is a very common way of thinking about stress. It is a view ascribed to by many managers and health care personnel.

A second view is that organizational influences exert a significant effect that should be considered along with the personal perceptions and attitudes. This is the view taken by this text, based on 30 years of consulting for organizations as well as on research on workplace stress. This broader view focuses on stressors such as time demands and job control. In this view, stress management strategies must target these organizational influences as well as the worker's personal perceptions and attitudes.

## LONG-TERM STRESS MANAGEMENT STRATEGIES

### Environmental Stressors

Certain work environment factors have been shown to cause feelings of loss of control and powerlessness among workers in certain jobs. Highly stressful environmental conditions that foster feelings of loss of control, helplessness, and hopelessness are associated with high levels of cortisol—the so-called stress hormone—and catecholamines, which contribute to heart disease, clinical depression, and neoplasm formation (i.e., tumors and cancer). Conversely, employees who are motivated and seek productive results are likely to experience a "strong sense of personal control, accompanied by a sense of accomplishment and job commitment" (Girdano, Everly, & Dusek, 2001, p. 190). Physiologically, these employees have suppressed or low levels of cortisol production.

Research on the causes and effects of loss of job control employs the term *job strain* to describe the particular stressors of a given job. Any job can be characterized by both its psychological work demands—such as the required speed and intensity of the job—and its control or decision latitude. The greatest job strain occurs in jobs that have high demand and low control, such as nursing assistant, police or security officer, and switchboard operator. The least job strain occurs in top executives, including senior health care managers, and in architects, who have considerable control over their jobs.

Karasek and Theorell (1990) reviewed the health effects of job control and noted that the risk of poor health associated with low job control is about the same as the risk of heart disease associated with smoking and elevated cholesterol levels. Workers with low job control were five times more likely to develop heart disease and three times more likely to develop hypertension than those with high job control. These authors also described other stress-related effects of low job control. Table 1 is an adaptation of Karasek and Theorell's model.

Until the advent of managed care, the occupations of physician and, to a lesser extent, nurse were considered high-control, high-demand jobs (Category I), meaning that individuals holding these jobs had relatively high levels of decisional control over their work. For all practical purposes, physician's decisions about which laboratory tests to order, which surgical or nonsurgical treatments to provide, and which medications to prescribe were seldom if ever questioned. Managed care has considerably decreased the level of decisional control with the requirements of medical necessity and authorization of services. Requesting authorization from HMO personnel—who are not physicians—has effectively "moved" the occupation of physician into Category III: low control, high demand. Now physicians must seek authorization for treatment they wish to provide a patient, and are aware that they must justify the requested treatment according to the HMO's criteria of medical necessity. This loss of decisional control not only has resulted in in-

**Table 1.**   Job stress: Impact of levels of demands and control on job and health

| Category | Variables | Description |
| --- | --- | --- |
| I | High control–high demand | High level of job commitment and job satisfaction |
| | | Immune system remains intact, that is, low cortisol levels |
| | | Low rates of physical and psychological illness |
| | | Example jobs: senior health care manager |
| II | High control–low demand | Least pathogenic job category; tends to be stable and low challenge but satisfying |
| | | Example jobs: medical librarian |
| III | Low control–high demand | Most pathogenic job category; very high risk job; high catecholamine and cortisol levels; highest rates of physical and psychological illness |
| | | Example jobs: nursing assistant, police officer, switchboard operator |
| IV | Low control–low demand | Second most pathogenic job category; boring, repetitive |
| | | Example jobs: janitor, security guard |

*Source:* Karasek and Theorell (1990).

creased job strain and stress but also accounts for the decrease in job satisfaction experienced by many physicians today. It may also account for the increasing number of physicians who are retiring from medical practice 10–20 years earlier than did physicians 20 or more years ago.

Recently, corporations have directed efforts at increased job control through participative management, team development, and job redesign on the assumption that increasing job control increases employee stress resistance. Unfortunately, health care organizations have not been very proactive in such efforts.

## INDIVIDUAL EXERCISE: ENHANCING JOB CONTROL

Consider your current job in terms of its psychological demands and level of control or autonomy. If you are overstressed, and your job control is low, consider the following:

1.   Talk to your immediate boss about ways of increasing decision making about deadlines, performance standards, flexibility in work hours, and the like.

2.  In some instances, increasing decision latitude will not be sufficient. Job redesign may be in order. Although a worker may have some input into this process, it usually involves a major commitment from management and possibly a union representative as well as skilled job redesign consultants.

3.  If there appears to be little change possible, you might consider a job or even a career change.

## Time Stressors

Time management is an essential skill and strategy of stress management. Why? Because, effective time management is a powerful strategy for gaining control over one's job. Although it is not the only solution to the workplace stress experienced by managers, it can go a long way toward reducing a considerable degree of stress. It is a truism that managers who effectively manage time experience less stress and are more productive than managers who do not.

Managers are increasingly aware of the cost of time. They and their units are being held accountable for their use of time: Goals are clearly defined and penalties are incurred for missed deadlines. Corporate culture can have an important influence on how employees use their time. In too many health care organizations, working long hours is equated with working hard. Leaving on time may be interpreted by others as lack of responsibility and commitment. Interestingly, research is clear that working longer hours may actually decrease efficiency and productivity.

Few managers readily admit that large parts of their working day are wasted. The only way for managers to make better use of their time is to analyze how they use it now and then to consider ways in which they can reallocate it more effectively. There are always competing demands on a manager's time. It is very easy to spend too much time on routine tasks, such as reading mail, at the expense of high-priority, productive tasks. Each manager must consider the following questions: How do I divide up my day at the moment? Do I prioritize my work so that I tackle important and urgent projects first, or do I concentrate on completing enjoyable tasks first? Am I distracted by telephone calls, or do I have a system for dealing with them? Do I waste a lot of time? The following exercise can provide answers to these questions.

## INDIVIDUAL EXERCISE: TIME LOG AND TASK PRIORITY PROFILE

1.  Maintain a daily log of how much time you spend on particular activities. Such a log provides a starting point from which you can assess areas to improve. The length of time for keeping a time log is dependent on the nature of your work. If you work on a monthly cycle, keep the log for 2 or 3 months. A 2- or 3-week log is reasonable if your work cycle is weekly. List each activity you engage in from the beginning to the end of each work day.

2.  Next, analyze your time log.

    a.  Begin by dividing each recorded day into 30-minute time blocks and categorizing each 30-minute block according to the nature of the primary task that you performed, such as meetings, reading and replying to mail, helping colleagues, or making phone calls. Then calculate the amount of time spent on each type of task.

    b.  Next, calculate the percentage of your time spent on each task. This provides a baseline of your working day and allows you to assess how you can allocate your time more effectively. Look at the categories into which you have allocated your tasks, then divide them into three groups: $R$, or routine tasks (e.g., quarterly administrative reports); $O$, or ongoing tasks (e.g., organizing a meeting); and $D$, or developmental tasks that would further enhance your job and career (e.g., networking and making new contacts).

    c.  Next, calculate the percentage of time spent on each of the three types of tasks: $R$, $O$, and $D$. Research indicates that effective managers spend only 15% of their time on $R$ tasks, about 60% of their time on $D$ tasks, and 25% of their time on $O$ tasks. However, the typical manager's time allocation to these three tasks is just the reverse: 60% on $R$ tasks, 25% on $O$ tasks, and 15% on $D$ tasks!

3.  Having established your time allocation for the three sets of tasks, consider whether the time allocations meet your expectations for an effective workday. Might you be spending excessive time on R tasks at the expense of the more important D tasks? Look at the distribution of these two sets of tasks during a typical day. You

may need to reorganize your work day so that you are able to work more consistently and efficiently and, thus, more productively.

4.  Finally, consider how closely your work pattern is to the ideal 15% R, 25% O, 60% D. If you find that you are spending too much time on one group of tasks to the detriment of others, work out how you can reorganize your daily schedule so that your time is distributed more efficiently. For example, if you find that you are spending time on tasks that could easily be done by one of your staff, delegate those tasks. This way you can concentrate your energies on the areas in which you are not spending enough time.

## SHORT-TERM OR IMMEDIATE STRESS MANAGEMENT STRATEGIES

### Relaxation and Mindfulness

Relaxation techniques counteract the negative effects of stress by inducing its opposite state, relaxation. When a state of relaxation is achieved, the body is calmed: heart rate and blood pressure are reduced, the heart beats more effectively, and breathing decreases as oxygen demand is reduced. However, although our bodies may be calmed and relaxed, our minds may be chronically distracted with a chaotic mixture of repetitive thoughts, worries, daydreams, and impatience. Chronic distraction is an early warning sign that you are overstressed. Present moment awareness—also called *mindfulness*—is the opposite of distraction. The mind becomes calm and focused while the body is relaxed. Relaxation and mindfulness are thoroughly discussed in Borysenko's (1988) text, *Minding the Body, Mending the Mind.* This state of relaxation and mindfulness can be achieved by practicing the following strategies on a regular, daily basis.

#### INDIVIDUAL EXERCISES

#### Rapid Relaxation

This exercise takes 3–4 minutes. You might want to tape record the following description as a script. Allow about 10 seconds to pass on the tape at pauses.

When you have found a comfortable position for your body, take a very long, deep breath and fill your lungs. As you are breathing in, tense every muscle in your body. Hold your breath in, and study the tension in every part of your body.

*(pause)*

Now exhale, breathe out, and allow your entire body to relax.

*(pause)*

Feel the relief as the relaxation spreads all over and as you let go more and more.

*(pause)*

Now breathe in again, expanding your abdomen, and then filling your chest and lungs with air. Hold the breath.

*(pause)*

Now, let it out slowly.

*(pause)*

Then continue to breathe normally in and out.

*(pause)*

As you breath in, think the word *in,* and as you breath out, think the word *out.*

*(pause)*

Let go of all of your muscles so that you feel pleasantly heavy and calm. Each time you exhale, feel yourself breathing all of the remaining tensions out of your body. Continue this relaxing sensation for a little longer.

*(pause)*

Now allow your mind to come up with a word or phrase that describes your present relaxed state (e.g., "relaxed," "calm and comfortable"). Say [your cue word] to yourself each time you exhale for a moment or two.

*(pause)*

Repeat it to yourself whenever you feel this relaxed. The more you do this, the sooner the word or phrase can evoke the feelings whenever you desire. When you are ready to stop, take a deep breath and open your eyes as you exhale. Feel awake, alert, and nicely relaxed.

*(pause)*

Now stretch your body before getting up. Then slowly stand up and resume your normal activities.

### Mindfulness

Choose at least one activity each day to practice mindfulness. For example, if you are taking a walk for exercise, walk mindfully and resist the urge to solve a problem or worry about some concern. Absorb yourself in the feel of your shoes touching the pavement, the sound of birds chirping, the blowing wind and the rustle of the trees, and so forth. Put up a few signs around your home or office as reminders. The practice is easy, but remembering to practice is the real challenge. This exercise activity should last at least 5 minutes each time you do it for skill learning to occur.

## Breathing as a Stress Breaker

Surprisingly, although we each breathe about 20,000 times every day, most of us halt our breathing for several seconds or more at the start of and during a stressful situation. Dacher (1991) reported that this reduces oxygen to the brain and can result in feelings of anxiety, anger, and panic and a general sense of loss of control. Yet, even in nonstressful moments, most of us breathe inefficiently and unhealthily. We engage in shallow, upper chest breathing. Such inefficient breathing results in fatigue, diminished brain power, and weakened health. With a minimal amount of practice over a few weeks, it is possible to significantly and permanently improve the way one breathes.

### INDIVIDUAL EXERCISE: DEEP ABDOMINAL BREATHING

Here is a fast, simple exercise to improve your breathing:

1. Sit or stand with good posture—your head up, neck long and relaxed, chin slightly in, shoulders broad and loose, and back straight.

2. Place your hands lightly around the sides of your lower ribs with the fingertips pointing in toward the front centerline of the body, and with your thumbs to the rear.

3. Slowly inhale. As the abdomen expands slightly downward and forward (with the lower back staying flat), feel your lower ribs move out to the sides. Then, as you complete the breath in, feel your chest expand comfortably.

4. Exhale slowly, releasing muscle tension. Repeat this pattern for 2–3 minutes. Do the exercise several times each day.

## One-Second Emergency Destressor

In *The Performance Edge,* Dr. Robert Cooper (1991) described a simple stress-breaking strategy called the Instant Calming Sequence (ICS), which can effectively neutralize negative stress in less than 1 second. This five-step strategy—continue breathing, present a positive face, adopt a balanced posture, set off a wave of relaxation, and maintain mental control—will help an individual remain calm and in control of his or her thoughts, feelings, and actions in the midst of almost any stressor or high-pressure situation. The strategy can almost miraculously reverse physical and mental responses to negative stressors.

We can all imagine ourselves being stressed by negative criticism while engaging in sports competition, making a speech, closing a sale, or hearing bad news. We respond with shallow, halting breaths; a worrisome or frightened facial expression; slouched posture with tensed neck, back, and abdomen; and negative thoughts and feelings streaming though us. The calming sequence reverses these responses: uninterrupted deep breathing in place of the halting, shallow breaths; a positive, slightly smiling face instead of the worrisome look; full balanced posture and a wave of relaxation in place of the tensed slouch; and mental control replacing negative or fearful thoughts.

### INDIVIDUAL EXERCISE: INSTANT CALMING SEQUENCE

1. Select a stressful problem situation and vividly imagine the circumstances. Roll the slow-motion mental videotape backward in

your mind's eye until you catch the very first signal that the problem is starting to distract or hurt you. Stall the mental videotape right there.

2.   Picture yourself effortlessly and successfully going though the ICS: 1) continue breathing, 2) present a positive face, 3) adopt a balanced posture, 4) set off a wave of relaxation, and 5) maintain mental control.

3.   Now repeat the process a little faster. Practice the sequence a number of times each day, using different stress cues, while increasing the vividness of the mental images and the speed of your ICS response.

If at first you have difficulty with any of the steps, practice them one at a time until they become comfortable. If you get partially into the ICS and find yourself starting to lose control, back the sequence up and slow things down. Be absolutely certain that you freeze the image of the stress cue at the first instant—don't let the stressful image keep rolling to the point at which you become anxious. The goal of this practice is to automatically slip the ICS into the situation right behind the first signal of stress. This can make all the difference in the world in the outcome. When rehearsing very intense situations, you might try lightening the image of the stress signal (by seeing yourself move farther away from it in your mind or by dulling the vividness of the scene) until you're at ease with using the ICS to handle it. Refer to Cooper's book for further information on learning ICS.

## Using Rest Breaks to Destress

A normal part of everyone's daily sleep–wake cycle is a series of rest–activity cycles of approximately 90–120 minutes. During the first hour or so of each cycle, we experience a period of heightened physical and mental alertness and energy in which our skills, memory, and learning abilities are heightened ("peaks"). For the next 15–20 minutes, our performance drops to low levels ("troughs") during which we may yawn, become easily distracted, and feel like napping. It is during this down period that body–mind revitalization can occur, if we allow it. Unfortunately, most of us override this signal for rejuvenation, setting the stage for stress ranging from fatigue to psychosomatic problems. Research reported in Ernest

Rossi's (1991) *The 20-Minute Break* shows that even heeding this signal for a few minutes during the down phase of our 10 or more daily rest–activity cycles greatly enhances physical and mental well-being and increases resistance to stress.

## INDIVIDUAL EXERCISE: THE 3-MINUTE STRESS BREAK

We feel better and work more efficiently when we're not fighting our body rhythm cycles but rather take advantage of our natural peaks and troughs. So, plan important meetings and highly demanding activities during your peaks, and less demanding activities, such as opening mail, during troughs. When you first recognize yourself going into an energy trough, and it is possible and safe to do so, let yourself go with the flow: "Phase out" for 2 or 3 minutes while sitting at your desk or in an easy chair. Daydream, take a few deep refreshing breaths, or just "be." Then stretch a little and return to your task refreshed. If such a short rest break "phase out" is not possible, you might momentarily shift to a less demanding task, such as routine filing or reorganizing tasks, making a personal phone call, heading over to the water cooler, or talking to colleagues. As you return to your regular task, you should feel more refreshed and destressed. Refer to Rossi's book for further information on learning this strategy.

*Justin, Manager of Patient Accounts, arrives at the medical center 1 hour later than usual on Monday morning. He was delayed because of a flat tire on his way to work. As he enters the patient accounts department and checks his voice mail, he finds a message from Samantha, his secretary, saying she has a bad cold and won't be in today. She also mentions that she has not finished the overhead transparencies and handouts he needs for his presentation at the reaccreditation planning team meeting for the upcoming Joint Commission visit. The hospital's chief executive officer and chief financial officer are very worried about both the accreditation visit and accounts receivable. Justin has been under the gun for the past 3 months because of delays in Medicare reimbursement that have created a cash flow problem for the hospital. He knows that he has data to present that could greatly relieve their concerns. The problem is that he cannot possibly finish preparing those materials in time for the meeting, which is scheduled to begin in 20 minutes. He checks and learns that the meeting cannot be postponed because of the preparation team's very tight meeting schedule. Justin begins to experience panic-like sensations as he considers what he might do. Unfortunately, this is not the first time his staff has let him down in a pinch.*

## GROUP SKILL DEVELOPMENT EXERCISE

Divide into groups of four to analyze the previous case example. Allow up to 60 minutes for this exercise: up to 30 minutes in small groups and up to 30 minutes for the large group component.

1. One participant in each group reads the case example aloud. Then all members of the small group write down their initial reactions to Justin's dilemma and their plan for dealing with the stress.

2. Have each small group participant describe his or her initial reaction to the case example, followed by his or her stress management plan.

3. Compare both the reactions and the stress management plans. Some participants will propose personal or immediate stress management coping strategies, whereas others will propose organizational or long-term strategies. Note whether the focus is on environmental or on time stressors. Discuss the viability of each strategy proposed.

After 30 minutes, return to the large group and discuss the focus on either environmental or time stressors, the viability of both long- and short-term strategies, and the prospect of implementing both short- and long-term strategies simultaneously.

## SELF-ASSESSMENT OF SKILL 12: MANAGING STRESS AND TIME EFFECTIVELY

**Directions:** This assessment will help you evaluate your level of skill and attitudes regarding handling stress. Use the following statements to assess your attitudes and skills by circling the number that is closest to your experience: 1 = never, 2 = sometimes, 3 = often, and 4 = always. Respond in a way that reflects your skills today, rather than those you hope to have in the future. Answer as honestly as you can. Instructions on scoring and interpreting the results are provided in the analysis section at the end of the assessment.

1. I feel that the role I play within my organization is important.     1  (2)  3  4

2. I feel reasonably calm and centered even if I am under pressure.     1  2  (3)  4

3. I have a close relationship with someone who mentors and advises me.     1  (2)  3  4

4. I make it a point to exercise and work out regularly.     1  2  3  (4)

5. I undertake only as many tasks as I can handle at once.     1  2  (3)  4

6. I maintain balance in my personal and professional life by pursuing hobbies and interests.     1  2  (3)  4

7. I know and practice several immediate stress reducers such as mindfulness and deep breathing.     1  (2)  3  4

8. I deal with tasks by prioritizing my work load.     1  2  (3)  4

9. I can say "no" to requests and demands.     1  (2)  3  4

10. I do not feel I need to finish all uncompleted tasks each day.     1  2  (3)  4

11. I would say that, for the most part, I am able to cope with my work load.     1  2  (3)  4

12. My work life does not take priority over my family and home life.     1  2  (3)  4

13. The meetings I organize achieve their
purpose and finish on time.     1   2   (3)   4

14. I open my mail as soon as it arrives on
my desk.     1   2   (3)   4

15. I skim any relevant newspaper and
magazine articles.     1   (2)   3   4

16. I decide how many times I can be
interrupted in a day.     (1)   2   3   4

17. I close my office door when I want to
think strategically.   N/A   1   2   3   4

18. I limit the duration of my telephone calls.     1   2   (3)   4

19. I allow a colleague or secretary to screen
my telephone calls.   N/A   1   2   3   4

20. I skim internal memos as soon as I
receive them.     1   2   (3)   4

21. I keep the contents of my in-box to a
manageable size.     1   2   (3)   4

22. I specify which 20% of my tasks will
produce 80% of my results or outcomes.    (1)   2   3   4

23. I make a list of things to do each day.     1   2   (3)   4

24. I keep work to a certain number of hours
every day, and no more.     1   2   (3)   4

25. I delegate tasks to colleagues that I could
do myself.   N/A   1   2   3   4

### Self-Assessment Analysis

Add your circled scores together to arrive at your total score. Then refer to the following scoring ranges to identify your level of skill performance and attitudes toward managing time and handling stress.

You may want to refer back to sections of this chapter for suggestions on increasing and honing your stress and time management skills.

76–100 You appear to have highly developed stress and time management skills and attitudes usually associated with high productivity, job satisfaction, and personal well-being. Continue to enhance and maintain these skills.

51–75 You appear to have reasonably well-developed stress and time management skills but certain areas could be improved. By further developing your stress and time management skills, you can achieve greater productivity, job satisfaction, and personal well-being.

25–50 Your stress and time management skills appear to need improvement. It may also be that some of your attitudes toward stress and time management may hinder productivity, job satisfaction, and personal well-being. You might focus on the improving selected skills and attitudes (i.e., items that you scored as 1 or 2).

What about your capacity for handling environmental stressors as compared with time stressors? You can determine this by computing your subscore for items 1–12 and your subscore for items 13–25. The first subscore reflects your capacity for managing environmental and situational stressors, whereas the second subscore reflects your capacity for managing time stressors.

## REVIEW ACTIVITIES

1. Describe your level of job stress and the overall level of stress in your health care organization.
2. Briefly define and distinguish structural, relational, and time stressors. Indicate the provisions that your organization has made to deal with environmental and time stressors. Suggest additional stress management strategies that might be implemented.
3. Distinguish long-term stress management strategies from short-term or immediate stress management strategies. Indicate the immediate stress management strategies you utilize to cope with stress. Indicate how you learned them and their effectiveness for you.

4. Describe your job and your unit in terms of the demand–control model of job stress (see p. 247 and Table 1), indicating the category (I–IV) that is most representative of both. What job redesign efforts have been made—or could be made—to increase decisional control in your unit?

## FOR FURTHER INFORMATION

Girdano, D., Everly, G., & Dusek, D. (2001). *Controlling stress and tension* (6th ed.). Needham Heights, MA: Allyn & Bacon.

This short, readable textbook on stress and its management, now in its sixth edition, covers every conceivable determinant and consequence of stress, and can serve as a ready reference for the various stress models and research studies.

Karasek, R., & Theorell, T. (1990). *Healthy work: Stress, productivity and the reconstruction of work life.* New York: Basic Books.

This resource features a popular treatment of the demand–control model of job strain by the originators of the model. It describes the early observations and research studies that led to the formulation of what many consider the best research-based theory of workplace stress.

Radmacher, S., & Sheridan, C. (1995). An investigation of the demand-control model of job strain. In S. Sauter & L. Murphy (Eds.), *Organizational risk factors for job stress* (pp. 127–138). Washington, DC: American Psychological Association.

This book reviews several research studies that validate the demand–control model of job strain and workplace stress. If you find the demand–control model compelling and useful, you may find this book to be an excellent compendium of the earlier studies in this area. It goes well beyond the information covered in the Karasek and Theorell (1990) book.

# Being an Effective Leader in Health Care Management

> *"No amount of human having or human doing can make up for a deficit of human being."*
>
> —*John Adams*

By learning and applying the various skill sets described in this book, one can embark on the journey of becoming an effective health care manager. The next challenge on this journey is to master these skills by appropriately and effectively applying them in everyday work experiences. Mastery and skillful application are the hallmarks of the shift from *becoming* an effective health care manager to *being* an effective health care manager. This shift from *becoming* to *being* is both a significant transition and a transformation in a manager's professional career. Describing and facilitating this transition is the focus of this concluding section.

## THE TRANSITION FROM BECOMING TO BEING

An analogy of this transition might be helpful. Presumably, an individual who is beginning medical school has the desire to be a physician. However, *being* a physician comes about only after several years of *becoming* a physician, a process that requires graduating from medical school and a residency program and passing a federal licensure exam. A medical license signifies that the individual is considered qualified for the independent practice of medicine. Similarly, *being* an effective manager comes about after a period of time of *becoming* an effective manager, a process in which the manager has gained sufficient mastery of the requisite leadership skills. Although there is no certificate or licensure signifying the transition from becoming to being an effective manger, managers intuitively know that they have achieved this transition. Those around them also recognize, at some level, that these managers are head and shoulders above others.

How long does the process take, and what is this transition like? The answer to the first part of the questions is: as long as necessary to achieve mastery of the various skill sets. The remainder of this chapter addresses the second part of the question and sketches an action plan for facilitating the *becoming* to *being* process.

## THE MEDICAL EDUCATION
## MODEL: FROM BECOMING TO BEING

How does a manager make the transition from becoming to being? Because the transition involves a process of growth and learning, an educational analogy may be useful in conceptualizing this process. The transition can be likened to the basic model of learning in medicine. The medical education model is an apprenticeship or preceptorship model of learning. Most graduate and professional training relies primarily on didactic instruction and the case method. However, clinical training in medicine is primarily a preceptorship model of learning based on observing and imitating a preceptor performing a medical procedure or skill and then practicing the procedure until mastery is achieved. The essential goal of medical education is to transform learners or apprentices into preceptors.

This form of learning is neatly summarized in the phrase "see one, do one, teach one." "See one" refers to the process of a learner observing a preceptor perform or demonstrate a given skill. The preceptor not only performs the skill but also models it for the learner. "Do one" refers to performing the skill just as the learner had seen the skill performed. This is called imitation learning. Under the guidance of a preceptor, the learner performs or imitates the observed procedure and receives corrective feedback to ensure that the procedure was done correctly. Subsequent monitoring and feedback permit the apprentice to develop further confidence and mastery so that, in time, the learner can perform the skill independently of the preceptor. "Teach one" refers to actually imparting the learned skill to another learner. To reinforce skill learning and to achieve mastery, the learner then teaches the skill to someone who needs to learn it. At the point that mastery is achieved—usually in the last phases of a medical or surgical residency—a transformation occurs from that of *becoming* to *being* a preceptor. To signify this change in status, a senior resident may be given the designation of Chief Resident or the academic title of Instructor, which is a junior faculty position on a medical school faculty. The transformation signifies that the transition from becoming to being has occurred. In short, *becoming* a physician involves "seeing" and "doing" or working to achieve mastery, whereas *being* a physician involves practicing, teaching, modeling, and mastery.

To keep matters in perspective, it should be noted that the mastery sought in medical education primarily involves technical medical skills and only secondarily relational skills (i.e., bedside manner). However, many would contend that effective leadership requires mastery of leadership skills in all four skill areas: operational, relational, analytic, and technical. Unfortunately, there is yet to be consensus that the goal of leadership or management education—whether in degree programs or other management training—is a minimum level of competence or mastery in all four skill areas. In fact, there is little consensus that competence or mastery of the technical skills of management is necessary.

## A LEADERSHIP MODEL: FROM BECOMING TO BEING

The transition from becoming to being an effective health care manager involves a process of transformation similar to that of physicians. Table 1 outlines both dimensions of this transition, *becoming* and *being*, and the following sections describe elements associated with these dimensions.

## The *Becoming* Dimension

*Preparing*    Preparation and planning are essential in the process of learning and mastering a skill. There are several methods of preparation, including formal ones such as workshops and courses, and informal ones such as visualization and developing job aids (e.g., outlines of strategies related to specific skills). The more specific the preparation, the more likely it will lead to improved skill performance. Effective preparation begins by assessing one's current level of performance and analyzing areas of strengths and areas requiring improvement. For example, a manager who needs to improve his or her skills in doing employment interviews recognizes that he or she would first analyze his or her strengths and weaknesses. If the manager finds that he or she has difficulty keeping a focus on candidates' capacity to meet job performance expectations and on asking and following up on tough questions, he or she would prepare for both. The manager would clearly define the performance standards for that given job and then develop job-related questions that would elicit candidates' capacity. Next, he or she would specify the kind of answers that would demonstrate candidates' capacity. This would be very useful in being able to ask follow-up questions. Specifying these questions in writing would round out this type of preparation.

*Rehearsing*    Rehearsal is another form of preparation. Rehearsal permits individuals to practice saying and doing what they intend to say and do when engaged in specific management

**Table 1.**    Comparison between the *becoming* and *being* dimensions

| *Becoming* dimension | *Being* dimension |
| --- | --- |
| Preparing | |
| Rehearsing | |
| Imitating role models | Being a role model to others |
| Being mentored | Mentoring others |
| Engaging in mastery practice | Engaging in masterful practice |

situations. Rehearsal can take several forms, such as visualization, simulation, or role playing. Following up on the example of skill improvement with employment interviews, the manager could prepare for an upcoming interview by role-playing the interview process. The manager might arrange with a colleague or an administrative assistant to play the role of the job candidate, and practice asking the questions that he or she had previously prepared and practice analyzing the candidate's responses. To maximize the value of the rehearsal, it is important to make the role play as realistic as possible, in terms of focus, intensity, and time frame. A manager who is uncomfortable asking tough questions and following up on them could make a determined effort to focus on this in the role play. By videotaping the role play, he or she could subsequently review and critique his or her performance both in specific areas and in general. For some individuals, this kind of feedback, called self-feedback, can be less threatening than third-party feedback from a superior or peer.

*Imitating Role Models*    Imitation learning abounds in management, which is to say beginning managers tend to act like the senior managers whom they know or report to. Without consciously deciding it, managers commonly take on the strategies that other managers utilize to handle common and uncommon situations and challenges. When it comes to developing mastery of the core skills sets, it is critical for managers to discern about which of these others to imitate and which to avoid. For example, the manager who is attempting to improve his or her interviewing skills is quite likely to find him- or herself in interview situations that involve three or four managers and a job candidate. In such situations, he or she would do well to take cues from managers who are good strategic interviewers.

*Being Mentored*    Those who are in the process of becoming effective managers often find that their journey is quickened by being mentored by a highly effective manager. Good mentors offer those whom they mentor—*protégés*—support and encouragement in solving their own problems and becoming more independent. Protégé managers who can develop relationships with mentor managers who have considerable mastery of operational, relational, analytical, and technical skill sets are very likely to find themselves developing and being challenged to master these same skill sets.

*Engaging in Mastery Practice*  Becoming an effective manager requires continual practice of the essential leadership skills. Managers who espouse the attitude that every management situation is an opportunity to grow and develop their skills, and who are in a work situation that fosters the development of these skills, can be expected to achieve a sufficient degree of mastery sooner rather than later. This, in turn, facilitates their transition from becoming to being an effective health care manager.

## The *Being* Dimension

*Being a Role Model to Others*  Being an effective manager represents the achievement of a level of personal and professional development that few attain. Effective managers have reached a plateau from which their vision of their role is considerably broadened. They view their role as more than simply making decisions, solving problems, and motivating employees to higher levels of performance and commitment. They can accept that they also have a responsibility for serving as a role model. Whereas previously this prospect may have seemed foreign to them, now it seems appropriate and natural. Being a role model to other managers, supervisors, and employees is a leadership function they can undertake without feeling phony or self-conscious.

*Mentoring Others*  Similarly, being a mentor seems reasonable and right. Because they themselves were mentored, either formally or informally, effective managers can now consider passing on the collected wisdom of what they have learned about relationships, corporate politics, and life. According to Erikson (1982), mentoring is a form of generativity or "giving back" to others. Although managers at any point on the continuum from becoming to being an effective manager can be called on to mentor, managers who are closer to the *being* end of the continuum tend to be mature and likely to give freely of themselves and their experience without expecting a return from the protégé or feeling unduly threatened at the protégé's promise and progress. Mentoring involves sharing observations, knowledge, and experience as well as giving the big picture and providing advice and suggestions when appropriate. It also provides a natural forum for affirming and reinforcing the positive qualities and skills of those who are mentored and often leads to long-term mutually beneficial relationships. Needless to say, the development of such mentoring relationships tends to be one of the more satisfying and gratifying tasks of a manager.

*Engaging in Masterful Practice*    Whether a manager who has mastered the various skill sets is 35 or 60 years old, he or she continues to practice the art of management but practices it in a masterful way. These managers typically experience a sense of ease and naturalness in dealing with situations and employees that was not previously experienced or appreciated. That is not to say that life and leadership are no longer challenging, but instead that these challenges can be met with a relaxed presence and confidence. Many such managers report that they feel less apprehensive and worried and are more likely to trust their intuition than previously.

## CONCLUDING NOTE

The journey of becoming an effective health care manager and the transition to being an effective health care manager do not occur as a result of attending a few workshops or even reading this book and completing all of the exercises and review activities. Like life itself, this transition is a journey of self-development and transformation. It is a journey that requires a burning desire and commitment to grow and develop. It is also a journey that can be facilitated to a greater extent when the individual manager finds a position in which there is a high level of "fit" among self, job, family, career, and organization, as well as by helpful and effective role modeling and mentoring. My best wishes to you on this challenging and exciting transforming journey.

## SELF-ASSESSMENT OF
## ESSENTIAL LEADERSHIP SKILLS: POSTTEST

**Directions:** This assessment will help you evaluate your current level of skill and attitudes regarding several leadership skills. Use the following statements to assess your attitudes and skills by circling the number that is closest to your experience: 1 = never, 2 = sometimes, 3 = often, and 4 = always. Respond in a way that reflects your skills today, rather than those you hope to have in the future. Answer as honestly and realistically as you can. Instructions on scoring and interpreting the results are provided in the analysis section at the end of the assessment.

## MOTIVATION

| | | | | | |
|---|---|---|---|---|---|
| 1. | I try to persuade and influence employees rather than force them to do what I want. | 1 | 2 | 3 | 4 |
| 2 | I design work assignments so they are interesting and challenging. | 1 | 2 | 3 | 4 |
| 3. | I strive to match an employee's ability and talent with job responsibilities. | 1 | 2 | 3 | 4 |
| 4. | Knowing that employees have different needs and wants, I try to personalize rewards and feedback. | 1 | 2 | 3 | 4 |
| 5. | I provide immediate positive feedback and other forms of recognition for work that is well done. | 1 | 2 | 3 | 4 |

## COMMITMENT

| | | | | | |
|---|---|---|---|---|---|
| 6. | Many of my professional needs are met in my current job. | 1 | 2 | 3 | 4 |
| 7. | I would not be satisfied working for another health care organization. | 1 | 2 | 3 | 4 |
| 8. | I try my best and give full effort in my current job. | 1 | 2 | 3 | 4 |
| 9. | Emotionally, it would be difficult for me to leave my current job. | 1 | 2 | 3 | 4 |
| 10. | Other health care organizations can't compare with mine. | 1 | 2 | 3 | 4 |

## TEAM PERFORMANCE

11.  I allow the team to have input in any decision that affects team performance.    1    2    3    4

12.  I strive to show team members that I trust them implicitly.    1    2    3    4

13.  I set high standards of team performance and outcomes.    1    2    3    4

14.  I strive to foster a culture that values teams and team development.    1    2    3    4

15.  I lay out a clear vision and specific short-term goals of what our team can accomplish.    1    2    3    4

## DELEGATION

16   I try to do only the work that must be done by me and delegate the rest.    1    2    3    4

17.  I am regarded by my superior as a good delegator.    1    2    3    4

18.  I delegate with the thought that it helps staff grow to their fullest potential.    1    2    3    4

19.  When I delegate responsibility, I make sure that staff have the full authority to perform the task properly.    1    2    3    4

20.  I review my job every 3–6 months to see whether I can increase my delegation to staff.    1    2    3    4

## COMMUNICATION

21.  I strive to be an "active listener" by using eye contact, head nods, smiles, "uh-huhs," restatements, and leaning forward.    1    2    3    4

22.  If staff haven't understood my message,
     it means I haven't communicated
     effectively.                                    1    2    3    4

23.  My staff members tell me about bad
     news (i.e., problems, mistakes, delays)
     as well as good news.                           1    2    3    4

24.  I draft reports that are clear, concise,
     persuasive, and well structured.                1    2    3    4

25.  Throughout my presentation, I make eye
     contact with all segments of the
     audience.                                       1    2    3    4

## NEGOTIATION

26.  In attempting to resolve a conflict, I look
     for common areas of agreement.                  1    2    3    4

27.  When there is conflict, I try to clarify the
     interests of both parties and create an
     agenda for resolving the dispute.               1    2    3    4

28.  I try to keep the discussion focused on
     problems rather than on personalities.          1    2    3    4

29.  I encourage parties to generate possible
     solutions and spell out the benefits of
     each.                                           1    2    3    4

30.  I help the parties to come to agreement
     on the best solution.                           1    2    3    4

## COACHING

31.  Being a manager means coaching
     employees.                                      1    2    3    4

32. I revise performance plans with the employees and provide additional coaching as needed.  1  2  3  4

33. I communicate a positive attitude when coaching to convey my belief in employees' ability to achieve their goals.  1  2  3  4

34. When coaching, my focus is on current performance and potential achievement.  1  2  3  4

35. My superiors consider me to be an effective coach.  1  2  3  4

## COUNSELING AND INTERVIEWING

36. During interviews, I put the individual at ease and attempt to maintain a relaxed, friendly tone.  1  2  3  4

37. I start interviews by being direct and specific about my agenda or my concerns.  1  2  3  4

38. I try to listen actively and use good eye contact and positive body language to communicate my respect, interest, and concern.  1  2  3  4

39. I view the outcomes and success of counseling as dependent on the individual's involvement, so I encourage his or her full participation.  1  2  3  4

40. To avoid any possible misunderstanding on my part, I check out my perceptions of the situation or concern with the individual.  1  2  3  4

## STRATEGIC THINKING AND DECISION MAKING

41.  I follow a multistep decision-making
     model to ensure a sound decision.          1    2    3    4

42.  I make my decisions in a timely fashion
     and ensure that they are implemented.      1    2    3    4

43.  My superiors consider me a strategic
     thinker.                                   1    2    3    4

44.  I combine analytical methods and
     creative approaches in making decisions.   1    2    3    4

45.  I constantly check to ensure that my team
     operates within the strategy.              1    2    3    4

## BUDGETING

46.  I develop my goals and objectives for the
     coming year before I prepare my budget.    1    2    3    4

47.  I adjust my budget periodically to correct
     for changes in projections.                1    2    3    4

48.  I study the budget manual and follow it
     closely in preparing my budget.            1    2    3    4

49.  I prefer a flexible budget so that my
     projections can be corrected for changes.  1    2    3    4

50.  I communicate budget issues directly
     with my staff and get their input.         1    2    3    4

## FINANCIAL AND HUMAN RESOURCES MONITORING

51.  I use management accounting reports to
     manage my unit.                            1    2    3    4

52.  I use benchmarks in monitoring
     performance.                               1    2    3    4

53. I use accounting ratios to analyze
financial information.     1   2   3   4

54. I know how my organization's mission
and goals relate to its overall financial
management.     1   2   3   4

55. I can read and analyze my organization's
financial statements.     1   2   3   4

## ORGANIZATIONAL AND PERSONAL RESOURCES AND "FIT"

56. I maintain balance in my personal and
professional life by pursuing hobbies and
interests.     1   2   3   4

57. I can arrange my work life so it doesn't
spill over into my personal life.     1   2   3   4

58. I have made the most of my talents and
abilities.     1   2   3   4

59. My values match the organization's core
values.     1   2   3   4

60. There is a good fit among me and my job,
family, and organization.     1   2   3   4

## TIME AND STRESS MANAGEMENT

61. I feel reasonably calm and centered even
if I am under pressure.     1   2   3   4

62. I undertake only as many tasks as I can
handle at once.     1   2   3   4

63. I know and practice several immediate
stress reducers such as mindfulness and
deep breathing.     1   2   3   4

64. I deal with tasks by prioritizing my work
    load.          1    2    3    4

65. I would say that, for the most part, I am
    able to cope with my work load.      1    2    3    4

## Self-Assessment Analysis: Global

Add your circled scores together to arrive at your total score. Then refer to the following scoring ranges to identify your level of skill and attitudes toward leadership. For the assessment as a whole, if you scored in the range

221–260      You are in the top quartile

191–220      You are in the second quartile

120–190      You are in the third quartile

119 or below    You are in the bottom quartile

## Self-Assessment Analysis: Specific Skill Sets

Now compute your scores for the specific sets of skills. Enter each score on the line provided.

1. _____ Commitment and Motivation

2. _____ Team Performance

3. _____ Delegation

4. _____ Communication

5. _____ Negotiation

6. _____ Coaching

7. _____ Counseling and Interviewing

8. _____ Strategic Thinking and Decision Making

9. _____ Budgeting

10. _____ Financial and Human Resources Monitoring

11. _____ Organizational and Personal Resources and "Fit"

12. _____ Time and Stress Management

### Interpretation of Scores

For each specific set of skills, the following scoring ranges suggest that

| | |
|---|---|
| 16–20 | You appear to have highly developed skills in this area. |
| 11–15 | You appear to have reasonably well-developed skills in this area. |
| 10 or below | Your skills in this area appear to need improvement. |

## FOR FURTHER INFORMATION

Kinlaw, D. (1999). *Coaching for commitment: Interpersonal strategies for obtaining superior performance from individuals and teams.* San Francisco: Jossey-Bass.

Chapter 6 of this excellent book is titled "Self-Development." The author offers several strategies and suggestions for improving and mastering the skill set of coaching, yet these suggestions appear to be applicable to many, if not all, of the skill sets.

# References

Albrecht, K., & Albrecht, S. (1993). *Added value negotiation: The breakthrough methods for building balanced deals.* Homewood, IL: Business One/Irwin.

Allen, J. (1997). *Nursing home administration* (3rd ed.). New York: Springer-Verlag.

Americans with Disabilities Act (ADA) of 1990, PL 101-336, 42 U.S.C. §§ 12101 *et seq.*

Baker, J., & Baker, R. (2000). *Health care finance.* Gaithersburg, MD: Aspen.

Beatty, R. (1994). *Interviewing and selecting high performers: Every manager's guide to effective interviewing techniques.* New York: John Wiley & Sons.

Beer, M. (1980). *Organizational change and development: A systems view.* Glenview, IL: Scott Foresman.

Betof, E., & Harwood, F. (1992). *Just promoted: How to survive and thrive in your first 12 months as a manager.* New York: McGraw-Hill.

Bienvenu, S. (2000). *The presentations skills workshop: Helping people create and deliver great presentations.* New York: AMACOM.

Birnbaum, W. (1990). *If your strategy is so terrific, how come it doesn't work?* New York: American Management Association.

Borysenko, J. (1988). *Minding the body, mending the mind.* Toronto: Bantam.

Bramson, R.M. (1981). *Coping with difficult people in business and in life.* Garden City, New York: Anchor Press/Doubleday.

Brownell, E. (1999, February). Say it right. *IIE Solutions, 2,* 26–27.

Buckingham, M., & Coffman, C. (1999). *First, break all the rules: What the world's greatest managers do differently.* New York: Simon & Schuster.

Camp, R., Vielhaber, M., & Simonetti, J. (2001). *Strategic interviewing: How to hire good people.* San Francisco: Jossey-Bass.

Chandler, A. (1962). *Strategy and structure.* Cambridge: MIT Press.

Cleverley, W. (1997). *Essentials of health care finance* (4th ed.). Gaithersburg, MD: Aspen.

Cooper, R. (1991). *The performance edge.* Boston: Houghton Mifflin.

Covey, S. (1990). *Seven habits of highly effective people: Powerful lessons in personal change.* New York: Simon & Schuster.

Dacher, E. (1991). *PNI: The new mind/body healing program.* New York: Marlowe.

Erikson, E. (1982). *The life cycle completed.* New York: W.W. Norton.

Fisher, R., & Ury, W. (1988). *Getting to yes: Negotiating without giving in.* Boston: Houghton-Mifflin.

Fournies, F. (2000). *Coaching for improved work performance* (Rev. ed.). New York: McGraw-Hill.

Gapenski, L. (2002). *Healthcare finance: An introduction to accounting and financial management* (2nd ed.). Chicago: Health Administration Press.

Gill, L. (1999). *How to work with just about anyone: A 3-step solution for getting difficult people to change.* New York: Fireside/Simon & Schuster.

Girdano, D., Everly, G., & Dusek, D. (2001). *Controlling stress and tension* (6th ed.). Needham Heights, MA: Allyn & Bacon.

Hackman, J. (1990). *Groups that work (and don't work).* San Francisco: Jossey-Bass.

Hanson, G. (1986). *Determinants of firm performance: An integration of economic and organizational factors.* Unpublished doctoral dissertation, University of Michigan Business School, Ann Arbor.

Herkimer, A., Jr. (1988). *Understanding health care budgeting.* Gaithersburg, MD: Aspen.

Hiebert, M., & Klatt, B. (2001). *The encyclopedia of leadership.* New York: McGraw-Hill.

Karasek, R., & Theorell, T. (1990). *Healthy work: Stress, productivity and the reconstruction of work life.* New York: Basic Books.

Katzenbach, J., & Smith, D. (1993). *The wisdom of teams: Creating the high-performance organization.* Boston: Harvard Business School Press.

Kaye, B. (2000). Career development: Anywhere, anyplace. In M. Goldsmith, L. Lyons, & A. Freas (Eds.), *Coaching for leadership: How the world's greatest coaches help leaders learn* (pp. 235–243). San Francisco: Jossey-Bass/Pfeiffer.

Kinlaw, D. (1999). *Coaching for commitment: Interpersonal strategies for obtaining superior performance from individuals and teams* (2nd ed.). San Francisco: Jossey-Bass.

Kouzes, J., & Posner, B. (1987). *The leadership challenge.* San Francisco: Jossey-Bass.

Levinson, H. (1981). *Executive.* Cambridge, MA: Harvard University Press.

Lowman, R. (1993). *Counseling and psychotherapy of work dysfunctions.* Washington, DC: American Psychological Association.

Macher, K. (1988, September). Empowerment and the bureaucracy. *Training and Development Journal, 42*(9), 212–215.

Manion, J. (1998). *From management to leadership: Interpersonal skills for success in healthcare.* Chicago: American Hospital Publishers.

Manion, J., Lorimer, W., & Leander, W. (1996). *Team-based health care organizations.* Gaithersburg, MD: Aspen.

McCubbin, H., & Thompson, A. (1989). *Balancing work and family life on Wall Street.* Edina, MN: Burgess International Group.

McCubbin, H., & Thompson, A. (1999). *The dynamics of resilient families.* Thousand Oaks, CA: Sage Publications.

Mintzberg, H. (1990, May 1). The manager's job: Folklore and fact. *Harvard Business Review,* 175.

Muchinsky, P. (1993). *Psychology applied to work* (4th ed.). Pacific Grove, CA: Brooks/Cole.

Nelson, R.B. (1994). *Empowering employees through delegation.* New York: McGraw-Hill.

Nowicki, M. (2001). *The financial management of hospitals and healthcare organizations.* Chicago: Health Administration Press.

O'Malley, M. (2000). *Creating commitment: How to attract and retain talented employees by building relationships that last.* New York: John Wiley & Sons.

Parker, G. (1996). *Team players and teamwork: The new competitive business strategy.* San Francisco: Jossey-Bass.

Parsons, P. (2001). *Beyond persuasion: The healthcare managers guide to strategic communications.* Chicago: Health Administration Press.

Quinn, R. (2000). *Change the world.* San Francisco: Jossey-Bass.

Radmacher, R., & Sheridan, C. (1995). An investigation of the demand-control model of job strain. In S. Sauter & L. Murphy (Eds.), *Organizational risk factors for job stress* (pp. 127–138). Washington, DC: American Psychological Association.

Roebuck, C. (1999). *Effective delegation.* New York: AMACOM.

Ross, A., Williams, S., & Pavlock, E. (1998). *Ambulatory care management.* New York: Delmar.

Rossi, E. (1991). *The 20-minute break.* Los Angeles: Tarcher.

Salmon, W. (1999). *The new supervisor's survival manual.* New York: AMACOM.

Salters, L. (1997, October–December). Coaching and counseling for peak performance. *Business and Economic Review, 26–28.*

Sperry, L. (1987). ERIC: A cognitive map for guiding brief therapy and health care counseling. *Individual Psychology, 44*(2), 237–241.

Sperry, L. (1993). *Psychiatric consultation in the workplace.* Washington, DC: American Psychiatric Association.

Sperry, L. (1996). *Corporate therapy and consulting.* New York: Brunner/Mazel.

Sperry, L. (2002). *Effective leadership: Strategies for maximizing executive productivity and health.* New York: Brunner/Routledge.

Stephenson, P. (2000). *Executive coaching: Lead, develop, retain motivated talented people.* French's Forest, New South Wales: Pearson Education Australia.

Tichy, N. (1999). *The leadership engine.* New York: HarperBusiness.

Tuckman, B. (1965). Developmental sequence in small groups. *Psychological Bulletin, 63,* 384–399.

Wells, S. (1998). *Choosing the future: The power of strategic thinking.* Boston: Butterworth-Heinemann.

Whetten, D., & Cameron, K. (2002). *Developing management skills* (5th ed.). Upper Saddle River, NJ: Prentice Hall.

# Index

Page numbers followed by *f* indicate figures; those followed by *t* indicate tables.